*Counseling
Children
through the
World of Play*

AACC
COUNSELING
LIBRARY

Counseling
Children
THROUGH THE
World
OF *Play*

DANIEL S. SWEENEY, PH.D.
Foreword by Dr. Garry L. Landreth

Tyndale House Publishers, Inc.
WHEATON, ILLINOIS

AMERICAN ASSOCIATION OF

AACC

CHRISTIAN COUNSELORS

The American Association of Christian Counselors

is an organization of professional, pastoral, and lay counselors committed to the promotion of excellence and unity in Christian Counseling. The AACC provides conferences, software, video and audio resources, two professional journals, a resource review, as well as other publications and resources. Membership is open to anyone who writes for information: AACC, P.O. Box 739, Forest, VA 24551.

"Who Will Save the Children?" from the album *Celebrate This Heartbeat,* songwriter Randy Stonehill. Copyright © 1984, Stonehillian Music (Adm. by Word, Inc.) and Word Music (A Div. of Word, Inc.). All rights reserved. Used by permission.

Chapter 15 is adapted from Daniel S. Sweeney and Ross Tatum, M.D., "Play Therapy and Psychopharmacology: What the Play Therapist Needs to Know," *International Journal of Play Therapy,* vol. 4, no. 2 (1995): 41-57. Used by permission of the Association for Play Therapy.

Material quoted from "Child-Centered Play Therapy," *Play Theory and Applications: A Comparative Casebook* is used by permission from John Wiley & Sons, Inc.

Material quoted from Garry Landreth's *Play Therapy: The Art of Relationship* (Muncie, Ind.: Accelerated Development, Inc., Publishers, 1991) is reproduced with permission of the publisher. All rights reserved.

The chart in chapter 1 is used by permission of David Finkelhor, Family Research Laboratory, University of New Hampshire. Originally printed in *American Psychologist* (March 1994): 176.

Photo credits: Jonathan Reynolds

Designed by Beth Sparkman

Edited by Lynn Vanderzalm

Library of Congress Cataloging-in-Publication Data

Sweeney, Daniel S.
  Counseling children through the world of play / Daniel S. Sweeney ; foreword by
  Garry L. Landreth.
    p. cm.
  Includes bibliographical references (p.) and index.
  ISBN 0-8423-0307-3 (hc : alk. paper)
    1. Children—Pastoral counseling of. 2. Children—Counseling of. 3. Play—Psychological
aspects. 4. Play therapy. 5. Church work with children. 6. Pastoral counseling. I. Title.
BV639.C4S94 1997
259'.22—dc20
                                                96-30453

Printed in the United States of America

04 03 02 01 00 99 98 97
8   7   6   5   4   3   2   1

CONTENTS

FOREWORD

Who will help the children? And how can children be helped if they are not understood? Someone must step forward and begin the process of awakening the Christian community to the unique needs of children and the dynamics of the way they communicate those needs through play. Children are persons created by God. Most church staff members and mental health professionals readily acknowledge that people below a certain age or height are indeed children, but few know how to communicate with the person of the child. The fact that an individual is only five years old does not in any way make that individual any less a person. And that person (child) is just as deserving of respect, recognition, affirmation, understanding, genuineness, and the right to be listened to as any adult person.

Daniel Sweeney has accepted the challenge, stepped forward, and provided penetrating and perceptive insight into the world of children. I encourage you to let go of previously held views and limited expectations of children and allow the pages of this book to take you on a journey into the lives of children. Yes, they are children, but they are much more! They are God's creation—his best! To respond to children as anything less than God's best creation is to inhibit and interfere with God's intended purpose for children. Can a Christian parent, a committed church staff member, a caring teacher, a loving day-care worker, a spiritual choir leader, a Sunday school teacher interfere with God's plan for a child? Absolutely! And that person may not even be aware of having done so. When adults are not sensitive and appropriately responsive to the inner person God has created in children, then God's purpose for the child may be stifled for that moment.

Play is the most natural thing children do, and if adults want to make significant emotional contact with children, they must understand the meaningful messages in children's play. Play is not simply play. It is the child's way of communicating that which cannot be verbalized because words are simply inadequate. If we are to be helpful to children, we must be willing to go to their level, see what they see, experience what they experience, feel what they feel, and wonder as they wonder. This can be done only by entering into their world of play. Only then will we be in contact with the inner world of the child.

Daniel not only tells the reader how to make this kind of significant contact, he skillfully shows you, in simple language, how to engage in the process of being with children and communicating with them on their level. This book will change what you do with children.

God has given us an awesome responsibility to nurture and develop the children he has placed in relationships with us. The pages of this book open the door to the inner world of children and provide a haunting reminder of missed opportunities to respond to children in more developmentally facilitative ways. Each one of us enjoyed playing long before we learned how to sit still and work. I believe God has a purpose in that. It was preparation for how we should be communicating with and relating to children. Children speak volumes in their play. This book will help you develop and utilize the play language of children to help them grow in ways God intended. This is a very practical book, containing information that can be immediately applied in relationships with children in homes, counseling, classrooms, and church programs.

Dr. Garry L. Landreth
Regents Professor and Director
Center for Play Therapy
University of North Texas

ACKNOWLEDGMENTS

When I first began writing this book, I was convinced that the Christian counseling community needed a book like this. I believed that I had something to communicate, but I was not sure that I could do it. I deeply appreciate those who believed in me even when I did not believe in myself.

When all is said and done, my accomplishments, degrees, and publications do not define who I am as a person. Being a husband and father and being a child of God are the truly meaningful aspects of my life. I all too often forget that being a husband and parent is more important than such temporal things as getting published. I am so grateful to my wife, Marla, for her patience, tolerance, understanding, and encouragement. You are truly beautiful. My children—Jessica, Michele, Renata, and Josiah—are incredible. Thank you for tolerating the many hours that Daddy spent in the "computer room." I cannot express with words what being your father means to me.

What can I say about Dr. Garry Landreth? He has inspired me just as he has inspired thousands. I have learned so much from just being around him. His work is more than amazing; it is anointed. His name is mentioned many times in this book; I believe he is a pioneer in his writings and thoughts on children and play therapy. Garry, your love for the world of children and for your family and friends (I feel privileged to be numbered among them) is so special. I won't let the fire die.

My appreciation goes to Dr. Gary Collins and the American Association of Christian Counselors. Gary initiated my involvement in this AACC Counseling Library. Many people have helped me in the various stages of writing and reviewing the manuscript for this book. My thanks to Dr. Garry Landreth, Dr. Linda Homeyer, Dr. Gary Kirksey, Mrs. Mary Mock, Dr. Paul Warren, Dr. Angela Sabates, Dr. Grant Martin, Dr. Lee Carter, and my wife, Marla. Your suggestions and support were great. Dr. Ross Tatum did a wonderful job in writing with me the chapter about medications. A special thanks to Keith Wall, whose editing and suggestions (and patience) were invaluable.

Many thanks go to Lynn Vanderzalm, my editor at Tyndale. I have learned so much about writing, editing, and publishing. Apart from deadlines (I am not sure I met a single one!), I actually enjoyed much of the process. Your work has been wonderful!

The photographs in the book are of volunteers and not of clients. My thanks to my own family and friends for your willingness to contribute. I also greatly appreciate those organizations that have provided permission for various materials to be reprinted.

I have felt so supported by my friends at the Center for Play Therapy and my "family" at Newchurch Christian Fellowship. Thank you, Larry Ford and Kelly Elliott, for everything.

Most important, I must acknowledge and thank the Giver of life, who has sustained me and my family through the writing of this book and the recent years, which have been so rough. My words and my writing are so incomplete and imperfect. Yet God has been so faithful. He truly uses the weak to accomplish his purposes. I pray that God will use this book to touch people and help children.

WHO WILL SAVE THE CHILDREN?
Randy Stonehill

Cry for all the innocent ones
Born into a world that's lost its heart,
For those who never learn to dream
Because their hope is crushed before they can start.
And we shake our fists at the air
And say, "If God is love, how can this be fair?"

But we are His hands, we are His voice,
We are the ones who must make the choice.
And if it isn't now, tell me when?
If it isn't you, then tell me,
Who will save the children?
Who will save the children?

We count our blessings one by one,
Yet we have forgotten how to give.
It seems that we don't want to face
All the hungry and homeless who struggle to live.
But heaven is watching tonight,
Tugging at our hearts to do what's right.

And we are His hands, we are His voice,
We are the ones who must make the choice.
And if it isn't you, then tell me,
Who will save the children?
Who will save the children?

As we observe them through our TV screens,
They seem so distant and unreal.
But they bleed like we bleed, and they feel what we feel.
Oh, save the children.
Save the children.

Now we decide that nothing can change
And throw up our hands in numb despair.
And we lose a piece of our souls
By teaching ourselves just how not to care.
But Christ would have gone to the cross
Just to save one child from being lost.

And we are His hands, we are His voice,
We are the ones who must make the choice.
And it must be now, there's no time to waste.
It must be you, no one can take your place.
Can't you see that only we can save the children?
Save the children.
Save the children.
Please save the children.
Randy Stonehill, used by permission. © 1984

Introduction

When I began to take my relationship to the Lord seriously during my first year of college, I decided to serve in the children's ministry at church. I worked with a class of two- and three-year-olds; three of us in charge of thirty-five bundles of energy. It was insane. But I loved it! As I grew older, however, I became more "sophisticated" and took on greater responsibilities in the church. I didn't have time for children's ministry. Years later, I wondered how I ever had the patience to work with such an unruly and undisciplined population. I thought, *I must have been nuts. How could I have enjoyed serving that age group?*

It's not surprising, then, that when I first became a counselor, I never intended to work with children. I found so many fascinating and stimulating areas of counseling and psychology. I was being challenged by the people who came to me for counseling at my church. I felt I must get further training, which I did—but not with children! That was someone else's job! I had my eyes on bigger and better areas of ministry and vocation.

Now, years later, as I focus on this book and the importance of ministering to and counseling children, I am challenged to acknowledge my former attitude. I had loved working with children when I first became a Christian. I could even say it was one of my "first loves." My hope and prayer is that for many of you reading this book, working with hurting children is indeed a love and a calling. Undoubtedly, loving and ministering to children are close to the heart of the Father.

I did return to my first love—working with children—as a pastoral counselor with a local church. I fumbled my way through several years until I began to work in the area of foster care and residential treatment. I was still using cognitive approaches ("talk therapy"), but I was beginning to employ some games and art-therapy techniques. I was more successful but still did not feel that I was reaching my child clients. I spent a few years working in the area of forensic psychology, providing crisis-counseling services for psychiatrically impaired incarcerated adults. This experience solidified my belief that early childhood intervention could circumvent some of the adult problems I was encountering. Returning to the field of therapeutic foster care, I stumbled on play therapy as an approach for treating children. I was hooked!

In some ways, it was such a simple concept that I wasn't sure how it worked—using play as a means to communicate with children. The idea that children do not have the verbal and cognitive skills that adults have and therefore do not communicate in the same way as adults made sense to me. If the natural medium of communication for children is play, then it must follow that counseling should focus on children's communication medium and be at their level instead of forcing them to rise to an adult level. Could it be that using adult counseling techniques with children was one of those square-peg-in-a-round-hole things?

I strongly believe in working with children by entering their world (the world of play) rather than forcing them to enter mine (the world of thought and talk). You know, of course, from the title that this book focuses on using play as a means of touching and healing the wounded child. I will go into greater detail about this concept as the book unfolds, but let me give an example of how children speak through play.

Several years ago, my daughter Michele was going through a difficult stage and was being a challenge at home. This was, naturally, a concern to me—after all, it wouldn't do for the daughter of a therapist and church counselor to have such troubles! We had recently had another child, which meant Michele had lost her baby position. As you might expect, she was feeling displaced, and her behavior was making this clear. Soon I got the bright idea, *I'm a play therapist, so why not bring Michele into the playroom and let her express herself through play? Maybe I can even videotape it and have a good example to use in my play therapy training.* OK, I admit, I still was not quite with the program (focusing on the child and not myself). But eventually, I got a clue!

Michele engaged in "garden variety" play for much of the session—nothing extraordinary. However, when I gave her the five-minute time-limit warning before the end of the session, her play changed. This shouldn't surprise many counselors, since clients frequently "dump" issues at the end of a session. Michele proceeded to get a dollhouse from a shelf, place it in the middle of the playroom, and play house. She selected a few dolls and said: "This is the mama doll. This is the daddy doll. And this is the baby doll. The mama is cooking in the kitchen. The dad is reading the newspaper. And the little girl is building a shed in the yard because there's no room in the house." (By the way, I was offended by her reference to the dad doll, since I rarely read the paper until after the kids were in bed!)

It doesn't take a play therapy specialist to figure out what Michele was saying through her play. The issue wasn't that I was reading the paper or that Mom was cooking; it was that she felt we didn't have enough time for her. The girl doll building a room outside of the house couldn't have displayed a more graphic scene of feeling displaced and left out. Michele was able to express herself through play in a way she could not possibly have done through talking.

Children simply do not say to their parents, "Mom, Dad, I am feeling very displaced by the birth of my new sister, and I am experiencing acute emotional neglect. Sibling rivalry issues are intensifying, and I could really use some intervention right now." The way children let us know about these issues is by acting out. When hurting children respond to their emotional pain with inappropriate behavior and are referred to counseling, they desperately need the freedom to express themselves in their own language—the language of play.

In my quest to learn more about the world of children and play therapy, I have had the honor and privilege of working with Dr. Garry Landreth at the University of North Texas. I currently work as the assistant director of the Center for Play Therapy, which Dr. Landreth directs. The University of North Texas program is the largest play therapy training center in the world. Dr. Landreth believes that it is his calling and mission to make this world safer for children. I share that calling, as I'm sure many of you do. My thoughts about children as well as my personal faith journey have been profoundly influenced by Dr. Landreth, who is my mentor, colleague, and friend. I hope that many of you will have the opportunity to learn from him as you continue to grow as child counselors.

Like Dr. Landreth and many of you who work with children, I have an abiding concern about the welfare of children in our world. Newspaper and television accounts provide daily reminders that children are not valued in our society as they should be. You have probably seen and heard firsthand how children are treated with disregard or even contempt. From violence, abuse, and neglect to the sad state of the education and welfare systems, we see how children are frequently mistreated. It is not just a political problem; it is a moral catastrophe. Yes, we must address ecological and financial concerns for the sake of our children's future, but it is more important that we attend to the hearts and souls of God's little ones.

Although a great deal of lip service is given to children's issues, children are simply not honored in today's society, certainly not as God intended. The current focus on "family values" in today's political and social arena testifies to this. Forming committees and increasing funding do not honor children; giving time, building relationships, and entering the child's world do. Children are all too often ignored, and the child's world is too frequently misunderstood.

This low priority may also be reflected in the mental health field and possibly in Christian counseling circles as well. One of the licenses I hold is from the state of California as a Marriage, Family, and Child Counselor (MFCC). A requisite for this license is a master's degree in psychology or counseling, and the course requirements are spelled out in the licensing legislation. Only one course in child counseling is required, yet I am licensed in California to diagnose and treat childhood disorders. It is clearly unethical for psychotherapists to practice outside the scope of their license or expertise, but these requirements arguably do not give the licensed MFCC therapist the necessary training. Shouldn't helping hurting children be a higher priority?

I have had the opportunity to present workshops on child-counseling issues at a number of Christian conferences. On several occasions, my presentation was the only one related to children. At the Second International Congress on Christian Counseling in 1992, well over one hundred fifty workshops were presented on various aspects of Christian counseling, but only six addressed child-counseling issues. At the International Congress on the Family in 1995, only one of twelve workshop tracks addressed children's issues, and even this was combined with parenting and adolescent presentations. Shouldn't helping hurting children be a higher priority?

I recently sent a letter to a national Christian organization that provides counseling education, and I advocated more training opportunities for those working with children. I made my case for the importance of ministering to the youngest members of society and their families. The response I received was disappointing. I was told that participants in the counseling program are asked to evaluate the training and make suggestions for specific issues they would like to see included. The organization's letter said: "Although the counseling of children and children's issue has been mentioned, it has not been high on the list of their perceived needs." The letter went on to state that the training organizers "try to keep in mind what participants are requesting in light of what they have already received in their schools." As noted, the academic requirements for counselors do not seem to emphasize child psychology or psychopathology. Is it true that Christian counselors do not perceive training about children's issues to be important? Shouldn't helping hurting children be a higher priority?

Christian bookstores and book catalogs are filled with books about counseling, self-help, and parenting. These are important. Nevertheless, very little training material is available for Christians counseling with children. Shouldn't helping hurting children be a higher priority?

If the Christian counseling community gave greater emphasis to child counseling and children's issues, perhaps we would see less need for counseling adults. As counselors, shouldn't it be our goal to put ourselves out of business? It may never happen, but how wonderful if it did!

One reason I am convinced about the effectiveness of play therapy is because of what it has taught me about other areas of my life. My training and experience in child play therapy have made me a better father, husband, counselor, and person. My hope is that those who read this book will not only learn how to enter the lives of children and bring healing to their hurts but also learn something about themselves, about life, and about God. It would indeed be a blessing if we all could be more in touch with the child within us, for that's where God's kingdom is revealed.

This book is not intended to be just a bookshelf resource for Christian counselors who happen to have a child come up on their caseload. It is intended to help the person working with children to gain a broader perspective of the child's world and to gain further insight into entering that world. From psychologists, social workers, and family therapists to pastoral counselors, group-home staff, and children's-ministry workers, readers will find on the following pages truths that will help to touch hurting children.

Although we will discuss specific techniques and childhood disorders, understand that I am much more interested in the *process* of making contact with children. I believe that counseling is about *relationship*. It is *relationship* that brings people into God's kingdom, and it is *relationship* that brings healing to the emotionally wounded. If a counselor knows all there is to know about child development, child psychopathology, and child therapy techniques yet does not know how to make contact with children, how much benefit can there be? Relationship begins with making contact. Techniques cannot accomplish this.

What about this term I use—*making contact?* I like this phrase not only because it is common in play therapy literature but also because it conveys what Christ's ministry was all about. Scripture often tells us that Jesus was "moved by compassion" and that the "power of God was present" to heal. This does not speak of technique (how) but of relationship and motivation (who and why).

Perhaps I can give a childlike illustration of what I mean. One of our family's favorite books is *The Velveteen Rabbit.* If you are familiar with the story, you will remember that the Rabbit is having a conversation with the Skin Horse about what it means to be *real.* The Skin Horse explains that *real* is "a thing that happens to you. When a child loves you for a long, long time, not just to play with, but really loves you, then you become Real." The Rabbit wonders if it hurts to be real and what he would look like after becoming real. The Skin Horse responds, "These things don't matter at all, because once you are Real you can't be ugly, except to people who don't understand."

Becoming *real* is a crucial issue for children who are hurting. It is in the process of *making contact* with these children that we help them become real. Children need to know and believe that once they are real, they can't be ugly (or incomplete or labeled or damaged) except to people who just don't understand. It is an honor for any of us to be a part of this process.

I can't promise that reading this book will make you a great child counselor. I can, however, promise this: If your view of the world of children and the language of childhood grows, as I believe it can, you will be far better equipped to make this world better and safer for children. It has long been my hope and prayer that child counseling and children's issues will become the priority that I believe God intends. If this book can be a small part of that process, I will be truly grateful.

PART ONE

Entering the Child's World

1/ THE CHILD'S WORLD

Know you what it is to be a child? It is to be something very different from the man of today. It is to have a spirit yet streaming from the waters of baptism; it is to believe in love, to believe in loveliness, to believe in belief. —FRANCIS THOMPSON

Spending time with children is delightful! Their perspective of the world is very different from the perspective of grown-ups. Children view the world without the cynicism, suspicion, and mistrust that many people acquire by the time they are adults. That's why it is so refreshing for adults to spend time with children—their simple, untainted outlook is captivating.

Recently, my five-year-old daughter, Renata, reminded me of how innocent and unpretentious children are. Although my family and I live in Texas, we do not have Texan accents, and beyond saying "y'all," we do not use any common southern phrases. That's not true of our friend Becky, who peppers her conversations with regional terms and colloquialisms.

After spending several hours with us one day, Becky gathered her children to leave and called out, "Okay, kids, get your things together. We're *fixin'* to go."

She was holding Renata at the time, and my daughter looked at her with a quizzical expression. Then she asked, quite seriously, "Is your 'to go' broken?" A child's perspective is, indeed, different from that of adults!

Because the outlook, viewpoint, and insights of children are so fundamentally different from those of adults, it's no surprise that the counseling techniques we use with them are not the same as those used for adult therapy. To bring healing to hurting children involves much more than theory or methodology. Healing also involves *empathy*, understanding our clients' world. Part of empathizing with our young clients is learning—or relearning—to see the world as they see it. In their text *Counseling Children,* Charles Thompson and Linda Rudolph aptly note: "How wonderful it would be to return to the carefree, irresponsible days of childhood, with no financial worries, job pressures, societal problems—so the fantasy goes. Unfortunately, childhood is not the carefree, lighthearted, playful time remembered by many adults. Normal child development involves a series of cognitive, physical, emotional, and social changes . . . and the accompanying stress or conflict may lead to learning or behavior problems. . . . Add the stresses and conflict of a rapidly changing society—a society even adults find difficult to understand—and the child's world does not look so appealing."[1]

It is well worth the child counselor's time to consider the nature of the child's world. Think about how a small child perceives an adult—a monster with a small head. That's because adults are so tall, and their heads are so far away. Yet most child counselors greet their little clients while standing up and extending a hand of greeting. Then when the children don't want to leave their parents in the waiting room, counselors wonder why. Wouldn't it be great if training in child counseling insisted that counselors meet the child on his or her level by crouching down in the waiting room? First impressions do make a difference.

As we begin to look at the world of children from their perspective, we as adults also gain a new perspective of our own world.

Developing a fuller and deeper appreciation for the child's world enables us to become better parents and counselors. Consider what one of our U.S. presidents, Herbert Hoover, had to say about children:

> The older I grow, the more I appreciate children. Now, at my eightieth birthday, I salute them again. Children are the most wholesome part of the race, the sweetest, for they are freshest from the hand of God. Whimsical, ingenious, mischievous, they fill the world with joy and good humor. We adults live a life of apprehension as to what they will think of us; a life of defense against their terrifying energy; a life of hard work to live up to their great expectations. We put them to bed with a sense of relief—and greet them in the morning with delight and anticipation. We envy [in] them the freshness of adventure and the discovery of life. In all these ways, children add to the wonder of being alive.[2]

Wouldn't it be wonderful if it did not take us quite so long to arrive at such a fresh and genuine view of children and childhood? If you gain nothing more from reading this book than a broader understanding of the child's world, I will consider it a success. To that end, let's take a look at what the Bible says about children and then examine the world in which today's children grow up.

CHILDREN, THE BIBLE, AND SPIRITUALITY

This is not a book about Christian counseling of children. Rather, it is a book about counseling children by entering their world (which is what Christ did for us), using a basic approach that is compatible with Scripture. Although as a Christian I am strong in some areas and deficient in others, following Christ is not a role I play only while in church or when I am called on to do "Christian counseling." It is—or at least should be—a way of life, a grid through which I view the world around me. This in turn means aligning my counseling approach, techniques, and orientation with God's Word.

As I study Scripture, I find that what it says about children is primarily descriptive. As author and theologian William Hendricks notes: "Children are for real. They are people, even if people in the miniature. If there is but one way to God, they too will come by the message of Christ. It is instructive, and somewhat surprising, what the Bible says about children. Most of the biblical references to children are descriptive of some particular child. . . . An interpretation of biblical references to children would reveal the following conclusions. The childhood of important biblical figures is noted. Instruction of children by precept and example is commanded. There is a great compassion for the young displayed in biblical literature. As a whole, Bible references to children are descriptive rather than theological."[3]

Even though the Bible does not discuss children and childhood at length (and, of course, does not mention counseling children), the Christian counselor should not feel limited in his or her ability to minister to children. Harvard psychiatrist Robert Coles correctly notes that "the entire range of children's mental life can and does connect with their religious and spiritual thinking."[4] Significant truths about child development and child psychology can and should be practiced in treating children. At the same time, scriptural truths about children (for example, that all children are born into sinful humanity) are not recognized in the field of psychology in general.

My basic supposition is that the Bible is all truth but not all truth is in the Bible. While the law of gravity is not explicitly stated in Scripture, I do not have difficulty believing it is truth. Though we must guard against heresy, we must also recognize the validity of some psychological truths that are not mentioned in Scripture. My approach to treating children is based on child-centered play therapy, which is compatible with biblical principles and has been proven effective even though it is not specifically addressed in God's Word.

William Hendricks suggests that "Christian theology should not ignore or deny the insights of developmental psychology as to how much and what types of cognitive and affective experiences a child may appropriate at a given age. . . . Simply stated, developmental psychology can advise the sciences as to how the child learns and at what ages various types of learning usually occur. Christian theology must always insist on defining her own content."[5] Scripture provides us with this content.

The Bible includes several references that show us how the Creator feels about children. Clearly, children hold a special place in God's heart. King David tells us that children are a "heritage from the Lord . . . a reward from him."[6] Jesus instructed his disciples: "Let the little children come to me, and do not hinder them, for the kingdom of heaven belongs to such as these."[7] The Lord further instructs us that in order to enter his kingdom, we must be like little children.[8] The value of childlikeness in the pursuit of God is frequently mentioned in Scripture.[9]

This childlikeness in the approach to relationship with God is illustrated in these comments by Robert Coles, as he discusses children and spirituality:

> It is hard, I think, for those of us whose religious life is merely a part of what we do, one of many commitments, to put ourselves in the shoes of people for whom the phrase "God's presence" has an utter, rock-bottom psychological reality. . . . In such people, I have felt, spirituality makes up the very warp and woof of psychology. . . . God's parenthood [is felt] so deeply and continuously that their every emotional moment seems God-connected. . . . No wonder such children ask so many favors of Him; turn to Him with passion and disappointment; beseech Him openly and in the secrecy of their private moments (not to mention their half-forgotten dreams); rail against Him or, more consciously, obliterate Him with doubt. When [a little girl] told me . . . that "God is in heaven, but He is in my mind, too," she was perhaps making the definitive

analysis of the relationship between young spirituality and young psychology—a fusion. Let others visit God on Sunday for an hour, or have their discreet moments of engagement with Him, spiritual in content, psychologically significant; for her, God is just what she once characterized Him as being, "a companion who won't leave."[10]

THE CHILD'S WORLD IS UNSAFE

Children grow and develop where they feel safe. This is why a major goal for the child counselor should be to provide a healing environment marked by safety and stability. Unfortunately, the world beyond your counseling office is not safe for children. Abuse, neglect, violence, abduction, drugs—the list goes on. To be reminded that a child's world is unsure and unpredictable, we need look no further than the national divorce rate, which continues to be around 50 percent. Since divorce doesn't happen without trauma, how many children are affected? Thousands per day.

What is more, children themselves don't view the world as safe. In fact, they are frightened about what the future holds. In 1995, Barna Research conducted a nationwide, random-sample survey of 1,023 children, with some alarming results. According to the survey: 47 percent of children report dim expectations about life, stating that they anticipate being unhappy in the future; 65 percent think their parents might die; 57 percent fear doing poorly in school; and 54 percent fear they might get AIDS. As a group, children aged ten through thirteen believe they are more likely to become victims of abuse or to die than they are to begin drinking or smoking.[11] Since children do not grow and progress when they do not feel safe, it is no wonder so many children and adolescents in our society are troubled.

The March 1990 issue of *Redbook* featured an article entitled "Are Kids Growing Up Too Fast?" in which Dr. Lee Salk was quoted as saying, "Children are being shortchanged. We hurry them toward independence before they're emotionally ready. We rush them out of childhood."[12] Speeding children into adulthood not only makes this world unsafe for them, but it is also a national tragedy with serious consequences. Television, the nation's leading baby-sitter, contributes to this. Several years ago, the National Coalition on Television Violence reported that the average child will see 52,000 murders and attempted murders on television by age eighteen. When you factor in cable TV and VCR viewing, the number increases to 72,000.[13] Since no efforts to restrict television violence have succeeded, it is likely this number will continue to rise. Dr. Ellen Wartella, research professor at the Institute of Communications Research, says, "Children see world events on the news; they're privy to the lives of adults through television programming and advertising. Even during the Saturday-morning children's hour there are announcements about drugs, alcohol, AIDS. Television *is* changing the nature of childhood."[14]

Redbook goes on to discuss parents who encourage children to grow up ahead of schedule. Fred Rogers of *Mister Rogers' Neighborhood* (who, by the way, is a superb model for a child therapist) commented about the irony of hurrying children into adulthood: "If we really want children to succeed and be productive people, we'll respect them as human beings and let them grow at their own pace." [15] As children feel society's push to grow up too fast, they lose their innocence. Commenting on the current trend to educate preschoolers about sexual abuse, Dr. David Elkind says, "Reading a book about sexual abuse to a three-year-old gives her the message that it's up to her to take care of herself. But there's no way she can protect herself against an adult, and she shouldn't have to think about this danger."[16]

Redbook's report stated that five- and six-year-old girls worry about getting fat, that significant numbers of twelve-year-olds are having sexual intercourse, that pediatricians are reporting stress-related behavior and health problems (elevated cholesterol and blood pressure, headaches, and stomach problems) in children as young as three years old, and that suicide rates among children are increasing at an alarming rate.[17]

In an article in *American Psychologist,* David Finkelhor and Jennifer Dzuiba-Leatherman state, "Children suffer more victimization than do adults, more family violence, and some forms virtually unique to children, such as family abduction."[18] The authors divide child victimization into three typologies: (1) *pandemic victimizations,* which occur to a majority of children in the course of growing up and include sibling assault, physical punishment by parents, theft, vandalism, peer assault, and robbery; (2) *acute victimizations,* which are less frequent and include physical abuse, neglect, and family abduction; and (3) *extraordinary victimizations,* which are even less frequent and include homicide, child-abuse homicide, and nonfamily abduction. The following chart indicates the frequency of these victimizations.

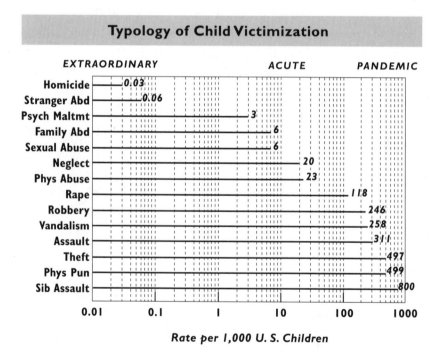

Typology of Child Victimization

EXTRAORDINARY　　　　ACUTE　　　PANDEMIC

Homicide	0.03
Stranger Abd	0.06
Psych Maltmt	3
Family Abd	6
Sexual Abuse	6
Neglect	20
Phys Abuse	23
Rape	118
Robbery	246
Vandalism	258
Assault	311
Theft	497
Phys Pun	499
Sib Assault	800

0.01　　0.1　　1　　10　　100　　1000

Rate per 1,000 U. S. Children

Note: Abd=abduction. Psych Maltmt=psychological maltreatment. Phys=physical. Pun=punishment. Sib=sibling.

Used by permission, David Finkelhor.

CHILDREN NEED COMPASSIONATE COUNSELORS

In the introduction to this book, I suggested that Christian counseling has not given child counseling the importance that I believe it should receive. Within this concern, perhaps we should ask the question: Is there a need for greater mental health interventions for children, or is it such a specialized area that only a handful of experts should be concerned? The secular psychological and psychiatric literature seems to indicate that children are getting short-changed—that is, they are not receiving the kind of therapy that would maximize healing and growth. I have no reason to believe that the situation is much different in the Christian counseling community.

According to the U.S. Office of Technology Assessment, some 12 percent of children living in the United States, or 7.5 million children, are in need of mental health care.[19] In another report, research psychologist June Tuma indicated that from 15 percent (9.5 million) to 19 percent of the nation's children suffer from some level of emotional disturbance.[20] From 3 percent to 8 percent of these are seriously emotionally disturbed children.[21] Additionally, of these children needing treatment, somewhere between 70 and 80 percent are not receiving adequate mental health services.[22] In a survey of children's mental health needs and services conducted in a large metropolitan area, 38.5 percent were found to be at risk of psychiatric disturbance. Only 11 percent of these children received treatment in a mental health setting, fewer than in schools (37 percent) or medical settings (13 percent).[23] Surely, this level of need and available service is similar in cities and towns throughout the nation.

Despite the obvious need and current deficiency in meeting that need, training of child therapists continues to be inadequate. A little more than 10 percent of psychiatrists are committed to working primarily with children, and less than one percent of psychologists have a similar devotion.[24] Tuma reported that the clinical training received by the respondents to a survey she conducted was "less than ideal" preparation for working with children: "The most frequently listed deficiency of the training respondents received was that graduate programs did not train psychologists as child psychologists. . . . There were five categories of deficiencies listed by respondents: too few developmental and clinical child courses, too little child assessment and therapy training, too little experience with children within a variety of settings, too little supervision, and too much emphasis on techniques suitable only for adults."[25]

If the secular mental health community is ill equipped to deal with children's issues, are Christian mental health providers stepping into the gap? Not as well as they should. Although we would like to think that church attendance and involvement in faith-oriented activities ameliorate mental health difficulties, we must be willing to consider that people involved in these very activities sometimes hide emotional and behavioral problems to avoid embarrassment or accusation. Frequently, the Christian community reinforces the idea that Christian children, like their parents, are not supposed to have problems. But if there are emotional and psychological issues that need to be addressed, where do these children go?

Despite feeling the need for more child counselors, I also believe that the situation is improving. Dr. Grant Martin, as guest editor for the first issue of the *Journal of Psychology and Christianity* dedicated to children's issues, writes: "For a variety of reasons, adult theory, research and clinical practice took the majority of our attention during the past 20 years or so. . . . But now, I would submit, we have more clinicians and researchers interested in children. Certainly the needs of children continue to be of urgent importance. As a result, the data base is developing for us to launch a multitude of theoretical musings, research proceedings and clinical findings regarding children."[26] I agree. Certainly, God's grace, as well as his heart for children, should empower those of us already working with children. As we look at the hurting children who come through our doors, we most definitely need that grace—especially if we want to extend God's love to those troubled, struggling children. To help them is to understand them. To understand them is to enter their world.

CHILDREN LONG TO BE HEARD

It is because children yearn to be heard that they sometimes make themselves "heard" through inappropriate and even obnoxious behavior. Consider the phenomenon commonly called "the terrible twos"—when toddlers seem to have an uncanny ability to drive adults crazy. Could this experience result from children's frustration at not being able to express themselves clearly and the dismay over not having adults understand? I think so.

What about the frustration that adults encounter in these circumstances? Surely, you have experienced the perplexity of not understanding a child's demands. Being misunderstood or not being able to figure out a puzzling situation is a common human experience. That is why taking time and making the effort to learn about the child's world are so important; that is why we must view the world through children's eyes.

I discovered this anonymous story, which illustrates the child's unique perspective on the world:

A college professor sat in his living room, totally absorbed in a heavy theological tome. His wife was vacuuming upstairs, and his three-year-old daughter was supposedly happily ensconced in the backyard sandbox. Her screeching "Let me in!" and her simultaneous clawing at the screen door raised her father's eyes from his text.

Annoyed, he called to his wife to let in the "little darling." By now, of course, the child was crying, and the vacuum upstairs bellowed on and on. It was useless! Knowing he had to attend to the brat, the professor slammed down his book, stomped to the back door, opened it abruptly, and spoke in harsh tones: "Well, come in."

The sobbing daughter cried at the top of her lungs, *"No!"*

The father, now completely disgusted, responded too quickly. "All right then, stay out!"

But the little girl, still sobbing, shot back, "No!"

The father now knew he had her locked on the horns of an Aristotelian dilemma. Already tasting pedagogical and parental victory, he smugly said through an artificial grin, "Either you must come in or you must stay out. Which will it be? There is no other alternative . . . *dear.*"

With that, the tears magically disappeared as the child gazed calmly into the summer sky and whispered quietly to her father, "But, Daddy, don't you see the pretty clouds?"

When we invest the time and energy in children, we will be able to see the clouds. But that is not the only benefit. When we enter children's world, we will be better able to minister to them. The care and treatment of children is both a scriptural mandate and a moral imperative. Those in the Christian counseling community, therefore, should not only pursue opportunities for training and growth in the field but also seek to educate colleagues, parents, and those in ministry about the importance and benefits of working with children. I would echo the call of a group of psychiatrists in a professional journal several years ago: "We must communicate with our colleagues who principally treat adults, affirming the fact that most mental disorders have their origins in childhood. This being the case, projected costs for mental health services for children and adolescents should take into account the likely benefits of effective interventions in childhood on later costs to society when these children reach adulthood. . . . We suggest that differences in emphasis, approach, or philosophy—even among child and adolescent psychiatrists—not divert us from working for our common goal; advancing the treatment and well-being of children who suffer from emotional and behavioral disorders."[27]

Advancing the treatment and well-being of children should, in fact, be a goal of the mental health community, and it should be a goal for all helping professionals in the Christian community. Yes, the child's world is sometimes bleak and scary, but we serve a Lord and Creator who "works for the good of those who love him."[28]

We should never give in to discouragement when children with whom we are working do not make the swift progress we hoped for and anticipated. If we have tried, in the love of Christ, to touch their lives by entering their world and ministering to them, positive change of some kind will surely occur. Hurting children cannot encounter the love of Christ without experiencing some healing.

Play is child's work, and this is not a trivial pursuit.

—*ALFRED ADLER*

2/ CHILDREN COMMUNICATE *through* PLAY

Consider the play of the child, and the nature of the Kingdom will be revealed. Christ is that fiddler who plays so sweetly that all who hear him begin to dance. —ROBERT E. NEALE

Would any counselor attempt to establish a therapeutic relationship with a client who spoke a different language? I should hope not! It would be at best foolish and at worst unethical. But consider this: The counselor who employs traditional cognitive therapies might as well be speaking a foreign language when attempting to make contact with a child. The natural medium of communication for adults is verbalization, but for children it is *play*.

Children do communicate through play, whether or not adults can interpret or understand the play. One example is Larry, a former client. When he came to me for therapy, he was six years old and lived with his mother and older sister. His parents had split up because the father had physically abused the children and mother. Larry's primary presenting problem was severe separation anxiety; he simply refused to leave his mother's side. He would not go to school, and he would not sleep alone.

Family therapy had helped the mother and sister cope with their difficult experiences and changes, but Larry continued to have problems. Another therapist had recommended to Larry's mother some behavioral interventions, which failed to help. The books to which she had turned for answers also had offered no solutions.

Although Larry was extremely resistant to entering the playroom at first, he eventually acquiesced. His play was not extraordinary. In fact, he did not speak to me throughout the entire therapeutic process. But after six sessions, his mother reported an almost complete cessation of the separation difficulties. Somewhere within the process of being able to express himself in play, Larry was able to emerge from his fixed place of confusion and hurt and move toward healing and emotional health. It is unlikely that trying to get Larry to talk about his troubles would have done any good; indeed, it was unnecessary since the process of play effectively brought healing.

As Larry's case illustrates, play is the way children process and express their emotional lives. Play is the most important and most natural activity of childhood. Scripture recognizes the importance of play: "The city streets will be filled with boys and girls playing there." [1] This picture of the restoration of Israel prophesied in the Old Testament points to play as a primary and expected enterprise of children. Children need play to develop physically, emotionally, socially, and spiritually.

Dr. Garry Landreth, director of the Center for Play Therapy at the University of North Texas, makes the following comments about children and play: "Children's play can be more fully appreciated when recognized as their natural medium of communication. Children express themselves more fully and more directly through self-initiated spontaneous play than they do verbally because they are more comfortable with play. For children to 'play out' their experiences and feelings is the most natural dynamic and self-healing process in which children can engage." [2]

Counselors who understand the importance of play to children are well on their way to understanding their young clients. For children, play is as natural and spontaneous as any other daily activity. A child needs to play as much as he or she needs to sleep and eat. Nancy Curry and Sara Arnaud discussed three assumptions about child's play in a recent article:

1. Play is a lawful, predictable phenomenon that shows clear developmental regularities, although the degree to which these regularities are expressed is greatly influenced by the child's environment.
2. Play serves to integrate complex cognitive, emotional, and social elements in the child's thinking and behavior.
3. Disturbances in play often reflect disturbances in the child's personality and social functioning.[3]

The counselor who recognizes these dynamics is in a much better position to enter into the child's world and establish the therapeutic relationship necessary to bring healing to the emotionally disturbed child. But when the counselor bombards the child with probing questions or says, "Tell me how you feel about that," the child is at an immediate disadvantage. It simply isn't fair. That is using a language the child doesn't yet speak fluently.

When I conduct training in child counseling and play therapy, I include a simple exercise to make this point. I ask the class or group the following question: "Is there anyone here who would be willing to stand up and share with the rest of us your most embarrassing and traumatizing sexual experience?" Of course, I never have any volunteers. After the nervous laughter has subsided, I make the point: "This is exactly what we are asking the child who has been molested to do when we say, 'Tell me what happened to you.'" This is intrusive at the least and likely retraumatizing and counterproductive. The therapeutic distance and safety of counseling children through the world of play avoids these potential dangers. More than this, however, it honors the child client.

THE IMPORTANCE OF PLAY

Play therapists Charles Schaefer and Kevin O'Connor list several elements typical of play behavior: play is pleasurable; play is intrinsically complete; play is person-dominated rather than object-dominated; play is variable across situations; play is noninstrumental; play does not occur in novel or frightening situations; and play has a flow.[4]

While play is certainly not limited to childhood, it is nevertheless the domain of children. The play of adults is most often marked by seriousness and competition. The play of children, internally and intrinsically motivated, is usually free of the demands that adults place on amusement and recreation. In their book *The Power of Play,* Frank Caplan and Theresa Caplan summarize several unique attributes that children find appealing about play:

1. Play is a voluntary activity by nature. In a world full of requirements and rules, play is refreshing and provides a respite from everyday tension.
2. Play is free from evaluation and judgment by adults. Children are safe to make mistakes without failure and adult ridicule.
3. Play encourages fantasy and the use of imagination. In a make-believe world, children can exercise the need for control without competition.
4. Play increases interest and involvement. Children often have short attention spans and are reluctant to participate in a lower interest, less attractive activity.
5. Play encourages the development of the physical and mental self.[5]

In the face of trauma, children play; it is their way of comforting themselves and bringing some meaning to their experience. Many of us recall the near tragedy in Midland, Texas, some years back, when eighteen-month-old Jessica McClure fell into an abandoned well shaft.[6] The nation was riveted as television news crews chron-icled the rescue. When rescue workers finally made contact with Jessica, she was softly singing to herself in her darkened captivity.

History shows that children of every era have played, frequently to make sense of their tragic world. For example, in the Nazi concentration camp in Auschwitz during the Holocaust of World War II, children played while preparing to die and while witnessing the horrors of war.[7] From the Black Plague of the Middle Ages, we get the child's game "Ring around the Rosie."[8] The "rosie" refers to the red blotches and lesions from contracting the plague; the "pocket full of posies" refers to the flowers for the dead and the practice of putting flowers into the pockets of plague victims to ward off the smell of death; and "ashes, ashes, we all fall down" alludes to the imminent death of the plague-stricken and the practice of burning the bodies of plague victims. Children not only use play to comfort themselves but also need play to make sense of and bring some order to a nonsensical and out-of-control world.

Play forms a valuable bridge between the subjective and the objective, between the concrete and the abstract, and between the nonverbal and the verbal. Psychoanalyst and developmental psy-chologist Dr. Erik Erikson suggested that children use play "to make up for defeats, sufferings and frustrations, especially those resulting from a technically and culturally limited use of language."[9]

Denise and Mark Weston, in their book about play and parenting, summarize the importance of play: "The instinctive method chil-dren use for solving problems and mastering conflicts is *play*. Play is the all-encompassing business of childhood—in it, children take charge of their world, sort out misconceptions, and re-create life experiences. For example, consider the child who is terrified of monsters he believes are lurking at night in the shadows of his bedroom. During the day, this same child draws monsters, pretends he is slaying them and even makes believe he is a monster. Without realizing it he is using various modalities of play to explore, to problem-solve, and eventually to overcome his terrors. He can do the same thing with his behavior problems."[10]

One of the most significant cases in the field of play therapy illustrates these dynamics. Virginia Axline's classic case of Dibs shows a five-year-old child who takes charge of his world, sorts out misconceptions, and re-creates life experiences.[11] Dibs's rather challenging behaviors ranged from mute and almost catatonic episodes in the classroom and at home to violent temper tantrums. He was thought to be mentally retarded or neurologically damaged. Dibs was a puzzle to virtually all of the adults in his life. Axline, however, saw great potential and courage in Dibs. As he began the process of play therapy, he became more emotionally expressive. Positive changes in his home and school behavior emerged as well. Dibs's activities in the playroom became more happy and included positive artwork and songs that he had composed. At the end of his therapy, standard I.Q. testing showed an overall score of 168. Beneath the emotional chaos and pain was a gifted and brilliant child who used the play process to master the world that did not understand him.

THE THEOLOGY OF PLAY

If therapists are to be instruments of healing and restoration for the wounded child, they must be willing and able to enter the child's world rather than force the child to enter the adult world. Scripture reminds us that to enter the kingdom of God, we must be like little children.[12] As a corollary, then, we might say that in counseling children, we need to enter their "kingdom" as "little children." Perhaps this is related to the apostle Paul's reminder: "I have become all things to all men so that by all possible means I might save some."[13]

Entering the child's world is directly related to the concept of empathy, which is arguably the most important tool a counselor has to employ. Empathy, however, should be more than a tool. It should be a lifestyle. In a paper Garry Landreth and I wrote, we asserted that play therapy is "a basic philosophy rather than simply a set of techniques to be applied when the play therapist decides they are needed . . . not a cloak the play therapist puts on when entering the playroom and takes off when leaving but rather . . . a philosophy resulting in attitudes and behaviors for living one's life in relationships with children."[14]

Empathy was, indeed, a lifestyle for Jesus Christ. In fact, the greatest act of empathy in human history was the Incarnation—the God of the universe entering our world. "Your attitude should be the same as that of Christ Jesus: Who, being in very nature God, did not consider equality with God something to be grasped, but made himself nothing, taking the very nature of a servant, being made in human likeness."[15] Could it be that by entering the child's world, we are learning more about Christ and becoming more like him?

Consider how Jesus might have interacted with children. He was obviously a busy man, thronged by people, always being watched. He did not put expectations on people (remember the woman caught in adultery?). Listening and demonstrating compassion were intrinsic to his nature. He called children unto himself. He paused—rather, he stopped—in the midst of the demands of the crowd and the disciples to spend time with some children. I do not envision Jesus giving children just a cursory acknowledgment, an obligatory pat on the head before he went on his way. Jesus must have honored children as he honored adults—with love, acceptance, and understanding. The Creator of children and the child's world took time to enter their world. We should do the same.

As important as entering the child's world is, however, it is not an easy task. Jurgen Moltmann, author of the translated book *Theology of Play,* appropriately suggests: "It is hard to answer a child's questions when we are no longer children. Still the adult world is unconsciously surrounded by the wondering and repressed questions of childhood."[16] It is not merely for the sake of children that we must attempt to enter their world, although this should be reason enough; it is also for what we may learn about ourselves and our Creator.

Children are involved in the process of creation through their play. Children at play create something from nothing. God the Father, Son, and Holy Spirit did the same thing ("In the beginning God created the heavens and the earth").[17] One author stated: "Hence the creation is God's play, a play of His groundless and inscrutable wisdom. It is the realm in which God displays His glory." [18] The creation involved in the process of play should not be a surprise because we are all made in the image of our Creator.[19] There are numerous points of contact between play and creation: "Like the creation, man's games are an expression of freedom and not of caprice, for playing relates to the joy of the Creator with His creation and the pleasure of the player with his game. Like creation, games combine sincerity and mirth, suspense and relaxation. The player is wholly absorbed in his game and takes it seriously, yet at the same time he transcends himself and his game, for it is after all only a game. So he is realizing his freedom without losing it. He steps outside of himself without selling himself. The symbol of the world as God's free creation out of His good pleasure corresponds to the symbol of man as a child of God. This is what Jesus meant when He turned from His disciples to the children: 'Truly, I say to you, whoever does not receive the kingdom of God like a child shall not enter it.'"[20]

CALLED TO PLAY

A call to full mature play has been given in those affirmations that proclaim that the chief end of man is to "Delight in the Lord" and to "Glorify God and enjoy Him forever." Unfortunately, many people ignore these admonitions.

Several thousand years ago, King David was bringing the Ark of God into a city. This was a serious and awesome responsibility.

Only a few months before, a man had died at the hand of the Lord for absentmindedly touching the Ark. Yet it is recorded that David played before the Lord. With much shouting and leaping, he displayed his melodious voice and grace of movement before God. His wife, and probably most of those who observed him, thought he was being irreverent and disapproved of his actions. But the Lord approved. He made David's wife barren for the rest of her days and blessed David (see 2 Samuel 6:21-23).

Two hundred years ago, when the church still sponsored the education of children, the following rule was created: "We prohibit play in the strongest terms. . . . The students shall rise at five o'clock in the morning, summer and winter. . . . The student shall be indulged with nothing which the world calls play. Let this rule be observed with strictest nicety; for those who play when they are young will play when they are old."

Unfortunately, the church and school were successful, and the children could not play when they grew into maturity. They could not permit themselves to be "irreverent." And like David's wife, their lives were made barren by the Lord. Despite a clear call, man has refused to delight in and enjoy His God.

—Robert Neale[21]

The therapist who requires a child to talk and verbalize emotions does an injustice to the young client. The apostle Paul tells us, "When I was a child, I talked like a child, I thought like a child, I reasoned like a child. When I became a man, I put childish ways behind me."[22] As an adult, a husband, a father, and a trained counselor, I have "put away childish things." My child clients, however, have not. The children I work with still talk, think, and reason as children. If I want to connect with them on a therapeutic level, I cannot forget this.

The therapist who insists on using traditional "talk therapy" with children is saying to them: "I am unwilling to enter your world of communication. I am an expert, and I know best. You must leave your world of play and come up to my level of communication and interaction. The responsibility is yours." But whose responsibility is it to meet the other in a therapeutic relationship? The counselor's, of course.

THE DEVELOPMENTAL IMPORTANCE OF PLAY

Psychologist Charles Schaefer, cofounder of the Association for Play Therapy, asserts that "one of the most firmly established principles of psychology is that play is a process of development for the child."[23] According to Piaget, play provides an "emotional laboratory" for children and is crucial to their development.[24] Play is where children learn about themselves, others, and the world around them. While developmental stages may vary according to theory and culture, the importance and inclusion of play as an element of developmental growth is universal.

The preoperational and concrete nature of children's cognition is incompatible with the formal operations of adult therapy. Children under the age of eleven or twelve do not have the mastery of language and abstract thinking necessary to process and verbalize thoughts. The developmental sophistication necessary for the abstract reasoning on which most verbal therapies are built is simply beyond most children. As Maria Piers and Genevieve Landau note, "What emotionally sturdy children do naturally—master fears through imaginative playing—is often difficult or impossible for severely troubled children to accomplish. Their anxiety may be so great as to paralyze their imaginations and inhibit their capacity to play." [25]

Piaget's research suggests that children are not developmentally able to engage in abstract reasoning until the age of eleven.[26] This suggests that it is difficult, if not impossible, to reach children's emotions through verbal communication techniques. Verbalization is symbolic and abstract in contrast to the concreteness of the child's world. *Play may be the only avenue children have to communicate the concrete nature of their world.* This was certainly the case for Dibs. His counselor, Virginia Axline, stated, "A therapist who is too literal-minded and who cannot tolerate a child's flight into fantasy without ordering it into adult meaningfulness might well be lost at times."[27] Perhaps this parallels Christ's warning: "Though seeing, they do not see; though hearing, they do not hear or understand."[28] Like the Lord's listeners, we sometimes miss the types and metaphors of a child's play.

Play is preoperational. In Piaget's theory, preoperational thought is that stage in which representational skills are acquired. Dr. Kevin O'Connor details several functions of play. It is (1) *biological,* such as hand-eye movement, expending of energy, and kinesthetic stimulation; (2) *intrapersonal,* including a child's need for function, mastery over situations, and mastery over conflict; (3) *interpersonal,* including a child's practice of separation and individuation, and learning of social skills; and (4) *sociocultural,* where children learn about culture and the roles of those around them.[29]

The preoperational nature of play and childhood cannot be overemphasized. When I think about preoperational thought in terms of development, I find it helpful to look at the term *preoperational.* In our technologically modern world, we talk about the concept of "operationalizing" a term or process. This means defining concepts in terms of identifiable and repeatable operations. This is fundamentally what occurs when a child learns the representational skills necessary for cognitive and verbal communication.

Play and language, however, are relative opposites. They are contrasting forms of representation. In cognitive verbalization, children must translate thoughts into the accepted medium (talk). The inherent limitation is that children must fit their world into this existing medium. Play and fantasy, however, do not carry this limitation. Children can create without the restriction of making their creation understandable. Play, therefore, does not lend itself to operationalism. It is *preoperational.*

The preoperational nature of play is detailed in Lawrence Frank's writings about the function of play in personality development. He suggests that play is one way children learn what cannot be taught through other means: "We might say that in play the child is learning to learn: he is discovering how he can come to terms with the world, cope with life's tasks, master various skills, techniques and symbolic processes in his way; then, having gained confidence in himself and his capacity to relate himself to the world, as he sees and feels it, he is ready to learn other tasks and accept less congenial patterns."[30]

The importance of play in the developmental process for children cannot be emphasized enough. The exploratory value of play behavior and experiences is key to this process. Landreth explains this further: "[Play] is the way [children] explore and orient themselves to the actual world of space and time, of things, animals, structures, and people. By engaging in the process of play, children learn to live in our symbolic world of meanings and values, at the same time exploring and experimenting and learning in their own individual way."[31] In play, children explore their creation and from this exploration discover their Creator.

Piaget further noted that play bridges the gap between concrete experience and abstract thought and described the corresponding importance of play's symbolic function.[32] The symbolic nature of play and play therapy is necessary for growth to occur. Symbolism is the beginning of faith, which is crucial to the development of spiritual awareness. Scripture tells us that faith is "being sure of what we hope for and certain of what we do not see."[33] Faith is initiated and develops within children through the symbolic function of play.

According to James Fowler, faith development is marked by the activity of the imagination. He states that "imagination is extremely productive of long-lasting images and feelings (positive and negative) that later, more stable and self-reflective valuing and thinking have to order and sort out. This is the stage of first self-awareness."[34] Play, it would seem, is a primary vehicle for this symbolic and imagination-filled exploration. Fowler goes on to assert that the school-age child develops faith in the "Mythical-Literal" stage, "in which the person begins to take on for him- or herself the stories, beliefs and observances that symbolize belonging to his or her community." [35] This parallels the interpersonal and intrapersonal functions of play noted above. Indeed, the numerous scriptural admonishments to have the faith of little children remind us that a child's faith development should be not only encouraged but also emulated.[36] As author Harry Van Belle says, "Never again can we experience the unconditional trust we feel during childhood. During the first twelve years or so we learn to rely on the constancy and solidity of our physical world; for example, we come to know that the world we cannot see in the dark is the same world we see when the light is on. During this time we also learn to have confidence in our own abilities. We gain the assurance that we are able to do what is expected of us, and we believe that those in whose care we are entrusted are reliable. Finally, if conditions are favorable we develop a basic trust in a providing God who surrounds the whole of our existence."[37]

But what if those people entrusted with a child's care are not reliable and the conditions of a child's upbringing are not favorable? This is where the counselor has the opportunity to provide a child with a therapeutic experience that honors children's natural medium of development and communication—*the world of play*.

If a child is to keep alive his inborn sense of wonder, he needs the companionship of at least one adult who can share it, rediscovering with him the joy, excitement and mystery of the world we live in. —*RACHEL CARSON*

PART TWO

Play As Therapy

3/ PLAY THERAPY
AS *a*
FOUNDATIONAL TREATMENT

*Enter into children's play and you will find the place where their
minds, hearts, and souls meet.* —VIRGINIA AXLINE

Mary Ann's case was challenging. Before the nine-year-old was
referred to the counseling agency where I worked, she had a long
history of mental health treatment. She had been sexually abused
by multiple perpetrators, treated in several different residential
settings, and was already receiving psychiatric intervention. Mary
Ann was considered seriously disturbed. She would often bark like
a dog and bite people. Her bizarre behavior had led doctors to treat
her with strong antipsychotic medication.

The staff members at our agency took a different view of her
"psychotic" behavior. Since Mary Ann had been brutally victim-
ized, why should it seem strange for her to do whatever was
necessary to keep people away from her? Her barking and biting
were indeed peculiar, but they served a useful purpose—they
protected her. We believed that although Mary Ann was obviously

a wounded and struggling girl with a poor diagnosis and prognosis, she needed a different treatment approach.

I cannot tell you that play therapy instantly cured Mary Ann. And I cannot report that play therapy was all she needed. But I can say this—it worked where nothing else had. Mary Ann regressed and acted out in the playroom. She was allowed to express herself in ways that she had never experienced. She played out her anxieties and victimizations, and she got better. Her acting-out behaviors subsided, and she began to interact with people in a more healthy, acceptable way.

After several months of play therapy, Mary Ann's psychiatric medications were discontinued. Her foster-care placement remained stable. Eventually, she was reunited with her mother. Yes, Mary Ann continued to need considerable intervention. Behavioral management, parent training, and group therapy were all part of her treatment program. None of these had any effect prior to play therapy, but once she began to experience the healing power of play, other components of her treatment started to help as well. Was it magic? No. It was essentially a matter of allowing a traumatized child to process unthinkable horrors in her own way, in her own time, and in her own language.

Although I strongly believe play therapy is the most appropriate foundational treatment modality for helping children, I know it is not a panacea for all childhood problems. After all, children's issues are often complex and multidimensional and therefore require a multidisciplinary approach. It is, however, my opinion that the basic principles of play therapy provide a strong foundation from which to minister to children. As I noted in the introduction, I am more interested in the process of making contact and building relationships with children than in providing a formula or technique for treating specific problems. It is the curative environment of play therapy—healthy relationships, safety, freedom to express emotions—that brings healing and restoration to our clients.

I was reminded of this a few years ago when I presented a paper at the annual conference of the Association for Play Therapy in Nashua, New Hampshire. The conference is always held in October, and that year, I spent a day touring the White Mountains. The fall colors were spectacular. As I soaked in the incredible hues bursting from the foliage, I thought about how the changing colors provided a metaphor of the play therapy process. When the trees change color, it is more than a botanical process; it is evidence of the Creator's design. God Almighty has placed in these trees something that responds to colder temperatures by changing the color of the leaves. When the environment changes, the trees change. In the same way, when we provide an environmental change for children through a play therapy experience, they will grow, change, and be transformed. It is a natural response to a new environment. The process by which creation grows and heals has been established by the Designer of all things.

Before examining counseling through play more closely, I should make a comment about the appropriate age limits for play therapy. Some therapists have used play therapy with adolescents and adults as well as children, but I generally work in the playroom with children between the ages of three and eleven. I have occasionally used play therapy with toddlers younger than three, and although it is challenging to understand their speech, it is a wonderful experience. I have also worked with teenagers in the playroom, particularly those who have been traumatized and are experiencing developmental arrest.

WHAT IS PLAY THERAPY?

Let's define what we mean by play therapy. Many counselors who work with children call their approach *play therapy* because toys and games are a part of the therapeutic process. I believe, however, that providing traditional, cognitive "talk" therapy and making toys available to children do not constitute play therapy.

Garry Landreth defines play therapy as a "dynamic interpersonal relationship between a child and a therapist trained in play therapy procedures who provides selected play materials and facilitates the development of a safe relationship for the child to fully express and explore self (feelings, thoughts, experiences, and behaviors) through the child's natural medium of communication, play."[1] Let's take a closer look at the specific elements contained in this definition.

1. The play therapy relationship is dynamic and interpersonal. In their book *Counseling and Children,* Walter Byrd and Paul Warren note that children can receive a "corrective emotional experience" from an interpersonal relationship with a caring counselor.[2] Play therapy should be primarily a child-centered process, with the therapeutic dynamics determined and orchestrated by the child. What other opportunity does the emotionally wounded child have to experience control and empowerment? A child-centered approach is nonintrusive. It allows for therapeutic distance and safety and thus enhances the relationship between therapist and client. The process should be active as opposed to passive, with the therapist exhibiting verbal and nonverbal involvement. Although the child takes the lead, the therapist must remain active and engaged.

2. The counselor should be trained in play therapy procedures. While this might seem to be an obvious point, we all know counselors who have attended a brief workshop on a therapeutic approach and then immediately began to incorporate the technique into their practice. Although their training and knowledge in the new modality is limited, the counselors readily integrate it into their work with clients. This is not only inappropriate, but it may touch the ethical issue of practicing outside the scope of one's expertise. It is my hope that this book will encourage counselors working with children to seek opportunities for thorough training in play therapy. There are numerous workshops available in play therapy and an increasing number of universities providing training in the field.[3]

Jesus Christ gave a wonderful model for training workers of all kinds, and those in the helping professions can especially benefit from it. Christ *taught* his disciples, *modeled* ministry for them, *released* them to minister, and *supervised* them. Training in play therapy optimally includes detailed training, practical modeling (including live demonstrations, role-playing, and laboratory practicum experiences), and supervised therapy sessions. Ideally, play therapy training should include live supervision and videotaping. Therapists hone their skills much more effectively when they can observe themselves on video. While it is preferable to have a highly technical setup (one-way mirrors, studio-quality audiovisual equipment, etc.), a camcorder mounted on a tripod in the corner of the room is certainly adequate.

3. *The play therapist should provide selected play materials.* It is not sufficient to provide a random collection of toys. Landreth reminds us that toys should be *selected,* not collected, and that play materials should be consistent with the rationale for therapy and should therefore contribute to accomplishing the therapy's objectives.[4] (We will discuss which toys to include in chapter 5.)

4. *The play therapist must facilitate the development of a safe relationship.* Facilitating does not mean initiating. Children who have been traumatized or are experiencing emotional turmoil feel disempowered and out of control. This is evident in their behavior and affect, which usually have led to the referral for counseling in the first place. Since few children refer themselves and are thus compelled to participate in a process that can be anxiety provoking, allowing them to lead builds confidence and self-esteem. The inappropriate acting-out behaviors of the hurting child will commonly subside as their needs for safety, security, and empowerment are met in the play therapy environment.

5. *Play therapy provides the opportunity for the child to express and explore self more fully.* Exploration of self should be a large part of any therapeutic process. This is not meant in a narcissistic way. Rather, a true self-exploration is a process that should lead a person to his or her Creator. We are made in the image of God. But when we lose that foundation of our self-image, we become susceptible to emotional and behavioral difficulties. The apostle Paul tells us that "since the creation of the world God's invisible qualities . . . have been

clearly seen, being understood from what has been made, so that men are without excuse."[5] Since the truth of God is implanted in his creation, to deny him is to deny part of ourselves. To deny a part of ourselves is repression, and with repression comes some level of delusion because we must take on a false belief to fill the void of that repression. Disbelief and the resulting inaccurate self-image contribute to pathology. Self-exploration, then, leads people to the Creator and ultimately to wholeness and health.

The responses of the counselor become a key element in this process. Play—including the reflection of both content and feeling—during the counseling session should be tracked by the therapist. The children who are brought to our offices frequently need to have their feelings—not to mention their existence as human beings—acknowledged and affirmed. Landreth notes that it is the therapist's responsibility to communicate four messages to the child: "I'm here. I hear you. I understand. And I care."[6]

6. *Play therapy enables children to use their own natural medium of communication—play.* "Given the opportunity, children will play out their feelings and needs in a manner or process of expression which is similar to that of adults. The dynamics of expression and vehicles for communication are different for children, but the expressions (fear, satisfaction, anger, happiness, frustration, contentment) are similar to that of adults."[7] If we do not understand children, perhaps it is because we are not speaking the same language. Jesus Christ posed the question to his disciples, "Why is my language not clear to you?" Then he answered: "Because you are unable to hear what I say."[8] Children struggle with the same frustration: "Why can't [won't] you understand me?" To understand, we must converse in their language, which is play.

One reason play therapy is so effective is that it honors children by meeting them on a "level playing field." Children lack the cognitive skills and abstract verbal abilities to communicate at an adult level. If the counseling relationship is to be truly egalitarian, the counselor should make the move. Child psychologist Haim

Ginott said that "a therapeutic relationship can be established and maintained only if the therapist understands the child's communication."[9] I might amend this slightly to say that "a therapeutic relationship can be established and maintained only if the child feels understood in the process of communication."

A BRIEF HISTORY OF PLAY

The use of play in the therapeutic treatment of children extends back to the first attempt at child psychotherapy, with Sigmund Freud's case of Little Hans.[10] Freud did not work directly with the five-year-old boy, but he advised Hans's father about different ways to respond to him. Freud used the father's notes about Hans's play as a basis for interpretation and counsel. Play was not directly used in the course of psychotherapy until 1919, when Hermine Hug-Hellmuth used play.[11] Landreth noted that Hug-Hellmuth called "attention to the difficulty of applying methods of adult therapy to children. It seems that the same problem we face now existed then, that of attempting to apply established methods with adults to children and discovering that child analysis was distinct and different from adult psychoanalysis."[12]

Hug-Hellmuth believed that play was essential for treating children. It was Anna Freud and Melanie Klein, however, who wrote a good deal about the use of play in psychotherapy. Anna Freud used play primarily as a means of forming a solid therapeutic alliance with the child client.[13] Melanie Klein believed that play could be used as a substitute for verbalization, replacing the psychoanalytic technique of free association.[14] The work of these three therapists dramatically changed the approach to working with children in psychotherapy.

The next trend in play therapy came in the late 1930s, when David Levy developed his approach called "release play therapy," a structured play therapy modality.[15] Kevin O'Connor suggested that counseling children from this perspective included three elements: a psychoanalytic framework, at least a partial belief in the cathartic value of play, and the active role of the therapist in determining the course and focus of the therapy.[16] Gove Hambidge went further with Levy's work: "While Levy made available materials that would facilitate re-enactment of a traumatic event, Hambidge directly re-created the event or anxiety-producing life situation in play to aid the child's abreaction."[17]

Jesse Taft, Frederick Allen, and Clark Moustakas adapted Otto Rank's philosophy of relationship therapy in their work with children and play.[18] The focus of relationship-based play therapy is the healing power of the therapeutic connection between the child and the counselor. "Through therapy, the child is given a chance to establish a deep, concerned relationship with a therapist in a setting that, simply because of the basic therapeutic agreement, is safer than any he or she will ever experience again."[19] Explanation and interpretation on the part of the therapist is not emphasized in this approach, which instead focuses on building the relationship and allowing the child to direct the play process.

In the 1940s, Virginia Axline adopted the person-centered work of Carl Rogers, applying a nondirective approach to play therapy.[20] Her approach is based on the belief that children have a natural striving for growth and that emotional or behavioral difficulties stem from a disturbance of this growth process. Axline stated, "A play experience is therapeutic because it provides a secure relationship between the child and the adult, so that the child has the freedom and room to state himself in his own terms, exactly as he is at that moment in his own way and in his own time."[21]

The field of play therapy has continued to grow over the last several decades, bringing forth numerous approaches, including child-centered play therapy, ecosystemic play therapy, Adlerian play therapy, cognitive-behavioral play therapy, Jungian play therapy, and developmental play therapy.[22]

Play therapy has been shown to be a potent treatment modality for a wide range of children's issues. "Play therapy has been demonstrated to be effective with children of all diagnostic categories except the completely autistic and the out-of-contact schizophrenic." [23] A large and increasing body of literature supports the efficacy of this approach. The Center for Play Therapy at the University of North Texas is a clearinghouse of play therapy literature, featuring more than two thousand journal articles and books about the field. The center publishes a bibliography of play therapy literature for clinicians or academicians.[24] Additionally, some colleagues and I recently published a book digesting play therapy research and case studies, ranging from acting-out children to withdrawn children. The book is a compilation of empirical and anecdotal evidence of the efficacy of play therapy.[25]

APPROACHES TO PLAY THERAPY

As noted, various counseling theories have been applied to the practice of play therapy. Let's briefly examine the three leading approaches—psychoanalytic, Jungian, and child-centered—and also explore directive versus nondirective approaches.

Psychoanalytic play therapy finds its roots in Sigmund Freud's case of Little Hans, as mentioned earlier. Anna Freud and Melanie Klein adapted the psychoanalytic approach to their work with children. Psychiatrist Aaron Esman, in his chapter about the psychoanalytic approach in the *Handbook of Play Therapy*, notes that Anna Freud used play as a means of promoting children's verbalizations, while Klein believed that children's play was equivalent to the free association of adult clients.[26] Esman asserts that Anna Freud's approach has dominated the psychoanalytic approach to play therapy in this country.

As with psychoanalytic work with adults, play therapy with children is based on the analysis of resistance and transference.[27] The role of the therapist is both to observe and to participate. The process moves from observation of the child's play and an establishment of the therapeutic alliance to more verbal interactions between the therapist and client, concentrating on the analysis and interpretation of metaphors in the child's play and daydreams.

The Jungian approach to play therapy is based on the work of Carl Jung and his personality theory of the ego, the personal unconscious, and the collective unconscious.[28] Jung referred to the primary organizing principle of the collective unconscious as the self. Jungian play therapist John Allan asserts that for the self to grow and for the ego to mature, a form of symbolic expression is necessary, and for children, this occurs through play.[29]

The Jungian play therapist is also both observer and participant, maintaining an "analytical attitude to reflect on and comment about the psychological issues with which the child is struggling."[30] John Allan and Keith Brown note that transference and counter-transference issues are key and that Jungian therapists should be aware of their own psyche during the play sessions and comment on the feelings within the course of play.[31] Interpretation is considered important and is facilitated by comments and questions by the therapist.

The child-centered approach is based on the client-centered work of Carl Rogers and was developed primarily by Virginia Axline.[32] The premise is that we all have within ourselves the ability to solve our own problems and that we have within us an innate striving for mature versus immature behavior (self-actualization). When this innate drive is thwarted, resulting in resistance and anxiety, an imbalance occurs. The goal of child-centered play therapy is to facilitate the resolution of this imbalance so growth can continue. The establishment of the therapeutic relationship and the communication of core conditions (genuineness, acceptance, and unconditional positive regard) within therapy promote this process. Play is used with children because it is recognized as the child's natural medium of communication.[33]

The role of the child-centered therapist is to facilitate the client's growth, and as such, the counselor does not lead or take responsibility for the direction of the play. Interpretation is not seen as a necessary condition for the child's growth. The child-centered therapist is not, however, a passive observer; rather, he or she actively facilitates the child's self-exploration and self-direction through reflection, encouragement, and involvement at the lead of the child. Garry Landreth summarizes the philosophy of this approach:

> The child, and not the problem, is the point of focus. When the focus is on the child's problem, the play therapist may lose sight of the child. Diagnosis is not necessary because this is not a prescriptive approach. The therapist does not vary the approach to meet demands based on a specific referral problem. The relationship that develops and the creative forces this relationship releases in the child generate the process of change and growth for the child. It is not preparation for change. Whatever develops in the child was already there. The therapist does not create anything. The therapist only helps to release what already exists in the child. In this process, the child is responsible for self and is quite capable of exercising that responsibility through self-direction, resulting in more positive behavior. In child-centered play therapy, the relationship, not the use of toys or the interpretation of behavior, is the key to growth. Therefore, the relationship is always focused on the present, living relationship.[34]

My approach is primarily child centered. While I do not see Rogerian theory as necessarily compatible with Scripture, I am attracted to the focus of child-centered play therapy. While all approaches to play therapy with children generally recognize that play is the natural medium of communication for children, that doesn't mean all approaches are child centered. The focus of child therapists, regardless of their theoretical approach, should be on the child rather than on the nature of the problem. What a child is capable of becoming is more important than what he or she has been in the past. "When we focus on the problem, we lose sight of the person of the child, and in the process communicate to the child that his or her problem is more important."[35]

I am less concerned about techniques and even theoretical approaches than I am about honoring children and making contact with them through the world of play. Direction and interpretation by the therapist have potential to take the focus off the child. Focus on evaluation, diagnosis, interpretation, and direction, while not inappropriate in itself, often serves to meet the needs of the therapist rather than the child. It is not that I am opposed to various child and play therapy techniques that I do not employ; I am opposed to prescriptive approaches that refuse to recognize the uniqueness of each child and directive techniques that impose the expertise of the therapist at the expense of the child.

Children deserve the same regard that adult clients do—to be recognized as children of God. God deals with each of us as individuals in relationship to him and does not use techniques. This is why we cannot put a theological box around his interactions with his people. A "technique" that honors this recognition or is led by the Holy Spirit is more important than counseling theory. Working with children, remember, is more than theory and technique—it is a way of being and relating to God's children.

THE BENEFITS OF PLAY THERAPY

Dr. Charles Schaefer asserts that "play has the power not only to facilitate normal child development but also to alleviate abnormal behavior." [36] Research confirms that children use play to develop language, cognitive, motor, and social skills. If play is one of the primary means by which children view and make sense of their world, then it follows that play should be beneficial in understanding and processing emotional pain and hindrances. Schaefer lists many therapeutic factors in the play therapy process:

1. *Overcoming resistance.* Play draws children, involuntary clients, into a working alliance.
2. *Communication.* Play is the natural medium of self-expression.

3. *Mastery.* Play satisfies children's need to explore and master the environment.

4. *Creative thinking.* Play encourages children to improve problem-solving skills.

5. *Catharsis.* In play, children can release intense emotions that have been difficult or impossible to confront.

6. *Abreaction.* Children can process and assimilate trauma by reliving it with an appropriate expression of emotion.

7. *Role-play.* Children have the opportunity to try out alternative behaviors.

8. *Fantasy.* Play enhances the use of the child's imagination to make sense of and overcome painful reality.

9. *Metaphoric teaching.* Children can experience adaptive solutions for their conflicts and fears through metaphor.

10. *Relationship enhancement.* Play facilitates a positive therapeutic relationship.

11. *Enjoyment.* Children fundamentally enjoy play.

12. *Mastering developmental fears.* Repeated play experiences help reduce anxiety and fear through systematic desensitization.

13. *Game play.* Games assist children in socialization and developing ego controls.[37]

Children recognize the uniqueness of the play therapy relationship. They know that the playroom is a special place and that the play therapist is a special person. I have had children tell me that the playroom is the one place where they can be themselves. Children also know what they need in the playroom. A colleague of mine had a graphic session in which a child "performed" a heart transplant. That was more than just play. It involved the child's communicating to the therapist what he needed. His heart had been damaged, figuratively, and needed to be repaired.

The play therapy process undoubtedly benefits the child. My

experience supports what Garry Landreth states that play therapy accomplishes for children. He asserts that play therapy helps the child

1. Develop a more positive self-concept
2. Assume greater self-responsibility
3. Become more self-directing
4. Become more self-accepting
5. Become more self-reliant
6. Engage in self-determined decision making
7. Experience a feeling of control
8. Become sensitive to the process of coping
9. Develop an internal source of evaluation
10. Become more trusting of self[38]

Play therapy's primary benefit is that it provides an experience of growth and healing in an environment that promotes these experiences rather than an environment that makes cognitive or psychic demands on the child. To be able to experience such an environment with a caring and supportive adult enables the child to discover and nurture internal strengths. This not only allows the wounded child to process conflict and turmoil within play therapy but also equips the child with coping skills and self-control, which can be translated into daily functioning.

THE HEALING POWER OF THE RELATIONSHIP

I have already stated that my primary concern is the *process* of child counseling rather than specific techniques or diagnostic prescriptions. The foundation of this process is relationship. *The alliance between the child and the therapist is the single most creative force in healing.* The Christian life is all about relationship. It is our relationship with the Son of God that brings about salvation and healing. We are called into relationship with other Christians. It is likely that most Christians reading this book came into relationship with God through another person, someone committed to prayer and evangelism through relationship. While the play materials used in play therapy are important, they are secondary. Any interpretation of metaphors in the play, while they are intriguing, are also subordinate to the therapist-child relationship.

Scripture has many reminders of the importance of relationship. The "one another" passages ("love one another," "encourage one another," "bear one another's burdens," "be hospitable to one another") remind us that relationship should be present, living, and active. As Garry Landreth states in *Play Therapy: The Art of the Relationship*, the therapist–child relationship should focus on

person	*rather than*	problem
present	*rather than*	past
feelings	*rather than*	thoughts or acts
understanding	*rather than*	explaining
accepting	*rather than*	correcting
child's direction	*rather than*	therapist's instruction
child's wisdom	*rather than*	therapist's knowledge[39]

Let's take a closer look at each of these aspects:

■ *Focus on the person rather than the problem.* This is in stark contrast to the medical model, which focuses on pathology. There is a significant difference between child counseling that emphasizes diagnosis and prescription, and the process-oriented, child–centered approach. The prescriptive approach is, by nature, problem focused. Clark Moustakas, in his book *Psychotherapy with Children*, suggests that most counseling relationships with children are problem centered.[40] This ought not to be so.

■ *Focus on the present rather than the past.* This is not to deny that a child's past is crucial to the presenting issue. Since children have the opportunity to actualize and feel the empowerment of leading the process, they can take the fantasy of play into the past. It is the therapist's task to *be with* the child in the present. It is difficult to attend fully to a client in the present if the therapist is focused on the past. As much as we would like to change the past of a child who has been traumatized, we cannot. The healing that God provides for a client does not change the past; rather, it changes the client's view of the past and his or her response to it.

■ *Focus on feelings rather than thoughts or acts.* Issues will come and go in the lives of the children and adults we treat. How people respond to these issues, particularly the emotional response, needs to be a focus in the treatment process. As children attempt to make sense of what has occurred in their lives, it is their emotional response that will dictate their behavior. It is, of course, behavioral concerns and problems that bring most children to therapy, so looking to the emotional need expressed in the behavior is crucial.

■ *Focus on understanding rather than explaining.* When clients of any age are experiencing difficulty, they need an empathic ear, not a problem solver. In my experience as a marriage counselor, I have found that husbands are frequently so focused on giving solutions for challenges faced by their wives that they forget to express care through listening. To communicate understanding to a child is a great expression of love and care. When I train counselors, I often remind them that it is more important that their clients feel understood than it is for them to understand their clients. That is, we may not fully comprehend the roots of an issue or all of the ramifications, but if we can make the client feel understood, healing will follow. This is a helpful reminder for me when I am struggling to figure out what a child's play might mean. If I can communicate those four messages mentioned earlier—"I'm here. I hear you. I understand. And I care"—the child will feel understood.

■ *Focus on accepting rather than correcting.* Children are regularly corrected by parents and teachers, and they do not need this experience in therapy. As therapists, we may need to educate parents about their style of correction, but it is equally important to train parents to be more accepting. Unconditional acceptance is what we have received from God, and this kind of acceptance has incredible healing power in the counseling relationship.

■ *Focus on the child's direction and wisdom rather than the therapist's instruction and knowledge.* When we trust children's wisdom to take the counseling process where they believe it should go, we provide them with a growing experience. What's more, therapists might hinder the counseling experience and even damage clients by foisting our "knowledge" on them. This brings to mind 1 Corinthians 1:27: "God chose the foolish things of the world to shame the wise; God chose the weak things of the world to shame the strong." In their innocence and simplicity, children have important things to teach us. A child's direction and perspective may appear to be foolish, but it is through opportunity and experimentation that a child matures and develops.

One laugh of a child will make the holiest day more sacred still.
—R. G. INGERSOLL

4/ WORKING *with* PARENTS

Parenting isn't for cowards. —JAMES DOBSON

Before we discuss the specific dynamics of a play therapy session, let's focus on the other important people in the child's life—the parents or guardians. In traditional therapy, the parents of clients may be only indirectly involved or not involved at all. In play therapy, however, parents will inevitably be a part of the process. After all, it is frequently parents who initiate counseling, drop off and pick up the child, and pay the fees. Furthermore, most parents want to monitor the progress of their child's therapy.

It is important to involve parents in the course of treatment. Parents who do not participate in the counseling process often become reluctant to continue because they feel uninformed. You may be a talented child therapist, and you may be successfully working with your client, but your goals will be undermined—or stopped altogether—if you intentionally or unintentionally leave out parents. If you can convince parents or guardians that they are

51

partners in the counseling process, you will sharply increase the likelihood of treatment success.

Play therapist Terry Kottman writes: "Parents are invaluable sources of information about the child's developmental history and interactional patterns. They can also provide support for changes the child makes during play therapy. As the child learns new ways of viewing self and others and new behaviors, her or his parent(s) can help the child apply these concepts and actions to situations other than the play session. Quite frequently the parent(s) also need to change the way they view themselves and their children and the way they behave in their interactions with one another and with their children."[1]

An important point needs to be made here. While consultation with parents and gathering information about the child are necessary, they should not change the general approach to working with the child. Regardless of the presenting problem, children still communicate through play. As Garry Landreth says, "No attempt is made to match a certain technique with a specific problem. The therapist's belief in the child is unwavering regardless of the specific problem."[2] Thus, the therapist can honor the child through the intervention, as opposed to applying a prescription for a particular diagnosis.

INITIAL MEETING WITH PARENTS

When a child has been referred for counseling, my first session is always with the parents, for intake purposes. Parents are most often the best source of information about a child's presenting problem, developmental history, and relational patterns. It is helpful to obtain a detailed history from the parents, along with feedback from the child's school, to gain a complete picture of the presenting issue(s). This information is important for reporting, making an accurate diagnosis for insurance, and assessing the possible need for referral. In these days of increasing litigation, it is also advisable to have prudently gathered thorough background information.

At one of the university clinics where I see clients, we routinely use assessment instruments, including the Child Behavior Checklist, the Parenting Stress Index, and some type of self-concept or self-esteem inventory such as Piers-Harris Children's Self-Concept Scale or Joseph Pre-School and Primary Self-Concept Screening Test.[3] I have also used the Family Environment Scale and the Porter Parental Acceptance Scale for further assessment.[4] Although I use such instruments primarily for research purposes, these and other psychological-evaluation tools can be helpful in diagnosis and treatment planning. See appendix A for addresses and lists of publishers from which you can order some of these assessment tools.

One danger in gathering this information is that it is tempting to rely on the assessment data rather than to use clinical skill and intuition. Remember, however, that it is not the diagnosis, treatment modality, or theoretical approach that brings healing to a client; it is the therapeutic relationship. It's possible that the "hard and fast" data could be an impediment to the therapeutic relationship, since most therapists have an inherent tendency to define and interpret. What's more, this tendency is frequently reinforced inside and outside the therapeutic community. Counselors and psychologists are constantly asked to interpret and evaluate a person's emotional and behavioral patterns. So it is only natural to enter the counseling situation with preconceived notions and interpretations based on the information we have gathered. This is a mistake, and it isn't fair to clients. Consider the following example:

> For two consecutive sessions, Paula busily arranged all the chairs in a tight cluster, bound them together with string, and covered the entire construction with paper. She left a small opening and crawled in and out with some nervous giggling. Armed with the knowledge of the pregnancy [of Paula's mother], the therapist "understood" the play as a symbolic acting out of fantasies about pregnancy and birth. After making

some observations to Paula about her manifest behavior, her pleasure and her "worried" giggle, he considers the best way for interpreting to her his "certain" interpretation of its latent meaning. However, since the second of these sessions is about to end, he decides to wait to deliver his interpretation until next week. In the intervening week, he meets with Paula's parents in a regularly scheduled interview. They tell him that three weeks earlier, the family had gone camping. They were pleased that Paula was able to manage this experience without significant fears and say, "That's something she couldn't have done a few months ago." They did note that *she was a bit anxious about sleeping in a tent* with them and her older brother, but she was easily reassured.[5] (italics added)

It became clear that Paula's play behavior was related to camping and the tent, not to her mother's pregnancy. It is certainly not difficult to form interpretations and offer them when we are "armed" with a great deal of information. When we take assumptions and preconceived ideas into the therapeutic relationship, we are interjecting too much of ourselves into the process and not allowing issues to unfold as play occurs.

One of the most important issues to address with parents is the treatment process. Few parents understand the basis of and reasoning behind play therapy. Some parents believe play is frivolous and are not interested in paying for their child to "play" with a counselor. Landreth asserts, "If parents do not understand how play therapy works, they cannot be expected to trust the process or to have faith in the therapist, and, if they do not, their negative attitude may affect the child's feelings about the session."[6] It becomes imperative, therefore, to educate parents about the purpose and process of play therapy. This need not be a lengthy apologetic but rather a brief explanation followed by an opportunity for questions.

Kevin O'Connor suggests that parents be informed of the counselor's theoretical orientation as well as the "pragmatics" of the treatment process. Parents will want answers to questions like these:

QUESTIONS PARENTS WILL HAVE

1. How often will the child be coming to sessions?
2. How long will each session be?
3. How much will each session cost?
4. Will we talk to the play therapist? When and for how long?
5. What will go on during an actual session?
6. Will we get to hear all about it?
7. When can we expect to see the effects of the treatment?
8. How will we know if treatment is working?
9. How long will treatment take from assessment to termination?[7]

An additional question that parents may have involves whether or not they may be able to observe a session through the one-way mirror or by closed-circuit camera. Although I have never had this request, in this age of abuse and exploitation (and the resulting paranoia), it would not seem to be an unusual possibility. My response to this would be that I have no objection to some concerns about a parent being able to understand the process. My preference would be either for the parent to be accompanied by a trained therapist who might explain the process or for the parent to observe me on tape in my presence prior to observing me live, so that I would be able to explain the process to them.

Some of these questions are easily answered and routinely discussed during the intake, while others are difficult to answer definitively at the outset of treatment.

At the Center for Play Therapy, we distribute a brochure that gives parents background information about play therapy. The first part of the brochure, excerpted from Dr. Landreth's book *Play*

Therapy: The Art of the Relationship, gives a brief overview of the process:

> Play therapy is to children what counseling is to adults. Play is the child's natural way of communicating just as talking is the adult's natural way of communicating. In the playroom, toys are used like words and play is the child's language. Children are provided special toys in play therapy to enable them to say with the toys what they have difficulty saying with words. When children can communicate or play out how they feel to a trained play therapist who understands, they feel better because the feelings have been released. As a parent, you have probably experienced the same thing when you were bothered or worried about something and told someone who really cared about you and understood; you felt better and could then handle the problem. Play therapy is like that for children. They can use the dolls, puppets, paints, or other toys to say what they think or how they feel.[8]

While it is helpful for parents to have printed material they can review at their convenience, it should not be a substitute for the therapist's taking time to explain the process. Parents may question whether or not their child needs play therapy or any other kind of therapeutic intervention. They may have been referred by their child's school or family physician. It is helpful to explain that most children experience some difficulty with behavior and emotions that cause concern for parents and teachers (not to mention the children themselves). Some children may need counseling to help them cope with the difficulty, and if the child has been referred for counseling, play therapy is an effective approach.

Parents may also need help in figuring out what to tell their children about coming in for counseling. I believe children initially need to know only that they will be coming to play in a special playroom. I prefer that parents do not tell their children that they have "an appointment with Dr. Sweeney." Children will assume that the counselor is a physician, and they know that the only time they go to the doctor is when they are sick. If a child wants to know why he or she is coming to the playroom, parents should simply say: "When things are hard for you at home (or at school), sometimes it helps to have a special place to play."[9] I sometimes suggest that the parents and child read the book *A Child's First Book about Play Therapy*.[10] I am not as interested in the content of the book as I am in the relationship-building dynamic that occurs between parent and child while they are reading together.

It is helpful to tell parents to dress their children in old play clothes for the sessions and to take their children to the bathroom prior to the session. Parents should also reassure their children that they will be in the waiting room during the session. Although some parents prefer to drop off their children for the session and pick them up afterward, I recommend that parents stay throughout the session. It can be quite distressing for children to be brought back to the waiting room only to discover that the parents are not there. At the University of North Texas clinics, we often encourage parents to consider pursuing therapy during the same time as the children's appointment. It is also helpful to encourage the parents not to pump the children with questions about the therapy afterward. By avoiding asking questions and by listening attentively to their child, parents communicate care and understanding.

Some parents may be concerned if their children become upset about the issues that are "stirred up" in the therapeutic process. Parents may have had a similar experience; following a session in which they were in counseling, they felt a sense of emotional turmoil. This is generally not a significant concern in play therapy. When I first began seeing foster children in play therapy, I was concerned that, following a session in which a child went "ballistic" in the playroom, the child would go back to the foster home and disrupt the family. This was not the case, however. Children intuitively know that the playroom is a place where negative emotions can be expressed and processed. The negative emotions and behaviors seem to stay in the playroom.

The playroom is a place where the children are in control, and when children are able to meet some of their emotional needs in the playroom (such as the need to be in control), they are actually less likely to express those emotional needs in a negative manner outside of the playroom.

If children do manifest some negative emotions and behaviors that seem to be related to the play therapy, it is the counselor's responsibility to process these with the parent. It is important to remember that not all "bad" behaviors that result from a therapeutic intervention are negative in the big picture. Take, for example, children who are withdrawn, unassertive, and dependent. If they suddenly get into a scuffle at school, something they have never done before, it is likely that the parents will be concerned. Although children need to be taught appropriate limits about such behavior, it can be seen as therapeutically positive that the children were finally able to assert themselves.

Part of the process of working with parents on these issues is providing them with training on the appropriate ways to respond to their children. If I am not able to engage parents in parent training as I might prefer (see chapter 10), it is still my desire to spend regular time with them each week to provide some modeling and training in active listening and building the parent-child relationship. If children bring up with their parents issues that have emerged in the counseling process, the parents will then be equipped to respond appropriately.

SHOULD PARENTS BE IN COUNSELING?

Often I recommend parent consultation and training as a crucial element for dealing with clients' presenting problems. When parents bring their children in for counseling, they are likely to be under some degree of stress and may be looking for the counselor to "fix" their children. With many of the behavioral and emotional problems for which children are referred, however, working with the parents (who spend far more time with the child than I will) may be a better investment of counseling resources. (I will discuss parent training in chapter 10.)

This approach is usually not the case, however, for children who struggle with more serious issues or who have experienced some type of trauma. The acute crisis that children (and their parents) are in when trauma has occurred normally necessitates direct intervention with the child. Many of the benefits of play therapy discussed in the previous chapter are crucial for children dealing with more severe issues, and the skill of the trained child counselor must be applied. In these cases, I will often look to "transfer" the case to the parents only after a course of play therapy, following the appropriate training of the parents.

Without doubt, parents should be an integral part of the counseling process, whatever the intervention. In most of my play therapy cases, I work concurrently with the parents and children and look to conclude the counseling process by moving into parent training. There are, of course, those cases in which I refer the parent(s) for therapy themselves. "Remember that it is the parents who brought the child to treatment and, at the point of referral, it is likely that the parents' emotional needs are at least as great as those of the child."[11] When parents have a better grasp of their own issues, feel better about themselves, and are less anxious, they are more likely to respond to parent training and to their children in a more positive manner. In these cases, I prefer not to be the therapist who counsels the parents in addition to the children.

Occasionally, parents will be resistant to pursuing counseling for themselves. Their attitude may be, *Counseling is fine for our son but not for us. After all, he is the one with the problem.* When this thinking is conveyed, I respond by saying, "Yes, that may be true, but you are the ones who have to live with this problem. Perhaps you can explore some things to help you deal with the problem a little better." I am not interested in overcoming resistance and defensiveness with an offensive attack. My goal is to bring the parents into the process. If I can present my position that we are all on the same team, trying to deal with an issue affecting the whole family, then I find that parents are normally much less wary of my attempts to involve them in counseling. If there are personal issues for the parents to address in counseling, they will emerge in the process. There is no need to hit the parents over the head with the issues.

While it is my preference to involve parents in the counseling process, I believe children should proceed with therapy even if their parents can't or won't participate. Although systemic interventions are most beneficial, working with only the children can still positively affect the family system. "To insist that children not be seen in therapy until their parents can be worked with is to deny the growth potential and coping ability of children and the ability of parents to alter their behavior in relation to the child's change in behavior." [12] If I am treating a child who has been physically or emotionally abused by a stressed single parent, I would certainly like to work with both the parent and child. If for some reason I cannot do this, I am confident that my work with the child will help the entire situation. As the child begins to process his or her issues through play, the acting-out behaviors for which the child was referred (and which have likely preceded the abusive experiences) will usually begin to subside. As these symptoms begin to subside in the home, my expectation is that the parent's stress level will diminish, and he or she will be less abusive. As this happens, the child will improve even more, with the combination of decreased tension at home and the therapeutic intervention. As this occurs and the parent's stress is further reduced, they may become more amenable to therapy themselves. While this cycle may not occur when there is deeper pathology or substance abuse with the parent(s), the intervention with the child usually has a ripple effect throughout the family system. It is possible, therefore, to have a systemic effect without treating the entire system.

To keep parents updated about the process and progress of play therapy, I speak with them briefly at each session and schedule a parent consultation every four to five sessions. During the consultations, we discuss aspects of the play therapy that may help the parents further understand the dynamics of their child's issues. I also provide the parents with suggestions to use at home. As previously mentioned, when appropriate, I look to "transfer" the case to the parents by transitioning my work from the child to the parent for parent training.

It is also helpful to involve the parents and other family members directly in the treatment process. As children begin to process relational issues through play, parents or the entire family might be brought into the counseling process. I prefer to keep a play-based modality so as not to disempower the child client, who has likely gained a sense of control through the expression of self through play. I commonly use one of the therapeutic techniques discussed in chapter 8, such as sandplay, art assessment and therapy, or puppet play. Simply having a family put on a puppet show is a wonderful way of assessing family dynamics and developing positive communication patterns.

I have no formula for when or how to involve the family in this way. I do so when the child's movement seems stalled or when the issues discussed in parent consultation appear to need processing by the entire family. It is important to note that I will bring family members into the session only with the child's permission, as this shows respect and honor.

INFORMED CONSENT AND CONFIDENTIALITY

Since children generally do not have the legal capacity to give informed consent for counseling, parents (or legal guardians) must give their permission for treatment to begin. Let's look briefly at some legal and ethical issues.

It would be shortsighted to assume that the parent who has brought the child in for treatment has custody of the child. It is definitely recommended that an informed consent be signed by the parent(s), including verification that the parent is the legal guardian.

In cases of legal separation or divorce, obtain copies of court orders detailing custody. With foster care, signed consent from the court-appointed guardian is necessary. Note that a friend or noncustodial family member (grandparent, aunt, uncle, etc.) cannot provide consent for treatment.

Informed consent is imperative in today's litigious society and should include material about the limits of confidentiality, possible benefits and risks of counseling, alternatives to treatment, and a release to record or videotape sessions, if appropriate. I also recommend using a professional disclosure statement and treatment contract. I have included in the appendixes some sample forms I use for informed consent, professional disclosure, and authorization for videotaping a session for training purposes. Appropriate releases should be signed and on file prior to discussing a child's case with *anyone* other than the parent.

Confidentiality is another important issue that should be discussed with the parent(s). Although younger children will not be able to comprehend the concept, older children do have some awareness, and the issue is best dealt with up front. Therapists should operate under their own professional code of ethics. For me, this means telling parents that the child's play session is confidential, in the same way that adult counseling sessions would be. However, I assure the parents that I will keep them informed of my general impressions and make parenting suggestions based on what I see in the playroom. Since parents are legally responsible for their children, it is a sensitive situation when they want to know precisely what is happening in the course of their child's therapy. "Where does the parent's right to know end and the child's right to privacy begin? This is a difficult question to answer, and the decision is always dependent on the parent's ability to use the information appropriately, the content of the information, the emotional vulnerability of the child, and the physical safety of parties involved."[13]

Parents sometimes will insist on knowing everything and will badger the therapist for details about their child's therapy. For example, I videotape all of my sessions, and some parents ask to watch the video. I generally discourage this because it is an invasion of the child's privacy, and most often the parent will not understand the process as it unfolds on the tape. My policy is that if parents insist on viewing videotaped sessions, I will set up an appointment to watch the tape *with* them. I do not consider it appropriate to hand over a videotape to parents with no explanation or consultation.

When parents badger me for information, I find it best to deal with the badgering as a counseling issue. I will discuss the child's case within the context of providing counsel for the parents. These types of parents are often the ones who believe that the child's problem is the child's problem and that the therapist's job is to fix the child. Labeling and pigeonholing of the child merely serve to perpetuate the problem and should be addressed. I will not deny the parent information, but the welfare of the child and family as a whole is the foremost priority.

Along these lines, a child's artwork or any craft created in the playroom should not be displayed. Although the intention may be to provide an encouraging experience for the child, it is, nevertheless, a violation of his or her privacy. Displayed artwork may also have the negative effect of causing one child to feel in competition with another child's art.

PARENT PROBLEMS AND PROBLEM PARENTS

Let's face it: Some parents are difficult to work with. When we encounter these troublesome parents, it's not surprising that the children are having problems at home. That makes it all the more important, therefore, to invest time and energy in these parents.

Therapists should follow some guidelines when they deal with and counsel parents. *First, be sensitive to the parents' needs.* Many parents feel overwhelmed with the responsibility of parenting and doubt their ability to parent. We have discussed how play therapy empowers children; let's not forget that it can do the same for parents. Empowered parents raise empowered children. Similarly, it is important to recognize, appreciate, and support the parents' position. Most parents make an honest attempt to raise their children well, and even if they miss the mark, it is not helpful to criticize or blame parents. For the therapist to come across as the *expert* does not help the counseling process; to do so will likely cause the parent to become defensive.

Second, model listening and parenting skills. If parents do not know how to listen to their children, model active listening during parent consultation or counseling. I have had parents watch my play therapy through one-way mirrors at the university clinic to show them how to attend to and reflect their child's feelings. Most parents who come in with their children are open to at least some parenting suggestions, even if they are unwilling to enter formal parent training. Modeling basic skills is an excellent way to accomplish this.

Third, remember that your role is temporary. It should always be a goal to build skills and foster independence for both the child and parents. Recognize the family dynamics and the role that the counselor and each family member play.

Fourth, make parent education a major part of the process of working with children. Many parents have unrealistic expectations of themselves and their children. Basic education about child development may be appropriate. Parents who rush their children to attain developmental milestones too early are setting up their children to acquire problems. Counselors need to be educated about development issues and prepared to share information with the ignorant or naive parent. Kevin O'Connor comments: "This may involve educating the parent to both developmental norms and the degree or manner in which their child's pathology relates to his overall developmental functioning."[14]

In his classic book *Between Parent and Child,* Dr. Haim Ginott discusses several parent types that he believes are likely in need of professional help. He identifies the following issues:

- *Overemotional parents.* These are parents who have not learned to place proper limits on the expression of their emotions. The children reflect the turbulence of their own parents.

■ *Overprotective parents.* These parents have a relentless concern for the child's functioning. They need intervention so that their children may become self-sufficient.

■ *Childish parents.* These are adults who view their children as playthings and eventually look to their children to parent them. Dr. Ginott asserts that these parents need help growing up.

■ *Alcoholic parents.* Children of these parents are subject to "sudden storms and periodic desertions." These parents most often need professional help to overcome their problems.

■ *Seductive parents.* Parents who need to develop "mature modesty" fall into this category. Poor sexual and relational boundaries negatively affect their children's development.

■ *Rejecting parents.* Physical or emotional abandonment by parents can cause pronounced damage to children. These parents push their children into autonomy early, which can foster a fear of failure and criticism.

■ *Overconscientious parents.* Being overly child centered upsets the balance of the family and the parents' marriage. Seeking to solve all of a child's frustration will only foster frustration for the family.

■ *Divorced parents.* Because divorce is a "soul-shaking" experience for all involved, parents must strive to overcome the inherent difficulties. Parents who use their children as weapons in a divorce do incredible damage to them.[15]

Since all children come with parents, it is our responsibility as counselors to recognize and meet the needs of parents. By honoring the parents, we honor the children.

To cease to be loved is for the child practically synonymous with ceasing to live. —*KARL A. MENNINGER*

5/ THE PLAYROOM
and
MATERIALS

The microsphere—i.e., the small world of manageable toys—is a harbor which the child establishes, to return to when he needs to overhaul his ego.
                                                        —ERIK ERIKSON

While it is your child-therapist relationship that will have primary curative value, it is important to consider the playroom and materials you make available to children. Since play is a child's natural medium of communication, toys are the words. The playroom is the child's world during the counseling experience.

THE PLAYROOM

As I outline my preferences for a playroom, I am aware of the limitations that many counseling practices and agencies have in terms of space availability. It is the rare child counselor who has the opportunity to work in a custom-designed facility. Although I strongly believe it is worth the investment to provide a quality playroom, a portable play therapy "kit" (which I will comment on later) will suffice.

Ideally, a playroom should be as free from distractions as possible.

This makes sense for any counseling room, but because children are easily distracted, a playroom that is removed from street and office noise is most desirable. It is best to have a tile floor in the playroom; linoleum can too easily be damaged, and carpeting will be quickly ruined if paints are used. Carpeting may also carry the message "Be neat," which can hinder free expression. Landreth suggests that the walls be painted an off-white color.[1] Nevertheless, I have had wonderful therapy experiences in a playroom with murals painted on the walls. The clinical staff of the agency where I previously practiced made recommendations to the painter, and all of the walls depicted various scenes. Some of my clients would engage in play involving the scenes on the walls, and others would not. The scenes did not appear to be either a distraction or a stimulating factor for the children. Whether you opt for scenes or a solid color for your playroom walls, it's best to use an enamel paint that can be easily cleaned.

An example of a child's using painted scenes also provides a wonderful illustration of how metaphors are evident in the child's play. Eight-year-old Tommy was an engaging boy in the playroom. His history as a foster child and his behaviors at home and school, however, presented quite a challenge to his teachers and guardians. A survivor of physical and sexual abuse, Tommy had multiple physiological and psychological difficulties, including learning disabilities, temper tantrums, and a bone-growth disorder.

Tommy's play was often wild and chaotic in the playroom. This was not surprising considering the wild and chaotic life he had experienced. Before Tommy was brought into the foster-care system, he lived with his mother and three siblings under a bridge. He had learned what to do to survive. I occasionally worried that his frenzied play in the playroom would transfer into his home or classroom. My experience told me, however, that the majority of children who express aggressive and reckless behavior in the playroom do not continue that behavior outside of the playroom. In fact, it is most often the opposite: As children have the opportunity to express negative emotions in the safe environment of the play-room, the need to act out beyond the playroom decreases, as do the disruptive behaviors.

In one session, Tommy decided to interact with the paintings on the walls. He took a plane and pretended to fly it in and out of the trees in the mural. He then flew his plane into an abandoned mine painted in a corner. Could this be a metaphor for reaching into his past, filled with darkness and desolation? Inside the mine, Tommy "found" some old dinosaur bones, which he pretended to strap to the top of his plane. Dinosaur bones? This might be a metaphorical representation of death and loss—issues that have been extinct (repressed).

My interaction with Tommy during this session was different from most other sessions. He was in a trancelike state for much of the session, which is not uncommon for children who have expe-rienced severe abuse. His voice was soft and low as he narrated his play. My responses to him were primarily verbal and nonverbal reflections. I simply tracked his activity, reflecting both the content and feeling of Tommy's play. He spoke softly, almost in a whisper, so I spoke softly. He gestured with his hands and arms, so I gestured as well. Interpretations or questions would have been inappropriate. Tommy was telling a story, and I was his audience.

Tommy flew the plane out of the mine, in and out of the trees, and landed it in the sandbox in the middle of the playroom. After "unloading" the top of his plane, Tommy announced that he had retrieved a dinosaur's hipbone, while simultaneously patting his left hip. What metaphorical meaning could this have? What might Tommy have been trying to communicate?

Although Tommy didn't realize it, I was aware of some of his past medical problems. Tommy had experienced hip-replacement sur-gery—yes, on his left hip. Certainly, I could have asked him about the experience and what it was like being in a full-body cast. His play experience, however, enabled Tommy to share with me, in his language, a traumatic event in his life. He used the painting on the wall, but more important, he shared and processed a previous medical trauma with a counselor who communicated understanding and acceptance. Through his play, Tommy expressed the beginning of the healing process.

In addition to the paint choices for the playroom, another important consideration is size. Landreth suggests that an ideal playroom is approximately 12 by 15 feet and has roughly 150 to 200 square feet of space.[2] The playroom should be small enough for the therapist never to be too far away from the children but large enough for them to retreat from the therapist if they need some space.

Ideally, the playroom will have a bathroom attached directly to the room because children often need to take rest-room breaks. I have also found that as some children begin to approach sensitive issues through play, they will need to go to the bathroom more frequently. This makes sense when you keep in mind that using the toilet is a comforting alternative to processing out-of-control issues and is an activity over which children can exercise control. The playrooms at the Center for Play Therapy at the University of North Texas have sinks with running water (only the cold water should be connected for safety reasons), which is a helpful feature. Water is an important "toy" to make available in the playroom, if possible, and it makes the cleanup process easier.

Again, as we discuss the conditions for a prototypical playroom, don't become dismayed at your own facilities. Often, school counselors must migrate between multiple school sites and carry a bag of toys wherever they go. The hospital-based counselor will move from one child's hospital bed to another with some sort of portable playroom. Your playroom space may be no larger than a closet. Although this may not be ideal, a variety of toys and an empathic play therapist can more than make up for the space deficiency. When it is not possible to use a separate playroom (for counselors who see both children and adults in their office, for example), it is imperative to reduce distractions for the child and ensure the confidentiality of the play therapy experience.

SELECTING PLAY MATERIALS

Since play is the language of children and toys are their words, selection of toys is an important part of designing a playroom. Toys are the tools of the play therapist. Toys should be safe for both the child and the therapist, which is why plastic and foam toys are recommended. After all, a plastic toy thrown by an aggressive child is less painful than a metal one. Toys should be as generic as possible so that children can project anything they wish onto a toy. It is difficult to project onto a Power Ranger anything other than its inherent intent.[3] A nondescript bendable figure such as Gumby can be used in a much wider variety of play themes. Garry Landreth notes that toys should be selected to facilitate several essentials in the play therapy process:

1. establishment of a positive relationship with the child
2. expression of a wide range of feelings
3. exploration of real-life experiences
4. reality testing of limits
5. development of a positive self-image
6. development of self-understanding
7. opportunity to develop self-control[4]

Landreth also discusses three primary categories of toys used in the playroom: real-life toys; acting-out, aggressive-release toys; and toys for creative expression and emotional release.[5] *Real-life toys,* such as a doll family and puppets, can represent the child's family. These toys can provide for direct expression of emotions, such as fear, anger, and anxiety related to the child's relationships. Toys such as a doctor's kit and a cash register enable the child to be industrious, exhibit nurture, and feel the empowerment of manipulating "real-life" materials in the freedom of play. These toys provide the therapist with multiple opportunities to make self-esteem-building responses, which we will discuss in the next chapter. *Acting-out and aggressive-release toys,* such as an inflatable bop bag, soldiers, guns, and knives, can be used by the child to express anger, rage, and frustration. *Toys for creative expression and emotional release* provide an opportunity for the children to express themselves through the use of imagination and fantasy. These include blocks, sand, water, clay, paints, crayons, and other art media. The generic nature of these materials allows free expression because there is no "right" way to play with them.

WHAT ABOUT TOY WEAPONS IN THE PLAYROOM?

It is my opinion that toy guns or knives in the playroom are not detrimental and do not increase the aggressiveness of children outside of the playroom. Although I do not have any toy guns in my home, I nevertheless find that my own children have made guns out of Duplo blocks, sticks, or a pointed finger. Where did they pick this up? I don't know, but all children seem to do this.

I feel that shooting is acceptable in the playroom because it is expressed in fantasy and symbolism. I do not permit children to shoot me (particularly with the dart gun), but if they are angry with me and want to shoot the bop bag and pretend it is me, that is acceptable. I do not believe that this encourages the child to be violent. There are other ways to express hostility and anger in the playroom, and the child is free to choose, since children are not directed toward or away from any toy. Limits are set only if a child uses a toy inappropriately. When the child uses a dart gun, for example, I will set limits, which is an important aspect of the play therapy relationship.

If you are uncomfortable having a toy gun or any other toy in your playroom, then do not include it. Your inability to communicate understanding and acceptance will be apparent to clients if they engage in play with a toy that makes you feel uncomfortable. I would suggest that you explore the issue, however, as I believe these toys can be helpful for children.

I have found the following toys to meet the previous criteria and provide an effective assortment of expressive materials for children in the playroom. Toys marked with an asterisk can be included in a portable play kit.

Toy List

Airplanes*
Animals*
   Wild
   Zoo
   Domestic
Baby bottle*
Balls (foam, plastic)*
Bat (foam, plastic)
Binoculars*
Bop bag
Blanket
Blocks (wood, foam)
Boats*
Boxes (small and large)
Bus (with people)
Camera*
Cars*
   Ambulance
   Fire truck
   Army vehicles
Chalkboard and chalk
Clay (or Play-Doh)*
Craft items*
   Glue
   Popsicle sticks
   Pipe cleaners
   Scissors (blunt), tape
Crayons and paper*
Dinosaurs
Doctor's kit*
Dishes*
Dollhouse
Dolls
Doll family (to fit in dollhouse)*
   Various ethnic groups
   Father, mother, boy, girl, baby
Drawing materials*
Egg cartons
Flashlight*

Food (plastic)
Gumby*
Guns (including holster)
   Cowboy gun
   Dart gun*
   Machine gun
Handcuffs*
Hand grenades
Hats
   Police helmet
   Firefighter's helmet
   Skipper's cap
Jewelry and purse*
Keys*
Knives*
Magic wand*
Masks*
Mirror
Money*
Musical instruments
Paints and easel
Pillow
Pots and pans
Puppets*
Refrigerator (wood, if possible)
Rope*
Sandbox
Stuffed animals
Soldiers*
Sunglasses*
Sword
Targets (Velcro)
Tool bench
Telephones (at least two)*
   Cellular phone
Tinkertoys
Walkie-talkies
Wristwatch*

If you are assembling a portable play kit, you do not need to have several of each item, as might be appropriate for the playroom. It is also nice to transport these toys in a cardboard box, which can double as a dollhouse or fort. If you use a portable play kit, set out the play materials before the session begins. This encourages the child to participate in the play process and sends the message that you care enough to prepare for the session.

A few final considerations about toy selection: Always have available in the playroom something that the child can break. This is why egg cartons are on the toy list (I prefer plastic foam egg cartons). If children have a need to express anger or frustration by breaking something, they can be directed to the egg cartons. Any emotion is acceptable in the playroom; it is the *expression* of that emotion that may have to be limited.

Generally, toys that become broken should be removed (always if the broken toy is sharp or otherwise dangerous). Nevertheless, unlike some other play therapists, I think it is acceptable, and perhaps even helpful, to have one or two broken toys in the playroom as long as an unbroken duplicate is also available. Some children feel "broken" themselves and can identify with a toy that has been damaged.

The toys should be placed on sturdy shelves in the playroom. The emotionally fragile child is less likely to rummage through a toy chest or box. Displaying toys on shelves sends an invitation to the child to interact freely with the toys. It is also helpful to categorize toys. Group hats together, as well as balls, craft items, and so on. When you display animals, separate the wild animals and dinosaurs from the domestic animals. It can be frightening for a child to reach for a kitten when it sits next to a menacing dinosaur. Another reason for categorizing and displaying toys is for the sake of consistency—children will know that every time they come to the playroom, the dolls will be in the same place. If several counselors use the playroom, take pictures of the room so that toys can be returned to the proper place after each session.

I have had the unfortunate experience of allowing other therapists to use my playroom as a baby-sitting room while I met with
parents or other clients. I do not recommend this because it is
difficult to preserve the playroom and materials when the therapist
is not present. If a child client is in the room at other times without
the therapist, it decreases the "specialness" of the play therapy
experience. It is better to have some toys available in the waiting
room.

Also, it is important to keep the playroom clean and well stocked
with disposable supplies, such as paints and paper. This shows respect
for the child client and respect for others who use the same room.

The playroom is a magical place for children. It may be the only
place where some children can freely and safely express themselves.
It is an honor to be with them as they process their issues and
confront their pain. It is challenging, to be sure, but watching
children grow and seeing the hand of God in the playroom is one
of the greatest experiences for any person in the helping profession.

You can discover more about a person in an hour of play
than in a year of conversation. —PLATO

6/ Conducting *a* Child Play Therapy Session

The therapeutic medium best suited for young children is play. In therapy, the term play does not connote its usual recreational meaning, but is equivalent to freedom to act and react, suppress and express, suspect and respect.
                                        —HAIM GINOTT

I recall a play therapy session with ten-year-old Amy, a sexual-abuse victim who had been transferred to me from another therapist in the community. She suffered from emotional and behavioral difficulties, and the referring therapist thought play therapy might be helpful.

At Amy's initial session, she entered the playroom, promptly sat down on a chair, and said in a questioning manner, "I suppose you'll want to talk about the molest?"

The question caught me off guard since very few of my sessions begin this way! As I paused to formulate my response, I thought what a shame it was that this child—even though she already talked like an adult—had such a concept of the counseling process. Here I was, a new therapist to her—a new *male* therapist, no less—in the first seconds of the first session, and she was disclosing a traumatic event in her life.

After a few moments, I responded by saying, "In here, you can decide to talk about whatever you would like, or you can choose not to talk at all." I think my response surprised her even more. After an awkward silence, because she didn't know how to answer or what to do, I said: "It's probably pretty strange being with a counselor who doesn't ask a lot of questions." With a big sigh, Amy responded affirmatively. Although it took her a while within that first session, she began to play, and the process developed rapidly after that.

The only thing that Amy had known about counseling was that it involved talking. After her initial surprise at my response, she was relieved not to have to process her trauma verbally. As Amy began to work through her feelings and experiences in the playroom, positive changes began to appear in her life. It was not my brilliance as a therapist (although it strokes my ego to believe it was) that brought about the improvement as much as allowing her to "talk" in her language and experience the understanding of a caring therapist.

When counseling children, you will choose a therapeutic style that reflects your theory and your personality. However, one principle is critical to the success of play therapy. From the initial contact in the waiting room through the session itself, child counselors need to be willing to step into the child's world and stay there. Unlike Amy's previous counseling experience, children should not be forced, encouraged, or nudged out of their world and into the adult world.

MAKING CONTACT WITH CHILDREN

As I mentioned before, making contact with children begins in the waiting room. In reality, though, the process begins with the therapist before he or she ever greets a new client. For the skilled counselor, play therapy becomes a lifestyle. To reiterate a point I made earlier, "Play therapy is not a cloak the play therapist puts on when entering the playroom and takes off when leaving but rather is a philosophy resulting in attitudes and behaviors for living one's life in relationships with children. . . . Play therapy is a complete therapeutic system, not just the application of a few rapport-building techniques."[1]

Making contact with children begins with the little things. Have you ever noticed that children often tilt their heads when they greet each other? Ethological research (the study of human and animal behavior) on children demonstrates this. Ethologist N. Blurton-Jones noted that children tilt their heads when looking and smiling at other children.[2] Other research posits that head and body cants are postures of submission and appeasement.[3] It would seem that tilting your head when greeting children is a nonverbal way of communicating acceptance and the message that the therapist is not a threat. When I interact with children, I usually tilt my head. My wife thinks it is a little strange, but when I make eye contact with a child—at church, in a shopping mall, at a restaurant—I will often tilt my head and smile. I will usually get a smile in return. Through this simple act, I will have made a small connection with a child.

Such seemingly insignificant actions are quite important for those who wish to enter into the child's world. I have seen many therapists walk into the waiting room, greet the parent(s) with a handshake, and then, while still standing, extend the same open hand to the child. When you consider the child's perspective, you realize how threatening this interplay can be. The child has been brought to counseling by a person (a large person) who has a great deal of power and control in the relationship. Now think about a stranger (the therapist) approaching the child in a strange place (the waiting room) and asking him or her to go to another strange place (the counseling room). Could it be another "giant" coming to make decisions for the child?

Think also how the child perceives the therapist standing up with an arm extended for a handshake. My three-year-old son, Josiah, often calls me a "giant daddy." Most, if not all, adults probably appear to be "giants" to children. Therapists are so tall, and the smile on their face is so far away. Surely, we do not want children to perceive us this way. George Orwell said, "Part of the reason for the ugliness of an adult in a child's eyes is that the child is usually looking upwards, and few faces are at their best when seen from below." Therefore, when we greet our small clients, let's get on their level.

Referral

Let me make an obvious point: Children are not in the counseling office because they have chosen to be there; children do not refer themselves to counseling. Most children are referred to mental health treatment for noncompliance—that is, they simply are not doing what their parents or teachers expect them to do. You have probably met parents who have sent the message: "My child has [or is] a problem. Please fix him [or her]." This attitude becomes a therapeutic issue to take up with the parents and perhaps the entire family. It is also important to realize that the decision to seek mental health intervention is much too difficult a decision for the child to consider. The very fact that we are talking about how children process emotions and communicate is enough to lend credence to this. The responsibility belongs, therefore, to the parents.

When I teach a parent-training group, I talk with each parent about the importance of working with the child who is currently experiencing difficulties in the family. Garry Landreth asks the question, "If your three children are playing in the backyard and one falls out of a tree and breaks a leg, which one do you bring to the hospital?" The point is that it is the parents' responsibility to seek medical attention for the injured child, just as it is the parents' responsibility to seek counseling for the troubled child. When a child is hurting, whether physically or emotionally, it is obviously not appropriate to leave the decision about treatment to the child. When parents make the decision to seek counseling for their child, for whatever reason, we need to support them.

Of course, there is always the possibility that parents are not making the right decision in bringing their children in for counseling. It may be that the parents are the ones in need of therapeutic intervention but are not able or willing to admit this. Perhaps the parents are bringing in their children as a punishment or a consequence for unacceptable behavior. I have even had parents in the midst of a divorce bring their children to counseling as a ploy to gain an advantage in a custody battle. The seemingly obvious solution to these dilemmas is to encourage the parents themselves to enter counseling. However, it could also be argued that children who live under such manipulation are likely in need of the freeing experience of play therapy, and it would be beneficial to work with both children and parents.

The Waiting Room

The waiting room is not the place to discuss the child's situation with the parents. Most of the time, the child is present, and too often, children have the demeaning experience of being talked about in their presence as if they were not there. If parents have something important to report, take the time to confer with them privately, being sure to send the message that they are an important part of the process. When you come to the waiting room, consider using the practical suggestions from *Play Therapy: The Art of the Relationship:* "Immediately crouch down and greet the child. The therapist will find it helpful to enter the waiting room, give the parents a short warm greeting, immediately crouch down, make eye contact, give a warm smile, and make an introduction to the child without giving the parent a chance to initiate conversation. The child is the most important person in the whole building at that moment. The therapist is there to build a relationship with this important little person, and to communicate the child's importance. Therefore, the therapist will not stand in the child's presence and discuss the child."[4]

Sometimes, when the parent has told me ahead of time about the child's reluctance to enter therapy and I expect some resistance in the waiting room, I will bring with me a small foam ball from the playroom. When I enter the waiting room and the child is predictably clinging to the parent's leg, I will crouch down a few feet away and roll the ball in the direction of the child. Almost all children will stoop to pick it up, and it is at this point that I have made contact. The connections will continue from there. For children who still refuse to go or who throw a temper tantrum in the waiting room, ask the parent to help you bring them into the playroom.

BEGINNING THE PLAY PROCESS

After making initial contact, I will tell children that it is time to go to the playroom and that their parents will be staying in the waiting room. *Tell* children that it is time to go to the playroom. Take care not to extend an invitation. If the counselor asks "Would you like to go and play with some toys?" or some similar question, anxious or resistant children might answer "No!" If necessary, have the parents accompany the child down the hall to the playroom. It is my preference to enter the playroom with the child alone, but if the child remains resistant, it is acceptable for the parents to come into the playroom until there is an appropriate time to leave.

This brings up the issue of safety. Feeling safe in the counseling room is a significant therapeutic issue. If children do not feel safe apart from their parents, then it will be difficult to explore issues without at least having the parents escort the children to the playroom. If the parents stay in the playroom, however, the children may not feel the freedom to explore issues. Another aspect here is that you may not feel safe (confident or competent) with anxious or resistant children, and you may be tempted to focus more on the parents than on the children. The issue of separation is a related one; it becomes more difficult for children to separate from their parents once they are already in the playroom.

Therapists caught in this situation should keep a few things in mind. Politely ask the parents to leave their children in the playroom even if the children are still crying. Although this is not the ideal way to begin therapy, it does provide a wonderful opportunity for you to respond to children's feelings with compassion and empathy. Thus, a bond can be established. Often, it is the parents who experience some sort of separation anxiety. Children do, however, have a keen sense of this and will pick up on their parents' discomfort. If it has become necessary for the parents to escort the child to the playroom, it is more beneficial to deal with the separation issue at the door than inside the playroom. Also, if the therapist is more comfortable dealing with anxious parents than an anxious child, this may be an issue to address in supervision.

If you plan to administer assessment instruments or to implement another technique, avoid using the play therapy room. The playroom and the play therapy relationship are special, particularly to the child, and we should guard against contaminating the process.

Once in the playroom, the therapist should introduce the child to the playroom and the process. I begin by saying something like, "Jason, this is our playroom, and this is our special playtime. You may play with these toys in lots of the ways you would like to." I want to communicate the uniqueness of this experience and let children know that the playroom is a place where they can make choices and lead the process. Notice that I don't say, "You may play with these toys in *any* of the ways you would like to." Such a statement would be untrue, since the child may not attack me with a toy or throw a toy at the one-way mirror. I do not begin with lengthy explanations, and I do not list a series of limits. Chapter 7 will discuss proper limit setting, but suffice it to say here that beginning a play session by telling a child what he or she *cannot* do would not facilitate a free and accepting environment.

Once I have introduced the child to the playroom, I sit down in a chair—one that is smaller than the average adult chair but is still comfortable. From that point on (really from the first moment I greeted the client but especially now), I do my best to communicate the four messages: "I'm here. I hear you. I understand. And I care."[5] It is best to sit in a chair for several reasons. First, if you decide to remain standing, you will perpetuate that "giant" issue that I mentioned earlier. Second, when you are standing, you may be tempted to follow the child around the playroom. As I noted in the last chapter, it is important to give children space in the playroom. Let the children decide how close to you they want to be. If the child chooses to play behind the sandbox or with his or her back to the therapist, the child probably has a reason for this. Children are intruded on enough without having a therapist trailing them around the room. It is still possible—and necessary—to give verbal feedback whether or not you can directly observe the child's activity.

I prefer to sit in a chair rather than on the floor because I want to communicate to the child that I am a caring and accepting adult and therapist, not a playmate who must be included in the child's play. By sitting on the floor, the therapist communicates, "I am here to play with you; include me in your play." However, it should be the child's decision to include me or not.

The therapist's body language in the playroom is important. Use basic attending skills, such as maintaining an open body posture and leaning forward. Being seated in a smaller chair and leaning forward (which brings your face closer to the child's level) conveys interest, involvement, and acceptance. Think about what thoughts this action brings to a child's mind: *Wow! I'm important enough that this nice adult is really paying attention to what I'm doing!* It is also important to shift your entire position—rather than just moving your head—when the child moves to another part of the playroom. Turning your whole body to face the child sends a much stronger message of involvement than simply turning your head. Landreth teaches the rule of thumb that the therapist's "toes should follow the nose" when attending to the child.[6] Also, I have found that many beginning play therapists are so focused on making the proper response that they forget to smile and relax. If you are concentrating so hard on your responses or on interpreting the child's play themes, it will be difficult to attend fully to the child.

How involved should a therapist be in the child's play? It is tempting to rush the rapport-building process by using some technique, such as the therapist engaging in some type of play, in hopes that the child will join in or initiate his or her own play activity, or by extending a verbal invitation to play when the child is not active. While some approaches to play therapy encourage greater interaction, the child-centered approach is careful to let the client lead the process. If you feel tempted to hurry into the play process, I encourage you to ask yourself, "Is my desire to get involved in the child's play meant to meet the child's need or my own?"

This doesn't mean that you shouldn't use a technique or be involved in the child's play. I tell the therapists I supervise that if they use any technique in the playroom, they should have both a theoretical and practical rationale for it. "Whether or not to participate in children's play is an important decision the therapist must make prior to the onset of therapy and, although largely a function of the therapist's personality, should be based on a rationale consistent with the therapist's objectives."[7] Specific techniques or direct involvement in the child's play guarantees nothing. Your message of care and acceptance, communicated through your verbal and nonverbal attitude, is the key.

There is no formula for determining how much or how little you should be involved in the child's play. Generally, the more involved you are in the play, the more challenging it will be to keep the client in the lead and thus facilitate the benefits of making decisions and learning responsibility and self-control. This is not to say that you should limit your involvement when the child requests your participation. Recognize, however, that many children feel obligated to include the therapist. Also, the request may reflect the child's need to be liked or the desire for someone else to make decisions. The immediate response of the therapist to participate in the play may eliminate the recognition and resolution of these dynamics.

Nevertheless, you can and should be involved in the child's play without jumping into the middle of it. Your attitude, and the communication of that attitude, is much more important than any participation. A child is looking more for acceptance and understanding from you than for your involvement in play.

If you decide to join in the child's play, keep a few things in mind. As noted, the client should continue to lead the play process. You must be adept at setting limits, and you should let the child choreograph the play. If the child asks you to paint a picture or do some other art project, the child may set up a competition over whose craft is better, or the child may attempt to copy your work. This would not promote the child's growth or foster the therapeutic relationship.

Another playroom issue we must address is cleanup after the session. Should the client help put the room back in order? My first response is, "No, that's what graduate students are for!" In actuality, however, this is another question that relates to the therapist's theoretical approach. The fact is, some children are quite messy in the expression of their issues. By allowing such children to leave without having them help clean up, we may be giving them a lesson we don't want to teach. Are the children getting away with something they shouldn't be able to get away with? I believe children do need to learn to pick up after themselves. This teaches them responsibility. But this ethic should be taught to children by their parents, not by the therapist. Therefore, the therapist should not require children to clean up the playroom. Some might protest: What about teaching children the consequences of their behavior? Shouldn't a child learn that a repercussion of making a mess is having to clean it up? My response is that a child should, in fact, be learning about choices and consequences in the playroom, but this is best learned through the process of therapeutic limit setting (see chapter 7).

Further, since play is the language of children and toys are their words, I do not ask a client to clean up his "language" or straighten up his "words." Here's another way of looking at it: Suppose you had an adult client who was working through a difficult issue, and this person wept and sobbed throughout the session. By the end of the hour, the client has used an entire box of tissues and has littered them all over the floor. Would you ask that client to pick up the tissues before he or she left? Probably not. Is it possible that we are doing the same thing to children when we press them into cleaning up toys?

A word of advice on messy playrooms: Be sure to give yourself plenty of time to clean up the room. My play sessions are generally forty-five minutes long, which leaves me time to clean up before the next session. If a child has been particularly untidy, you may want to end early so you have extra time to straighten up the room. Also, if you are planning to spend time with the parents after the play session, be sure to leave yourself extra time.

THERAPEUTIC RESPONSES

Let's face it, the way most adults interact with children is to solve their problems, deliver consequences, give directives, or ask questions. It can be a challenge to avoid these types of interactions in a counseling relationship. How the therapist responds to the child in the play session determines whether or not the session is therapeutic. Haim Ginott makes this statement about therapeutic responses: "The therapist must exercise great caution in formulating responses to the child's communication."[8] An obvious statement, yes, but it is filled with important points. Therapists must *exercise caution* in the playroom. The first dictionary definition of the verb *exercise* is "to make effective in action." Counselors must assure that their responses actively bring an effect. Responses should be carefully selected and purposeful. There is no room for casual or haphazard answers and actions. We are involved in touching the very soul of a hurting child. As such, responses should be *formulated*. And, of course, we need to remember the *child's communication* medium, which is play.

Since play is the language of children and toys are their words, counselors' primary goal is to respond to children so as to facilitate this process. That's precisely what play therapists should be—facilitators. It is not my job to initiate change in the lives of my clients—indeed, I could not. I can *assist* my clients in making change, and then when change occurs, I cannot possibly take credit for it. In this way, a facilitator in the playroom might be compared to a midwife, who does not cause the conception, gestation, or birth of a child. A midwife merely facilitates the birth process. Likewise, as a therapist, I am neither the cause nor the cure of a child's problems. Yet I can facilitate growth and healing.

Suspending the typical evaluative or directive nature of adult-child interactions and communicating understanding and acceptance to a child are the most healing things we can do. Consider the following story from *Play Therapy: The Art of the Relationship.*

> Rachel was a small first-grader who always walked the few blocks home from school. Her mother constantly reminded her that she was to come directly home immediately after school was over for the day. This was drummed into Rachel repeatedly, and her mother's concern was understandable when Rachel was a few minutes late getting home one day. Rachel's mother walked to the sidewalk and looked down the street—no sign of Rachel. She paced the driveway for ten minutes, and still no sign of Rachel. After fifteen minutes, Mother became almost frantic. Twenty minutes had passed when Rachel finally came into view. Mother was relieved, but then became quite angry. She yelled at Rachel in a loud voice, grabbed her by the arm, and ushered her into the house. After several minutes of being angry, Mother finally asked Rachel for an explanation. Rachel told her mother that on the way home she had passed by Sally's house and found Sally outside in the yard crying because she had lost her doll. "Oh," Rachel's mother replied, "and you stopped to find Sally's doll for her?" "No, Mommy," Rachel said, "I stopped to help Sally cry."[9]

Perhaps this is the essence of the therapist's role—to stop and help children cry, to provide for them a safe place in which to cry, and to *be with* them when they cry.

If our primary role is to be with children, is it appropriate to ask questions as part of the therapeutic process? Many counselors consider questions to be the best and most efficient way to glean information from the client. There may be some truth to this. But here again, we should ask ourselves: Am I looking to meet my need or the client's? What hurting children need from the counselor is not to be peppered with questions but to have their feelings affirmed. Still, asking questions seems to come naturally for most people. Think about the husband who arrives home to his wife, who has been taking care of the children all day and has had one disaster after another. What she needs from her husband is not questions about the problems she has faced. She does not need suggestions and solutions. She needs someone to listen and understand. She needs an empathic ear rather than inquiry and advice. A helpful reminder is that if counselors have enough information on which to base a question, they have enough information on which to base an empathic response.[10]

I illustrate this concept when I train counselors by asking a person what she had for dinner two nights ago. After she has given me an answer, I talk about that simple exchange. As I asked the question, I was looking at the person. At that point, the person usually breaks eye contact with me. Why? Because she had to think about the answer. That is what I'm getting at. When children are asked questions, they have to think. Thinking isn't negative at all, but healing occurs at the level of the heart, not the mind. Scripture reminds us: "Above all else, guard your heart, for it is the wellspring of life."[11] Our goal is to minister to "the wellspring of life."

Questions themselves are not inappropriate. Remember, however, that responses and reflections communicate understanding far more effectively than inquiry. The child who enters the playroom with a frown is more likely to let the therapist know what is going on if the therapist reflects the feeling rather than asks, "What's the matter? Why are you frowning?" The times I ask questions are when the client requests my participation in the play. For example, if the child has given me play money and asks me to buy something from her store, I will ask how much I should pay.

Responses in the counseling session will be therapeutic if they flow with the child's play. Children should not be interrupted by the therapist but acknowledged, affirmed, and encouraged. In time, responses will become as natural for the therapist to make as they are for the child to hear and accept. Often, beginning play therapists become frustrated when the responses do not come as naturally and quickly as they would like. Indeed, it is awkward! Learning proper therapeutic responses is like acquiring basic counseling skills; until you have thorough understanding of counseling techniques and experience in applying them, the process feels foreign and clumsy. I remind trainees about the learning curve that Thomas Gordon outlined in his Parent Effectiveness Training.[12] In the acquisition of new communication skills, one moves from being *unconsciously unskilled* (not skillful and unaware of not being skillful) to being *consciously unskilled* (not skillful but aware of the need to develop skills) to being *consciously skilled* (developing the skills but needing much conscious effort) to being *unconsciously skilled* (being skilled and having the responses flow without much thought). Therapeutic responses naturally flow with practice.

Responses need not be lengthy. In fact, when they are, it is usually because the therapist is struggling with what to say. This, in turn, will likely cause children to struggle to understand, partly because the play process has been interrupted. Responses should be brief and interactive. The therapist should be conversational, not mechanical; responding, not parroting; facilitative, not directive.

An initial goal in responding to children is to *track* their play behavior. This means to communicate to children verbally and nonverbally that you are interested in and involved in their play. If a child picks up a toy to use, you might comment about the selection and use: "Michele, it looks as if you've decided to use that in the sandbox." (Avoid labeling the toy until the child has, so you don't limit the potential uses of that toy.) Making this tracking statement communicates to Michele that you are interested in her actions and are following her play behavior. As with all responses in the playroom, the therapist should avoid speaking in the third person. There is a significant difference between "Michele really likes to play with those soldiers" and "You really like to play with those soldiers." Speaking in the third person depersonalizes children. Speaking directly honors children and gives them credit for what they are doing.

Therapeutic responses should *reflect* both content and feeling in the child's play. Content involves the observable activity of the play, and feelings involve the emotional energy attached to the activity. The concept that feelings and behavior are related and affect each other needs to be communicated to the child. For many of the children with whom I work, the reflection process affirms not only their actions and feelings but also their very existence. I find in the supervision of play therapists that identifying and responding to feelings is a challenging skill to develop. The playroom, however, may be the only place where children can have their feelings validated and encouraged. Feelings are not often affirmed for children in everyday life; feelings are often dismissed or ignored. Think about the small boy who has skinned his knee on the sidewalk and runs into the house, crying for his parents.[13] It is not uncommon for the dad to say, "Oh, come on, Son, that doesn't hurt." How confusing that statement must be for a little boy! He might think to himself, *It does hurt! But Daddy's big and smart, and he says it doesn't. It must not hurt.* Do you suppose a child who is raised with confusing messages like this, or is sent the message that certain emotions are unacceptable, will grow up having a skewed perception of the expression of feelings? Simply acknowledging children's feelings in the playroom affirms that feelings are OK. You may set a limit on the appropriate *expression* of feelings, but the feelings themselves are acceptable.

Reflection in the playroom needs to be more than verbal. Your facial expression and tone of voice are crucial. If the child is surprised by something in the play session, your verbal acknowledgment of that feeling should be accompanied by a surprised expression as well. If the child is excited, the therapist's posture and body language should convey excitement. This is not a time to be solemn; it is a time to be animated.

One precaution here: Do not lead the client with verbal or nonverbal messages. If the child lightly taps the bop bag and you say "You really smacked that!" in a loud and enthusiastic voice, the child will probably turn to the bop bag and really smack it. Thus, the child is following your agenda and not his or her own agenda. A similar miscommunication occurs with a therapist who is not at all animated or is even depressed. This therapist sends the message that spirited, energetic play is unacceptable. Counselors have such a position of power and authority with clients that if the therapist is having a bad day, the clients will believe that they themselves are having a bad day as well.

Therapeutic responses should facilitate children to be self-directive. Facilitative responses are freeing and carry only the expectation that the child will make choices and lead the play. Responses should affirm children's choices as well as their ability to master tasks through play.

HELPING CHILDREN MAKE CHOICES

The child-centered approach to play therapy is deeply rooted in basic Christian principles for living life. The way the play therapist relates to the child does not depart from those principles. Crucial to this approach in building an appropriate therapeutic relationship with the child is the consistent utilization of choice-giving by the play therapist. This choice-giving allows the child to engage in decision making which will affect how the child lives out his or her life at that moment. Children must be allowed to experience making choices if they are to discover what responsibility feels like.

A degree of responsibility is given when Jason asks, "Which toy should I play with first?" and the therapist responds, "In here you can decide what to play with first." When presented with a choice, the child is provided an opportunity to experience what decision making feels like and then the reality of living out the choice. St. Paul presented the Christians in Corinth with a choice. "Which do you choose? Shall I come with punishment and scolding, or shall I come with quiet love and gentleness" (I Cor. 4:21). . . .

This part of the play therapy process is considered crucial . . . in view of the fact that the child is being equipped to someday make life's most significant choice, that being the nature of the child's relationship with Jesus Christ. How can children make appropriate life-changing choices if they have not been given opportunities to experience what choosing feels like and then allowed to live with the consequences of their choices? God allows individuals to choose whether or not they will have a relationship with his Son. Can we do less for children?[14]

When children are struggling in the playroom—struggling to make choices, to express an emotion, to get a toy to work for them—it is tempting to jump to their rescue. There is a little bit (or a lot) of "rescuer" in all counselors. But resolving the dilemma for children is usually not therapeutic. Allowing children to struggle within the caring and accepting environment of the playroom is important, even necessary. If a child has trouble removing the lid from a can of Play-Doh and the therapist offers help, the child is robbed of the opportunity to struggle and be frustrated (which is a part of life). The therapist is robbed of the opportunity to affirm those feelings of frustration and the opportunity to make self-esteem-building responses when the child succeeds. Landreth suggests that when you do for children what they are able to do for themselves, you teach them that they are weak.[15]

Responses that build self-esteem are critical to the play therapy process. When you give children credit for something they have accomplished in the playroom, they feel good. It is therapeutic. I am talking about encouragement here, not praise. I do not endorse praising a child in the playroom. What? Not praise a child? Shouldn't all adults do this?

I see a difference between praise and encouragement. Praise focuses on the product; praise carries an evaluative component. Children who are praised rely on the praise to evaluate themselves; they cannot build trust in their ability to evaluate themselves. If children are not praised for something they have done, then what they have done is not good. Positive and negative perceptions about self and others are based on the degree and amount of praise received. Praise is also given only to products as opposed to process. A child might think, *When what I say and do is good, I receive praise; therefore I am good. When what I say and do is bad, I don't receive praise; therefore I am bad.*

Encouragement, on the other hand, is focused on the *effort.* Encouragement emphasizes the process, not the quality of the end result. The effort involved in the action can always be encouraged, regardless of the quality of the activity. Whether children fail a task or accomplish a task, their willingness to attempt a task is worthy of encouragement. While praise is by nature conditional, children can always be encouraged.

An example of this is when children in the playroom paint a picture and ask, "Do you like my picture?" The easiest response might appear to be, "Yes, I do. It's great!" However, this sets up the therapist as evaluator of children's creations. The children are then likely to follow this interaction with more pictures and more questions because they want to please the therapist. Responses of praise, therefore, will restrict the children's freedom, foster dependency on the therapist, direct the play process, and create an external rather than internal locus of evaluation. A more helpful response to the question "Do you like my picture?" would be for you to prize the picture with your voice tone (showing keen interest through inflection and intonation) and body language (leaning toward the picture and pointing to details). The verbal response might be: "I see you used lots of colors.

You painted the bottom green. That must be . . ." Let your voice trail off so the child can finish the statement—"grass!" Then continue: "Oh, yes, that's the grass! And up here [pointing], you used blue. That must be . . ." When you respond like this, you are not evaluating but are showing respect for the children's work. Most children will forget their question about whether or not you like their picture; they will feel honored by your interest in their creation.

Perhaps the best way to illustrate therapeutic responses in the playroom is to give a sample dialogue in the playroom.[16]

THERAPIST: Jason, this is our playroom, and this is a place where you can play with the toys in a lot of the ways you would like to.

The child-centered approach is permission-giving. It respects the child's ability to lead the process where it needs to go.

JASON: (looks around the playroom tentatively but does not move toward any toy or play activity)

We would expect Jason to be somewhat cautious. He likely has not been in a situation with an adult who has allowed him to have control and take the lead. This is a very different experience.

THERAPIST: Looks like you're wondering just what to do in here. This is your time, and in here you can decide.

Reflection of the child's actions and affect are key in the child-centered approach. The therapist's response is already promoting Jason's self-responsibility. Note also the use of the words "in here," specifying that the playroom is a special place in which the child is able to make such decisions.

JASON: I don't know what to do. (in a quiet tone, looking in the direction of the therapist but not making eye contact)

When Jason looks in the direction of the therapist, he is beginning to make contact. He is still somewhat apprehensive about the process, but is making movement.

THERAPIST: (also in a quiet tone) You're just not sure what to do. Sometimes it's hard to decide. This is a place where you can choose what to do.

Note the therapist's voice tone matches that of Jason. Empathic reflection involves more than words; it also includes voice tone, facial expression, body language, etc. The therapist's response places with Jason the responsibility to make choices and thus the opportunity to learn self-control and self-responsibility.

JASON: (walking over to the paints) Is it OK if I play with the paints?

Jason is still seeking permission and approval. As he makes decisions for himself, he will feel empowered, and will develop an internal source of approval rather than looking for external praise.

THERAPIST: Sounds like you have something in mind. In here you can decide.

Actually, Jason is not asking a question. He is saying that he wants to paint. By not answering Jason's question, the therapist continues to allow Jason to lead.

JASON: I think I'll make orange by mixing up the yellow and red. (picks up paintbrush and dips into yellow paint)

Jason has made his own decision and is perhaps testing the perceived permissiveness of the relationship by mixing the colors.

THERAPIST: Oh, so you know that yellow and red make orange. Sounds like you know a lot about colors.

By giving Jason credit for knowing his colors, the therapist is building up Jason's self-esteem. Self-esteem building responses and tracking (communicating through reflection that the therapist is paying attention to and invested in the child's play) are important therapeutic tools in the child-centered approach.

JASON: Yeah, it's my favorite color.

Jason acknowledges the therapist's response and adds a personal dimension.

THERAPIST: So you've got a plan to paint something with your favorite color.	*Shows understanding.*
JASON: (suddenly puts the paintbrush back forcefully in its holder, tears the paper off the easel, and groans) Oohh!	*Jason is upset with himself. This is likely a reflection of a basic self-perception that he has.*
THERAPIST: You didn't like how that turned out.	*The response conveys understanding and acceptance of Jason's dissatisfaction with his painting.*
JASON: I messed up! (angry voice)	
THERAPIST: You're really angry about messing that up.	*The focus is not on messing up the painting but on hearing and accepting Jason's feeling.*
JASON: Yeah, I guess so. (pauses) Can I try another one?	*The therapist's acceptance of Jason's feeling allows him to accept that part of himself and frees him to try again since he does not need to defend that part of self.*
THERAPIST: In here, that's something you can decide.	*Therapist continues to return responsibility to Jason.*
JASON: I guess so. (looking around the room)	
THERAPIST: Seems like you're still not too sure about this place.	*The therapist continues to look beyond Jason's action—to feelings and to intentions. It stands to reason that the playroom would be a strange place for Jason. It is a new experience.*
JASON: Uh-huh. (picks up another paintbrush and dips into the blue)	

THERAPIST: You've picked another color.

Tracking of play behaviors needs to continue throughout the session to show interest and involvement.

JASON: (starts to paint in broad strokes across the center of the paper)

THERAPIST: Using a lot of paint.

Therapeutic responses in the playroom should be short, succinct, and interactive with the child's feelings and actions.

JASON: Uh-huh. (switching paintbrushes)

THERAPIST: Hmm, another color—you're covering a lot of that paper with paint.

Note that the therapist is tracking without taking away the lead from the child. Had the therapist commented to Jason that he was painting "all" of the paper, it may have created an expectancy for him to indeed paint the entire paper, thus reinforcing Jason's already evident dependency.

JASON: Yeah, I'm gonna cover the whole page! (sounds happy and has a big smile)

This choice was Jason's alone. He has verbalized a decision.

THERAPIST: You've got a plan, and that makes you happy! (said with enthusiasm and with a smile)

Reflecting feelings is a challenge for many play therapists. Equally challenging is matching the child's affective state. A minimized affective response diminishes the effectiveness of the response and may communicate to the child that the emotion expressed is not appropriate. A response that exceeds the affective expression of the child may be equally leading, as it sends a message to the child that he or she should have the same emotional level as the therapist.

JASON: They'd never let me do this at school. (continues to cover the paper with paint)

THERAPIST: You've noticed that this is a different place.

The therapist responds to the activity of the playroom and not to the situation at school. This reflects the importance in the child-centered approach of remaining in the present and with the child.

JASON: You know, you talk weird.

THERAPIST: I sound kind of different to you.

Rather than responding to Jason's adjective ("weird"), the therapist responds to the underlying message.

JASON: Yeah—you don't talk like other adults. (paper is almost fully covered with paint—Jason looks at therapist) Do you like my picture?

A child should notice that the therapist is not like other adults!

THERAPIST: You used lots of colors in that painting. You put some green on the bottom, blue on that side (pointing), red over there (pointing), some brown near the top—you made it just like you wanted it to be. (shows prizing in tone of voice)

The play therapist does not evaluate but focuses on the effort rather than the product. This is a basic difference between encouragement and praise that is key in child-centered play therapy relationships. By focusing on the effort, the therapist can make self-esteem building statements without creating the leading and approval-oriented dynamic that comes from statements of praise.

JASON: I sure did! (said emphatically)

THERAPIST: And you're proud of your painting!

Continued reflection of feeling. It is likely that Jason has not felt the feeling of pride recently in light of his life circumstances. When he has, he has also likely not been readily affirmed, as in this time in the playroom.

It can be awkward developing these types of responses in a play session with children. I would venture to say, however, it's not as awkward as it is for children when they encounter a therapist who believes in "talk" therapy. "This new language of empathic responding requires effort and commitment on the part of the therapist and a sincere desire to understand and to be fully with a child in unobtrusive ways that sufficiently allow the child the freedom to be completely the person he/she is at that moment."[17]

ENDING SESSIONS AND MISSED APPOINTMENTS

Let's briefly look at two additional issues: ending play therapy sessions and handling missed appointments. The first is the matter of ending a play session. For some children, this is not a problem. For others, however, it is not easy getting them to leave the playroom. A consistent approach is obviously beneficial.

It is best to give the child a five-minute warning before the end of the session. This is only fair, particularly if the child is involved in a specific type of play or the construction of a craft. To say "Our time is up" and to leave the playroom do not honor the child or the process. I usually say, "We have five minutes left in the playroom today." I state it like this for a number of reasons. I say "we" instead of "you" because it emphasizes the relationship, which, as I have noted, is the key to the therapeutic process. It is not true that "I" have five minutes left (and the child will stay) or that "you" (the child) have five minutes left (and the therapist will stay).

Also, I do not say that we have "about five minutes left." What does "about" mean? Does a child have a clear concept of this abstraction? The manipulative child may take advantage of a time limit that is not clear. It is also important to say "today." The child's opportunity to be in the playroom is not complete until termination of the therapy. If the child is coming back for another appointment, it is important to be specific about "today." These specifics may seem like nit-picking and probably do not make or break the therapeutic process, but they do continue the important trend of being clear and consistent and honoring the child.

With some children who are fully engrossed in play, I may also give four-, three-, two-, and one-minute warnings. This will often decrease the frustration response for children who have a hard time leaving the playroom.

After you have announced the time limit, initiate the end of a session with a statement such as, "Our time in the playroom is up for today," which is consistent with the five-minute warning. At this point, it is extremely important for the therapist to *stand up*. It is an incongruent, and thus confusing, message to verbalize that the session is over but to send the nonverbal message that it is not by remaining seated. The therapist may need to take a few steps toward the door to reinforce the message.

Some children can be quite obstinate in their refusal to leave the playroom. This may be because they are having so much fun or because they have a need to push the limits. A manipulative child can come up with all sorts of resisting and stalling techniques. I recommend using the therapeutic limit-setting model discussed in the next chapter to deal with this. The child's reason for prolonging the session, however, is not the issue—the session needs to end. An aspect of the counseling process, indeed an aspect of life, is for children to develop self-control, to stop, to say no, to delay gratification.[18]

The second issue to address is missed appointments. When a client misses an appointment and the parent has not called to cancel ahead of time, a phone call from the counselor is appropriate. Of more concern, however, is when *you* are not able to keep an appointment. It is important to remember that the play therapy appointment may be for the child the most important hour of the week. Therefore, if at all possible, keep the appointment! If, however, you must miss an appointment, extend to the child the same courtesy you would extend to any adult client. If you are aware of an upcoming conflict, inform the child of the anticipated absence at the beginning of the preceding session. Remind the child (and the parent) after the session that it will be two weeks until the next session. If you will not be available even by phone, give the parents appropriate emergency-referral information.

One of the reasons for discussing the change in schedule with children is so they will not internalize the therapist's absence as rejection or punishment for something done wrong. If you are going to attend a conference or go on vacation, your client should be given a general explanation. Respect the emotional fragility of your clients.

In the event of an unanticipated absence due to an emergency, try to talk with both the child and the parents. Again, this honors the client. Children do not generally receive phone calls from adults, and it will probably be a special experience for them. It may also be helpful to send a note in the mail. It is important that the child not feel chastised by the missed appointment, regardless of the reason. Respect for the child and the child's feelings should be the rule of thumb in handling any changes in the therapeutic process.

Another way to foster respect and encourage the growth of clients is to set consistent limits. We will address this issue in the next chapter, as we continue to discuss how to conduct a play therapy session.

The best way of getting to know children is by observing them play. *—SØREN KIERKEGAARD*

7/ THERAPEUTIC LIMIT SETTING

Without limits, there could be no therapy.   —CLARK MOUSTAKAS

Setting limits is one of the most vital elements in child counseling, regardless of the therapeutic modality. Limits define the therapeutic relationship as well as all types of relationships. In one of the earliest publications about limit setting in child therapy, Dr. Ray Bixler suggests, "Restriction of behavior is one of the few universal elements in therapy. Limits have a role in all treatment methods, whether the client is adult or child, withdrawn or aggressive."[1] A relationship without boundaries is not a relationship; rather, it is an unstructured attempt at connection that cannot be made because the people have no specific rules for engagement. A world without limits is not a safe world, and children do not grow where they do not feel safe.

All relationships exist within the confines of limits and boundaries. The Christian life is defined by limits; it is a covenant relationship. Within this covenant, God has established his law, the purpose of which is to bring us into relationship with Christ.[2] The limits of this covenant relationship do not exist to restrict but to give freedom: "The relationship of the partners in the covenant is expressed by *hesed,* God's covenant loyalty. . . . Man's remembrance of the covenant expresses itself in action. Both partners—Yahweh and the covenant people, represented only by an individual—face one another. . . . They are thus in an active and real partnership, and so they both share in the covenant meal. It goes without saying that this strengthens the fellowship of those involved."[3] The therapeutic relationship also has limits, which again are not meant to restrict but to give the freedom for exploration. Indeed, therapeutic limits "strengthen the fellowship of those involved."

In counseling children, setting therapeutic limits is essential to facilitate the relationship. The counselor should be permissive and encourage free expression, albeit within the boundaries of acceptable behavior. Acceptance of all behaviors is not therapeutic, reasonable, or appropriate. A play therapy approach to treating children involves imagination and fantasy, but limits and boundaries must still exist. Therefore, consistent limit setting provides children with the opportunity to learn life truths in the counseling setting. Play therapy, like life, is a learning experience. Limits in the playroom provide for children what appropriate limits provide in the children's home—they teach children that they have choices, what it feels like to make choices and have responsibility, and what it is like to develop self-control.[4]

RATIONALE FOR SETTING LIMITS

Just as with any other therapeutic intervention with a client, setting limits should have a purpose and rationale. If you set limits with the intent to benefit children, those limits will promote growth and development. Here are some of the rationales for setting therapeutic limits:

1. Limits define the nature and boundaries of the therapeutic relationship. The nature of the counseling relationship with children is more than therapist-client or doctor-patient. The relationship in the playroom should be egalitarian while at the same time carefully structured. Structure is not restrictive; it provides definition. It is the therapist's responsibility to provide that structure. "Through the structuring statements of the therapist, the child gains an understanding of the therapeutic relationship and the nature of his freedom and responsibility."[5]

2. Limits offer both physical and emotional safety for children. A lack of limits is often the underlying cause of the emotional and behavioral problems that bring children to counseling. Acting-out children may be screaming for limits through out-of-control behavior. Where no limits exist, anxiety abounds. Anxious children do not exhibit emotional and behavioral control, and they often pursue any behavior that brings relief. Disruptive or attention-seeking behavior prevails in children who have not experienced the security of limits. The consistency and predictability of limits in the playroom bring a sense of security to the relationship and the setting. Limits provide emotional safety for the children and protect them from getting physically hurt.

3. Limits demonstrate the therapist's intent to provide safety for children. The emphasis here is on the word *intent*. If children are aware of the counselor's intent to keep them safe, it will be easier for children to identify with the counselor as an ally.

4. Limits anchor the counseling session to reality. The playroom should be a place where children can explore issues within the safety and therapeutic distance of metaphor and fantasy. It should not, however, be a place where children escape from reality to the point at which they no longer have a connection to the outside world. "The therapeutic experience should not be so unlike life outside the playroom that no transfer of experiences and learning will occur."[6]

5. Limits allow the therapist to maintain a positive and accepting attitude toward children. It is simply too much of a challenge for a therapist who has been physically hurt by children to remain accepting and understanding. I recall a session in which a child intentionally scratched me with a toy, drawing blood. I had not set a limit in time, and the results hurt! My responses to the child during the session following this incident were not harsh or dramatic, but when I reviewed the videotape later, I noticed my tone of voice reflected my irritation. It was clear that my level of acceptance for the child had diminished.

Haim Ginott summarizes this concept: "It is reasonable to assume that a therapist cannot remain emotionally accepting and empathetic when the child attacks him, tears his shirt, paints his forehead, or breaks his glasses. Such activities must be prohibited in order to prevent the arousal of anger and anxiety in the therapist himself. The ability of any person to tolerate aggressive attacks is not unlimited. The invoking of limits prevents the therapist from exceeding his own capacity for tolerance and enables him to remain consistently unperturbed and tranquil."[7]

6. Limits allow children to express negative feelings without causing harm and feeling the subsequent fear of retaliation. When you see children accidentally break a toy in the playroom and then recoil from the therapist with arms covering their faces, it is not too difficult to guess what likely happens to those children when an accident occurs at home. All feelings, positive and negative, need to be affirmed in the playroom—and the negative feelings are the most difficult for children to process. When children need to express a negative feeling and when they are given a clear and nonpunitive limit, the expression of that feeling becomes safe and acceptable.

7. Limits offer stability and consistency. Many of the children who are referred for therapy come from home and school situations in which rules and the enforcement of rules are inconsistent. Think of children who come from the alcoholic home in which unpredictability is prevalent. In this kind of home, what was acceptable yesterday is not acceptable today; the parent might be kind and accepting in the morning but cruel and caustic at night. Therapeutic limits that are set and enforced consistently (not punitively) offer the stability that many children rarely experience. Limits set in this manner show children that the process of therapy is neither rigid and threatening nor out of control and lacking boundaries.

8. Limits promote and enhance children's sense of self-responsibility and self-control. Through the reflection and acceptance of feelings, both negative and positive, children learn that the expression of feelings is OK. In commenting on limiting inappropriate expression of feelings, Dr. Garry Landreth points out, "Before children can resist following through and expressing feelings in ways dictated by first impulses, they must have an awareness of their behavior, a feeling of responsibility, and exercise self-control."[8] As the play therapy process creates this environment, it becomes possible to set limits that give children choices, and thus encourage children to make their own decisions and take responsibility for those decisions.

9. Limits direct catharsis into symbolic channels. This rationale, suggested by Ginott, notes that one of the primary aims of therapeutic limits is to promote emotional release through acceptable symbolic means.[9] Children may want to express emotions in a way that is inappropriate, but through the world of fantasy, they can act out their emotions. That which cannot be acted out in reality may be acted out in fantasy. For example, children who have been sexually abused and want to act out with the therapist (which is obviously inappropriate) can pretend with the dolls or animals in the playroom. Children who are angry and want to break a toy or hurt the therapist can destroy the egg cartons or hit the bop bag. The expression of emotion is always acceptable; the means of expression may need to be limited.

10. Limits protect the playroom. Unless you have a budget large enough to cover continual damage and loss, it is important to set limits to preserve the playroom and play materials. Although accidental breakage is acceptable, random destruction is not. This is why the playroom needs to be stocked with something that children can destroy; as I have mentioned before, plastic foam egg cartons work well. Although the playroom is a special place—a place to enter fantasy and process the wide spectrum of emotions—it must not be so removed from reality that the process ceases to be therapeutic. In the real world, children cannot randomly damage and destroy things, so neither should they do that in the playroom.

11. Limits provide for the maintenance of legal, ethical, and professional standards. Although children may be less inhibited than adult clients and although play therapy may provide a greater avenue for free expression than other approaches, some behaviors are simply inappropriate from a legal and ethical standpoint. Children cannot take off their clothes in the playroom. They cannot urinate or defecate on the floor. And they cannot fondle the therapist. You may be horrified at the thought of these activities occurring, but if the clients you work with have experienced trauma, these things can happen. It is the therapist's responsibility to set clear limits in such situations. To maintain professional standards that will protect you from liability, videotape the play sessions, especially with children who have been sexually abused. For example, as a male therapist, I will not work with a female client without videotaping the session.

LIMIT-SETTING GUIDELINES

Now that we have looked at the rationale for setting limits, let's turn our attention to the specific guidelines of establishing boundaries and limits. In one of her eight basic principles of play therapy, Virginia Axline states, "The therapist establishes only those limitations that are necessary to anchor therapy to the world of reality and to make the child aware of his responsibility in the relationship." [10]

- *The first guideline is that limits should be set only when they need to be set.* While I do have basic limits in mind going into every session, I do not set any limits until children have presented the need for them. To set limits before the process begins would hinder children's sense of freedom and self-expression. It is impractical for the therapist to try to list all of the possible limits that might be transgressed in the playroom, and to do so might instigate a power struggle with oppositional children. It is simply easier to set limits as needed rather than give an "incomplete dissertation" before the session.[11]

■ *Some limits are absolute.* The basic limits I keep in mind are common for most play therapists:

1. The time spent in the playroom is limited, generally forty-five minutes per session.
2. While recognizing that accidents happen, toys may not be deliberately destroyed.
3. Children may not do harm to themselves or other children.
4. Children may not do harm to the therapist.
5. Toys must remain in the playroom.

These basic rules are nonnegotiable and exist for the protection of the counseling participants and the playroom.

■ *Other limits are relative.* Psychologist Ray Bixler talks about relative versus rigid limits and advocates well-defined limits with "concrete demarcation" whenever possible.[12] However, the use of water, sand, clay, and paints may require some relative limits. In the playrooms at the University of North Texas, for example, our limit on water in the sandbox is two containers (otherwise the sand would turn into a muddy mess). Throwing balls in the playroom is generally acceptable, but throwing anything at the expensive one-way mirrors is not.

■ *Know your boundaries.* Each therapist will have different personal boundaries. Therapists should identify their boundaries and clearly set limits for children who attempt to cross those boundaries. As I pointed out in an earlier chapter, if you are uncomfortable with certain activities or toys (such as guns), you will communicate your discomfort to children in some way. It is better to not have such toys in the playroom or to set consistent limits so the message of care and acceptance is not compromised.

I will allow children to place handcuffs on me or even tie rope around me (not with my hands behind my back, though; I have to protect myself if need be). Other therapists, however, might have different limits. It is perfectly acceptable to tell children, "I choose not to be tied up." This clearly states the therapist's limits and models personal boundaries for children. If you find yourself setting numerous such limits, it would be wise to seek supervision or consultation to discover the source of your discomfort. You may uncover some issues that are affecting the therapy process.

■ *Know when to enforce limits.* We've already discussed that it is best not to declare a laundry list of limits at the beginning of therapy because this would be confining and restrictive to children. But neither is it wise to try to set the limit too late in the process. For instance, when a child is loading the dart gun and looking at you with a mischievous grin, that is the time to set the limit—not after the gun is pointed at you. If the dart gun accidentally or purposely shoots while you're hurriedly outlining the limit, the child may feel guilt or rejection at the unfolding of the incident. Author of *Partners in Play: An Adlerian Approach to Play Therapy,* Dr. Terry Kottman points out that the "primary skills for timing limit setting are the ability to watch and interpret the child's nonverbal cues and anticipate the child's behavior. Most of the time, if the child is about to do something that he or she knows might not be acceptable, he or she will telegraph this nonverbally."[13]

■ *Set limits a minimal number of times.*[14] A playroom free of extra distractions is helpful in this regard. Many children will be distracted by items such as telephones, desks, computers, and clocks. If you set a large number of limits, whether by necessity or because of your discomfort, children's opportunities to express and learn freely become restricted. However, with some children, of course, you will need to set limits more often than with others. Since each child is different, there is no exact minimum or maximum number of times a limit should be set. The concern, however, is that the session not be characterized by setting limits. It is difficult to build a therapeutic relationship when the therapist's primary verbalizations are about limits. A particular limit should not be repeated over and over (the therapeutic limit-setting model discussed in the next section will address this concern). Continually setting the same limit establishes an unhealthy pattern and does nothing for the therapeutic relationship and growth process.

- *Set limits that are total and enforceable.* Conditional limits are confusing and less apt to be heeded. For example, if children are gently tapping the therapist's leg with a block of wood and the tapping turns into hitting, when does the limit get set? If you set a limit that instructs children not to hit hard, when does it become too hard? One of my clients likes to use the doctor's kit on me, including checking my reflexes with a plastic hammer. I know this boy tries to push boundaries, so my limit is that the hammer may not *touch* me in any way. If the limit was that he could not hit me hard, he would hit as hard as he thought he could get away with. Likewise, if the limit was that he could not touch my knee, he would find another place on my body to hit. I do not want to get into a power struggle with this child. Once I have set the limit, it is set, and I will follow through.

- *Set clear, concise limits in a firm, matter-of-fact manner.* When outlining a limit, your tone of voice, facial expression, and body language should not change. I have supervised play therapists who were uncomfortable setting limits, and their uneasiness was reflected verbally and nonverbally. In cases like this, the limit setting is usually rushed, unclear, and incomplete, and the voice tone and body posture reflect discomfort. If the therapist has a need to be liked by children, limits will be difficult to set. If the therapist does not trust children, limits will probably be set too often. A question to consider: Is it possible for children to trust you if you do not trust children?

A LIMIT-SETTING MODEL
The limit-setting model taught by Garry Landreth at the University of North Texas is simple and effective. The model, detailed in

Landreth's book *Play Therapy: The Art of the Relationship,* is composed of three steps. When it becomes necessary to set a limit in the playroom, the therapist can remember the following sequence:

Acknowledge children's feelings, wishes, and wants.

Communicate the limit.

Target acceptable alternatives.[15]

When a limit is necessary, it is imperative that the therapist act (ACT). It is far better to *act* than to *react*, which is often too late or inappropriate. The therapist should be more of a thermostat than a thermometer when it comes to setting limits.[16] This means the therapist's limits should *set* the temperature rather than *measure* the temperature in the playroom. Let's look at the ACT model more closely.

Acknowledge children's feelings, wishes, and wants. If you acknowledge children's feelings, they are much more apt to hear the message of the limit. Children express emotional needs through their behavior, and to acknowledge that is to honor them. To affirm children's feelings and acknowledge this need does not encourage the behavior that requires a limit; rather, it reinforces the messages "I'm here. I hear you. I care. And I understand." Further, by affirming the need, you may deter the action since children's behavior might be a call to be seen, heard, and acknowledged.

Communicate the limit clearly. Concisely and precisely delineate what you are limiting. Unclear limits are less likely to be observed. If children are throwing sand in the playroom, say, "The sand is not for throwing." There are certainly other ways to set the limit, but I believe this wording is best. Stating the limit in other ways may send a message you don't intend:

- Weak and nebulous: "It's probably not a good idea to throw sand in here."
- Pluralized: "We don't throw sand in here." Therapists need

not bring themselves into the limit since they have no intention of throwing sand.

- Punitive: "You can't [or shouldn't] throw sand." This sends a negative message that their play is unacceptable.
- Authoritarian: "I can't [or won't] let you throw the sand." This sets up the therapist as disciplinarian.
- Shifting responsibility to someone or something outside of the playroom: "The rule is you can't throw the sand." It is the responsibility of the therapist—not some vague presence beyond the playroom—to set and enforce limits.

Target acceptable alternatives. The need to set a limit indicates that children have simply chosen an inappropriate manner to express a feeling (since all feelings are acceptable) or that they may not be aware of another way in which to express the feelings. This step, therefore, involves offering an alternative means for children to express themselves. If children want to paint the wall, offer them paper instead. If children want to throw sand, suggest that they throw a ball instead. If children want to hit you, offer the bop bag instead. Also, it is best to offer the alternative nonverbally—the therapist should point to the suggested option. Children will naturally follow the therapist's pointing finger. Not all children are auditory in their communication style; some are visual or kinesthetic. Just as a classroom teacher would not lecture exclusively but would offer visual and experiential stimuli, a therapist's verbal statement of the alternative is inadequate. Some examples of this process might be helpful.

1. *If the child is angry and wants to shoot the therapist with a dart gun,* the therapist might say, "John, I can see you are really angry at me and you'd like to shoot me. I'm not for shooting. You can pretend the bop bag is me and shoot the bop bag." Here, children are permitted to act out in the fantasy of the play that which is not acceptable to act out in reality. If children wanted to engage in overt sexualized play, the alternative might be to use dolls.

2. If the child is excited in the sandbox and begins to throw the sand around the room, the therapist might say, "Jessica, you look pretty happy playing in the sandbox. I know you are excited, but the sand is not for throwing outside of the sandbox. The sand is for playing with inside the sandbox." I would not set a limit on children who are playing in the sandbox and accidentally spill sand out onto the floor. But throwing sand in the playroom calls for a limit. If the children's desire is to throw something, I may direct them to a ball.

3. If the child wants to leave the playroom before the session is over, the therapist might say, "Tommy, our playtime is not done for today. It looks as if you really don't want to be here, but our time is not done. We have twenty more minutes, and then it will be time to go back to the waiting room." If children are going to leave the playroom, it is not possible to stop them. I do not advise the therapist to sit between children and the door, as this can be quite anxiety provoking for children. You have probably noted that I tend to use the child's name in the setting of limits. Most children will pause in their activity when a limit begins with the use of their name. In setting this type of limit, I have rarely had children leave the room prematurely.

4. If the child asks for or attempts to take a toy from the playroom, the therapist might say, "Joey, it sure seems that it would be fun to take that [toy] home with you to play with, but the toys are for keeping in the playroom. They will be here the next time you come to the playroom." Children may want to take the toy home as a token of a special time in the playroom. I would argue that what children take home in their hearts and souls is more important than what they might take in their pockets. Although it is tempting to allow children to take something with them, it is not a good practice to begin. Doing so would set a precedent, and children might expect to take something after every session. (It would also be expensive!) If the child has painted a picture, made a craft, or modeled a clay sculpture, it is appropriate for them to take the artwork out of the playroom.

5. If a child wants to play with the therapist's clothing, jewelry, and similar things, the therapist might say, "Robin, my watch is not for playing with." It is certainly okay to use the entire ACT model here, but I do not feel the necessity in this case. My watch is not for playing with, so I will simply state this.

WHEN CHILDREN VIOLATE BOUNDARIES

If you set limits in a clear, concise, and nonpunitive manner, the majority of children will respond to them. Some children will, however, break the limit. If children persist in their behavior even after you have established a boundary, you may need to take a fourth step: placing the toy off-limits for the remainder of the session. When children continue to use a toy in an unacceptable manner, the therapist should give them a choice of adhering to the limit or having the item placed off-limits for the remainder of the session. Landreth points out that this step should be carefully stated so that children know they have a choice and the consequence will be a result of that choice.[17] For example, if children persist in painting the wall, the therapist should say: "If you choose to paint the wall, you choose not to use the paints anymore today." A limit that is set in this way is neither punitive nor rejecting. The choice clearly belongs to the child. If the child chooses to paint the wall, then having the paints placed off-limits is not the therapist's choice. The ultimate limit is, of course, to end the playtime. If children do not respond to this fourth step, then I will repeat the fourth step with the consequence being the end of the play session: "If you choose to shoot me again, you choose to leave the playroom." In the thousands of play sessions I have conducted, fewer than five have ended early. Again, leaving the playroom is the child's choice and thus not a rejection or punishment by the therapist.

It is up to the discretion of the therapist as to when this fourth step should be implemented. I have found that the fourth step is usually not needed, especially if the limit-setting model is followed. Generally, I will set a limit two or three times before I consider setting this fourth and final step. If it becomes necessary to set the final limit and if children persist in breaking that limit, I have the responsibility to follow through. The manner in which I do this is simple. If I have set a limit for throwing a ball at me ("If you choose to throw the ball at me, you choose not to play with the ball anymore today") and if the child throws the ball at me anyway, I will say, "I see you have chosen not to play with the ball today." (Or, if the limit involves ending the session, I will say, "I see that you have chosen to leave the playroom for today.") Again, it is the child's choice, not the rejection of the therapist. Additionally, when I have set this final limit, I have not had difficulty with children refusing to give up a toy or leave the playroom. They may not be happy with me, but I then have the opportunity to reflect their anger and frustration at the results of the choice they have made.

This fourth step is simply an extension of "logical consequences."[18] Within this process, children learn that their behavior has consequences, a concept that many children are not taught at home or school. Through the limit-setting process, children learn that they do have choices and that their choices carry consequences. Learning to make choices and reap the consequences (whether positive or negative) is an important part of the therapeutic process, the parenting process, and spiritual growth. The nation of Israel was given such a choice: "This day I call heaven and earth as witnesses against you that I have set before you life and death, blessings and curses. Now choose life, so that you and your children may live and that you may love the Lord your God, listen to his voice, and hold fast to him."[19] In helping children learn to make choices and learn responsibility, we are helping them to grow up spiritually as well as emotionally.

A final issue on setting therapeutic limits is this: If you choose to set a limit in the process of therapy, regardless of the modality, you must be willing to follow through. You must see to it that children's choices are carried out. If you are not prepared to follow through on children's choices, you send the message that this place (the playroom), this situation (the therapy), and this person (you) are inconsistent, unreliable, and therefore not safe. Children, while not always happy with their choices, will respect the stability and security of an environment where limits are clearly stated and consistently enforced.

Limits exist in every relationship. . . . In psychotherapy, there must be an integration of freedom and order. . . . Limits provide the boundary or structure in which growth can occur.

—*CLARK MOUSTAKAS*

8 / Using Stories, Sandplay, and Art in Play Therapy

The imagination is more important than knowledge.
—ALBERT EINSTEIN

As we have seen, one of the benefits of play therapy is that the toys become the receptacles or symbols of the pain and thus provide a safe avenue for expression. Several other techniques successfully help children project their feelings and experience healing. Intra-psychic pain can be difficult for clients of any age, but it is especially difficult for children, whose verbal and cognitive skills are not well developed. Children, therefore, find a healthy release in projecting issues and emotions into and onto a metaphor or symbol.

While much has been written on projective techniques, I would like to highlight three techniques that I have found to be particularly helpful in my work with children. Remember, however, that this is a summary overview of issues and techniques on which entire books have been written. Before using these techniques, read extensively about them and get training to help you use them effectively.

STORYTELLING

Storytelling has been an art and a tradition throughout human history. It has been used as a technique for teaching and for passing on traditions. Parables, fairy tales, and poetry make use of metaphors to present ideas and concepts in a way that can be more clearly understood. Parents and grandparents use stories to teach as well as to comfort in times of crisis. Play therapists can use stories to teach and comfort as well, while providing the safety of therapeutic distance. The therapeutic use of stories can help children deal with intrapsychic conflict and developmental tasks.

Scripture carries admonitions to teach children through the parables of storytelling:

> O my people, hear my teaching; listen to the words of my mouth. I will open my mouth in parables, I will utter hidden things, things from of old—what we have heard and known, what our fathers have told us. We will not hide them from their children; we will tell the next generation the praiseworthy deeds of the Lord, his power, and the wonders he has done.[1]

> These commandments that I give you today are to be upon your hearts. Impress them on your children. Talk about them when you sit at home and when you walk along the road, when you lie down and when you get up. Tie them as symbols on your hands and bind them on your foreheads. Write them on the doorframes of your houses and on your gates.[2]

As we have discussed in previous chapters, children learn, explore, and understand through imagination and play. Using storytelling as a therapeutic technique should, therefore, flow naturally. In their book about using metaphors in therapy, Drs. Joyce Mills and Richard Crowley make a case for the therapeutic use of storytelling:

In most cases [children] prefer hearing stories to being talked at by some adult. . . . Part of childhood identity in our culture is woven out of bits and pieces of fairy tales, cartoons, and movie heroes that have most affected the child. . . . Given this natural receptivity to metaphor that characterizes childhood, we found that a conscious and directed application of a therapeutic metaphor via storytelling produced effective and gratifying results. Certainly storytelling is not a new or unique form of child therapy, but the particular combination of techniques used to create the story can result in something quite special. When this happens, the story as experienced by the child is an effortless flight into an inner world. As crafted by the therapist, however, the story is a complex interweaving of observations, learnings, intuitions, and goals which ultimately leaves the child with a very important message.[3]

The issues that victims of abuse or other trauma face are often acute and troublesome. The fear, anxiety, rage, and depression that result often exist within an environment that is unpredictable and hostile. These issues and themes can be presented in the form of stories with characters. Children relate to the characters and apply the story to their own situations at an unconscious level. The children's sense of isolation about their own problem is often replaced with a sense of a "shared" experience.[4] It is this sense of identification that activates the therapeutic effect and the healing power of metaphors. On an unconscious level, children create bridges of personal connection between themselves and the events of the story.

USING FAIRY TALES TO COMMUNICATE TRUTH

In her book *More Annie Stories: Therapeutic Storytelling Techniques,* Doris Brett suggests that fairy tales are a prime example of how stories communicate powerful truths to children.

Fairy tales deal with issues that are important to children. "Cinderella," for instance, is concerned with sibling rivalry. "Hansel and Gretel" focuses on the fear of being abandoned. "Tom Thumb" speaks of the terror, helplessness, and frustration of finding yourself in a world where everything is overwhelmingly bigger and more powerful than you. Fairy tales explore the themes of good versus evil, of altruism versus avarice, courage versus cowardice, kindness versus cruelty, perseverance versus giving up. They teach the child that the world is a complex place; that things happen that seem unfair and unjustified; that the odds against success may seem overwhelming at times; that fear, regret, and despair are as much a part of our world as joy, optimism, and confidence. But most important, they also teach the child that if you can just keep going, even though the situation looks hopeless, if you can stick to your moral standards, even though temptation beckons at every corner, eventually you will win.

As children hear these stories, they recognize at an unconscious level the echoes that resonate in their own lives. They can use the stories to work through some of their own fears and feelings about these issues. They also recognize the message of hope, a very important message. A child who does not have hope will give up the struggle and never succeed.[5]

Storytelling can be used in several ways within the counseling setting. Violet Oaklander describes how she uses stories: "The use of stories in therapy involves making up my own stories to tell to children; the children's making up stories; reading stories from books; writing stories; dictating stories; using things to stimulate stories such as pictures, projective tests, puppets, the flannel board, the sand tray, drawings, open-ended fantasies; and using props and aids such as a tape recorder, videotape, walkie-talkies, toy microphone, or an imaginary TV set (a large box)."[6] Oaklander's Gestalt techniques are dramatic and interactive, providing the opportunity for children to express themselves through the metaphors of stories, as well as incorporate dramatic play.

Child psychologist Richard Gardner has developed a mutual storytelling technique: "In this method the therapist elicits a self-created story from the child. The therapist then surmises its psychodynamic meaning and tells a responding story of his or her own. The therapist's story utilizes the same characters in a similar setting, but introduces healthier resolutions and adaptations of the conflicts present in the child's story."[7] While this approach can be effective, the counselor should be cautious about leading children where they are not ready or able to go. It might also be argued that the counselor's adaptation removes the value of the therapeutic distance that metaphor provides in storytelling.

John Allan, a Jungian play therapist, advocates the use of serial story writing, believing "that psychological or inner growth occurs when dreams or daydreams are made tangible through some form of creative expression, such as writing or painting."[8] This approach encourages children to create a series of stories over time. Allan advocates interpretation of the stories following Jungian guidelines: (1) every part of the story reflects a slightly different aspect of the writer's emotional life; (2) the emotions reach consciousness through the symbols used (i.e., the symbol is the container for a particular type of feeling); and (3) the mechanisms of repression and projection are frequently seen.

Mills and Crowley also take a primarily Jungian approach to storytelling. They advocate that counselors develop stories based on the children's experience and suggest the following basic ingredients of building therapeutic metaphors in stories:

1. Establish an overall theme of *metaphorical conflict* in relation to the protagonist.
2. Personify *unconscious processes* in the form of heroes or helpers (representing the protagonist's abilities and resources) and villains or obstructions (representing the protagonist's fears and negative beliefs).

3. Personify *parallel learning situations* in which the protagonist was successful.

4. Present a *metaphorical crisis* within a context of inevitable resolution, by which the protagonist overcomes or resolves his problem.

5. Develop a new sense of *identification* for the protagonist as a result of his victorious "hero's journey."

6. Culminate with a *celebration* in which the protagonist's special worth is acknowledged.[9]

Mills and Crowley apply these ingredients to the well-known fairy tale *The Ugly Duckling* and their own stories to illustrate the process. I like using this technique because it does not change a story that the children have made up and offers a possible therapeutic resolution that children can accept or reject because it remains within the context of metaphor.

Keep in mind several points when using storytelling as a therapeutic technique. Storytelling should make great use of imagery and the imagination. Obviously, stories need to be entertaining and arouse children's curiosity so that they stay attentive. Use of vivid and descriptive images should be a part of the storytelling process. Include various learning modalities—visual, auditory, and kinesthetic—in the stories. Related to this, it is also helpful if therapeutic stories involve the basic human senses (touch, taste, smell, sight, and sound). This process can be enhanced by props, such as stuffed animals, musical instruments, or dolls. It is also beneficial if the storyteller utilizes a range of facial and vocal reflections, varying intonation and inflection to match the content of the story. Finally, my preference in storytelling is to use animals rather than real persons as characters. Even if you change the names of people in telling a child a therapeutic story, the situation can be too close to reality and end up being recapitulating instead of healing. The therapeutic distance provided by metaphor and the use of animals provides the safety necessary for impacting the child's unconscious processes.

I sometimes use storytelling to break bad news to a child. Too often, when children experience the trauma of divorce, terminal illness, or placement in foster care, the news is delivered in the same way it might be told to an adult, albeit with simpler words. Using their experience working in a foster-care agency, some of my colleagues have written a short book about therapeutic stories that cushion the trauma of receiving bad news.[10] Karen Lanners and Ken Schwartzenberger suggest using a "bridge technique." This involves telling a story and then introducing the new information with the phrase "Just like the character in the story, I have to tell you. . . ."[11] The story touches children and prepares them to hear the bad news. While this does not remove trauma from the situation, it helps to ease the blow.

The clinical staff of the foster-care agency created the following story to inform two young children that the adoptive home they were to move into was no longer available to them. The news would be especially devastating to the children because this had happened to them once before.

Two caterpillars were looking for the right tree to climb, the right branch to crawl out on, and the right leaf to go to in order to spin their cocoons. These two caterpillars had to search several trees, several branches, and several leaves before they could find just the right one—the one that was safe to spin the cocoon. Sometimes these caterpillars thought they had found the right tree, only to discover it wasn't quite the right one. The right tree, the right branch, the right leaf was out there somewhere. And it was tough when they thought they had found it and then realized it wasn't quite the right one. When the caterpillars find the right tree, the right branch, and the right leaf, they will spin their cocoons and begin the transformation into butterflies [here the storyteller, using puppets, would transform the caterpillars into butterflies], which can happen only in a special and safe place, on the right tree. And just like the caterpillars in this story, sometimes it takes a while for children to find just the right home. . . .

Although this story didn't change the outcome for these two foster children, it did help to cushion the pain of the bad news. Stories can convey information metaphorically and thus help children understand at an unconscious level. Stories can teach, comfort, and provide healing for children while helping them maintain therapeutic distance.

SANDPLAY

Another projective play technique is sandplay, which enables children to process pain and trauma in a nonthreatening manner. John Allan notes that "sand often acts as a magnet for children. Before they realize it, their hands are sifting, making tunnels, shaping mountains, runways, and riverbeds. When miniature toys are added, a whole world appears, dramas unfold, and absorption is total."[12] Creating "worlds" in the sand tray not only gives the counselor a view of the client's world but also allows the child to bring some sense and order to the chaos of emotional turmoil and trauma.

Dr. Margaret Lowenfeld first developed the therapeutic use of the sand tray and miniatures in London in the 1920s.[13] She had read H. G. Wells's book *Floor Games,* in which Wells talks about his playing with miniature toys on the floor with his two sons.[14] Lowenfeld used a sand tray and miniatures with children, asking them to create "world pictures." This technique was later called the "Lowenfeld World Technique."[15] Dora Kalff, a Swiss Jungian analyst, adopted Lowenfeld's technique and developed a variation called sandplay.[16] In sandplay, "The child has the opportunity to resolve the traumas through externalizing the fantasy and by developing a sense of relationship and control over inner impulses through play."[17] Like the play therapy we have discussed in earlier chapters, sandplay allows children to "talk" about their issues without verbalizing their thoughts and feelings. Children approach and process emotional issues within the safety of the modality, managing their issues through the placement and manipulation of the sandplay miniatures.

Sandplay meets a number of emotional needs for children. Director of the Center for Sandplay Studies in New York, Lois Carey lists six therapeutic rationales that summarize the benefits in using this treatment modality.[18]

First, sand is tactile and provides a total kinesthetic experience for the child. I have had nonverbal children start playing with the sand in the tray and begin to talk. It is as if the sensation of the sand running through their fingers loosens their tongue. While this is neither my intent nor my goal, it is a therapeutic by-product.

Second, sandplay encourages verbalization in children with poor verbal skills and provides a safe place for children who use verbalization as a defense. Again, although verbalization is not necessarily a goal of the intervention, sandplay can give words to previously unspoken emotional issues. For children who use verbalization as a defense, it is important to remember that the fact that children are highly verbal does not mean they know how to express deep emotional needs.

Third, the size of the sand tray sets natural limits, which ultimately leads children to develop their own limit-setting skills. As discussed in the last chapter, therapeutic interventions should assist children in developing their own internal locus of control.

Fourth, sandplay allows children to have total control over the construction and action of the tray, thus increasing their sense of power. They can create and rule their own world.

Fifth, the sand tray and miniatures—rather than the counselor— become the object of transference. Negative transference issues— such as a boy who has been molested by an uncle and is in therapy with a male counselor—can be diminished or neutralized with this projective approach.

Sixth, sandplay may help children access deeper issues more quickly than through other treatment modalities. The sand provides a safe venue in which to disclose and process, and the sand and miniatures assist in making concrete that which is abstract.

Sandplay Equipment

The equipment necessary for sandplay may be basic or quite elaborate. My experience has shown that it is not necessary to apportion a great deal of office space or to spend thousands of dollars on supplies to provide a helpful sandplay experience. It may even be that large and elaborate equipment will be intimidating and overwhelming to children.

The basics include two sand trays and an ample selection of miniatures. The counselor who also conducts play therapy may want to consider a separate room for sandplay equipment because the techniques and tools differ.

The sand trays are normally 20" x 30" x 3" and half-filled with sand. It is best not to use playground sand, which often has small pebbles in it, or extrafine sand, which can be a problem for allergy-prone clients and therapists. The inside of the tray should be painted blue to simulate sky and water. The size of the trays is important because children need to be able to view the whole tray in a single glance. I recommend having two waterproof trays—one for wet sand and the other for dry. If you have only one tray and a child wants to use water in it, you will be stuck with wet sand for all of your clients for the next few weeks. The trays should be set on a stable surface, preferably on a table that is about average desk height, with some room around the base of the tray. Sometimes children place miniatures outside the sand tray, an important representation of how they view their family lives.

Like toys for the play therapy room, miniatures should be selected, not collected. It is not necessary to have hundreds of miniatures, but it is helpful to have a wide assortment of toys and objects. Some basic categories include:

- Buildings (houses, castles, factories, schools, churches, stores)
- People (various racial-ethnic groups, military, cowboys, sports figures, fantasy, mythological, different occupations)
- Vehicles (cars, trucks, planes, boats, farm equipment, military and emergency vehicles)
- Animals (domestic, farm, zoo, wild, marine, prehistoric)
- Vegetation (trees, shrubs, plants)
- Religious symbols (cross, Madonna, menorah, nativity)
- Structures (fences, bridges, gates, highway signs)
- Natural objects (rocks, shells, driftwood, feathers)
- Miscellaneous (jewelry, wishing well, treasure chest)

Miniatures should be grouped together by category and displayed on open shelves, if possible. Children are less likely to rummage through drawers or bins than they are to choose objects from a shelf. Categorization is important; the emotionally fragile child may not select a miniature rabbit if it is right next to a fire-breathing dragon.

As I mentioned, a simple yet broad collection is more than adequate. Building up a collection of miniatures can be quite expensive. But you may be able to find miniatures at garage sales and thrift stores. It is cheaper to buy a bride and groom from a wedding cake shop or a bridge from a discount aquarium store than it is to order miniatures from a sandplay catalog. The trays themselves can also be expensive, but they are relatively easy to make. I have built pinewood trays and then painted and waterproofed them. If necessary, use a plastic sweater box with a blue cover; place the blue cover under the clear plastic to simulate the blue bottom of the tray.

The process of sandplay varies, depending on a counselor's theoretical orientation and style. I recommend doing more extensive reading in the field (see Suggested Reading at the end of this book). I should also note that Jungian sandplay therapists advise beginning counselors to pursue sandplay themselves (facilitated by a qualified sandplay therapist) before using this treatment modality with clients.

Sandplay may involve creating a scene in a single tray during one session, several trays during one session, or a continual active drama with the miniatures throughout the session. Some children quickly construct their trays; others linger or use painstaking detail. This is essentially up to the client. Themes evident of the child's intra-psychic issues will emerge, whether or not the therapist is able to interpret them. The point is to provide a medium of expression and to communicate understanding. Now let's briefly explore how to use the sand tray and miniatures.

I introduce the sand tray and miniatures to children by suggesting that they look at the miniatures and then create a picture in the sand. Although I rarely encounter resistance from children, I have occasionally added that this is a type of counseling I use with teenagers and adults (which is true), and it is helpful for almost everyone. This always hooks in children and preteens because it appeals to their pseudomaturity.

How interactive should a counselor be as children begin to select miniatures and place them in the sand? That depends largely on the counselor's approach. This spectrum is similar to the range between a Jungian therapy approach and a Gestalt approach. Involvement may range from little interaction and comment to being active and making several comments and asking questions. It also depends on the children's development level and the issues with which they are struggling. Sometimes I make continual tracking and reflective comments, just as in play therapy. Other times I will say very little, with the intent to "honor and reverence" the construction of the tray, which is a key element of the Jungian approach. Most the interaction occurs at the completion of the tray, when I begin to ask a few questions.

I ask the children to tell me the title of their picture. Only rarely will children not be able to come up with a title. I then ask the children to tell me a story about the scene—essentially to describe what is going on. A great deal of information normally comes out in this story. The therapist might ask questions such as: "What about this figure here? What is she doing? It looks as if these two are saying something to each other—what could they be talking about? Are you in this picture? Do you know anyone else in this picture? What's going to happen next [if it is an action scene]? What [not who] has the most power here?" Other questions may come up within the process, but I try to keep them simple and open ended. I avoid questions that are intrusive or that jump to a conclusion.

Let me sound a warning about interpretation. It is, without doubt, fascinating and intriguing to observe the process of sandplay and to speculate about what the miniatures might mean or what a scene might be saying. It is often possible to interpret correctly what is laid out in the sand. This helps the counselor to know that children are making progress, but interpretation is not necessarily appropriate with children. The developer of sandplay, Jungian analyst Dora Kalff, cautions against interpretation, which is an appropriate warning.[19] It is worth reiterating that interpretation most often seems to meet the counselor's need rather than the client's need. Most often, interpretation is truly helpful when the child comes up with it. John Allan notes: "The crux of the sandplay is not that it must be interpreted but that it must be witnessed respectfully. The counselor's attitude for the process is 'active being' rather than direction and guidance."[20] Essentially, if you are able to communicate those four messages—"I'm here. I hear you. I understand. And I care."—during the process, you have created an environment for growth and healing.

Many counselors have found it helpful to take slides or pictures of completed sand trays. This provides a visual and chronological record of the therapy process, and these can be discussed with clients during and at the end of therapy to review progress. It is also beneficial to videotape the sandplay sessions for supervision purposes and your own growth as a counselor.

John Allan discusses common sandplay stages that are helpful in assessing the progress of therapy.[21] The first stage is *chaos,* in which children may "dump" miniatures into the sand, often without apparent deliberate selection. The chaos evident in the sand reflects the chaos and emotional turmoil in the children's lives. The next stage is *struggle,* in which there are often battle scenes. These include armies battling, knights jousting, monsters fighting, and so on. At the beginning of the creation of these scenes, often the two (or more) opposing sides in the fight will annihilate each other. In fact, in the early stages of sandplay, it is typical that no one survives battles or accidents. Eventually, a transition occurs whereby one side begins winning, normally good over evil. The third stage is *resolution,* in which life seems to be "getting back to normal." The scene in the tray shows more order and balance. Children deliberately select and carefully place the miniatures, and children see themselves in the trays, often in the role of helper. This is usually a sign that termination is appropriate, with the confirmation from parents and teachers that change outside the counseling room has occurred as well. The duration of treatment is not uniform. That is, some clients may progress through the stages in just a few sessions; others will take longer. In his book *Inscapes of the Child's World,* John Allan discusses sandplay as a technique to use in a school setting, noting that the average length of therapy is eight to ten sessions.

Sandplay can also be used in other ways. I have occasionally applied it diagnostically, with the request that a child do a Kinetic Family Drawing in the sand with the miniatures.[22] I will simply ask children to create in the sand a scene of their family doing something. The activity depicted is entirely up to the children. I have also used sandplay with couples and families because it provides an excellent picture of family communication and dynamics. In this situation, I will either use the same instructions as an individual sandplay session or specifically ask the family to construct a tray of some family activity.

Sandplay is a powerful and effective intervention, which, like play, often transcends age and cultural barriers. It can provide a wonderful tool for the counselor working with children.

ART TECHNIQUES

Although I am not a registered art therapist, I have found art techniques extremely valuable for counseling children. To make contact with and garner information from children, many counselors use art, such as the House-Tree-Person test (this test involves asking the client to draw a house, a tree, and a person, which are then interpreted by the therapist according to established guidelines). Many different art materials may be used to impact the emotional world of children and families. I do not, however, *require* children to draw a picture any more than I would require children to play in the playroom; rather, I *invite* children to participate.

Several years ago, I attended a lecture by a nationally recognized expert on child sexual abuse. He told the audience that he required sexually abused children to draw a picture of their perpetrator during the first session. The children were *required* to draw their perpetrator? Weren't these children forced by their perpetrator to do things they didn't want to do? I cannot agree with potentially revictimizing a victim by requiring such a recapitulating experience.

Still, crayons and paints can be a nonthreatening means of connecting with children. Gerald Oster and Patricia Gould describe the benefits of this technique: "For most people, drawings are a less common avenue of expression and therefore less likely to be controlled, allowing more pre- and unconscious material to be revealed. In that drawings provide a platform for individuals to expand their repertoire beyond their usual narrow sphere of senses, unexpected things result, providing a springboard for discussion and learning. Drawings also provide a vehicle for gaining insight into underlying conflicts, ego strength, and character traits. This allows people in treatment to better understand themselves and enhance their appreciation of how they function as individuals and within their family and job/school setting."[23]

Let's briefly explore a few art-therapy applications that can be used with children and families. While many child counselors routinely use various art techniques, I use them primarily when I am away from my play therapy facilities or when I am working with a family for assessment purposes.

An art intervention that I have used with success is Joyce Mills's "pain getting better" technique.[24] Here, the counselor asks the child to make three pictures. The first is a drawing of how the child's pain looks. This can be either emotional or physical pain, and the picture helps the child disconnect or dissociate from the pain. The second drawing depicts how the pain looks "all better." This plants the unconscious seed that "all better" is, in fact, a potential reality. The third picture, which Mills calls a "metaphorical bridge," shows what will help change picture one into picture two.[25] The intent here is to enable the child to activate unconscious resources and potentials for healing to occur. For children whose situations seem chronic and catastrophic, this series of pictures can be a powerful beginning to a positive counseling experience.

John Allan advocates a technique called serial art drawing, in which the therapist asks the child to create a picture in each session over the course of the counseling relationship.[26] Allan describes the advantage of this approach: "When a child draws in the presence of the therapist on a regular basis, then the healing potential is activated, conflicts [are] expressed and resolved, and the therapist can gain a clearer and more accurate view of the unconscious. . . . The piece of paper becomes the 'safe place' onto which projections are placed. . . . With this safe expression, movement occurs in the unconscious and new images (feelings) are produced."[27]

The therapist's primary role is to *be present* with the children while they draw. Often, children are quiet during the drawing process, and it is important to honor their silence by refraining from intrusive comments. Questions asked about the drawing after it is complete should be simple, open ended, and phrased so the children may reject them altogether. Questions should remain within the context of the drawing and refrain from taking abstract leaps, which are usually beyond the children's developmental capability to answer. The important element is the process itself. Approach interpretation cautiously.

Another use of art is family art therapy and assessment. Along the same lines as Virginia Satir's sculpting (a family therapy technique in which the relationships between family members are illustrated through the creation of a physical "picture"), using art and drawing in the counseling process reveals a great deal about family dynamics.[28] The materials for this technique can be as simple as a large piece of newsprint placed on the wall of the counseling room or a large white board, if one is available. A five-by-eight-foot drawing surface is best.

Instruct the family to pick a color (I prefer colored markers over crayons) to use throughout the drawing exercise. First, ask the family to draw a picture together without saying anything to each other during the process. When the family is done with the drawing, ask them to describe and title the picture. The family dynamics that arise during the creation of the picture will also be evident during the explanation. The family then draws another picture together, during which they may talk and change colors if they wish. If I have the opportunity to see the family of a child I am treating in play therapy, I will often use these techniques as a means of assessing family dynamics as well as not removing my client from the realm of projective and play-based treatment.

ASSESSING FAMILY ART

The process by which the family creates the artwork is important. Helen Landgarten suggests a series of questions that the counselor should keep in mind during the family interaction:

1. Who initiates and ends the artwork, and in what order did the rest of the family make their contributions?

2. Which members' suggestions were utilized and which were ignored?
3. Which participants remained in their own space versus those who crossed over?
4. Did anyone "wipe out" another person by superimposing their image on top of someone else's?
5. Who made friendly contact gestures and who made hostile ones?
6. Did any member send out a "leave-me-alone" message?
7. Where is each person's contribution (central, end, corner, all over)?
8. How much space did each individual occupy?
9. Who functioned dependently and who independently?
10. Who contributed content that was either provocative or emotionally laden, and how did the rest of the family respond?
11. Did a leader evolve?
12. Who contributed the most and who the least amount of art?
13. Did the interaction take on structure, or was it chaotic?
14. Did the members take turns, work in teams, or work simultaneously?
15. Was the working style concordant or discordant?[29]

We could discuss many other forms of expressive and projective treatments, some of which I have used and others I haven't yet tried. Some of these include clay work, doll and puppet play, sculpture, and collage. If you decide to use one of these techniques, have a specific goal and purpose in mind, know the therapeutic rationale for the technique, and receive appropriate training and supervision in its application.

Projective counseling techniques use a wide variety of expressive media. The various materials used—sand, water, paint, clay, crayons, stories, and so on—are means to facilitate the expression and processing of inner issues. Making use of imagination and creativity, these techniques can effectively assist in the process of transformation, healing, and growth.

The dynamic principle of fantasy is play, which belongs also to the child. . . . The debt we owe to the play of imagination is incalculable. —*CARL JUNG*

9/ ISSUES *in* COUNSELING CHILDREN *through* PLAY

I love little children, and it is not a slight thing when they, who are fresh from God, love us. —CHARLES DICKENS

Counseling children, like parenting children, is simultaneously one of the most rewarding and most challenging endeavors a person can undertake. Our hearts soar as wounded children make breakthroughs in the healing process, and our hearts ache for wounded children who seem stuck in a cycle of hurt. To maintain balance, we must remember that God loves children and that he is in control.

Even though God ultimately brings restoration to our wounded clients, we must fully apply our skills, training, and insight to be effective tools in the healing process. We must be as prepared as possible to address all of the issues that might arise in the course of therapy. This chapter suggests several strategies for addressing issues such as the stages of treatment, assessing progress, working with other professionals, group play therapy, using prayer in counseling, and termination.

STAGES OF TREATMENT

The process of play therapy should be fluid, so it is difficult to discuss precise stages of treatment. Nevertheless, it is helpful to consider some generalities about the progression of treatment. The process of play therapy—like the growth and maturity of children—is developmental and evolves at different rates for different clients. Child psychologist Mary Haworth suggests: "The disturbed child may become fixated at one stage or level or may regress to earlier infantile levels. Often, therapeutic progress can be measured by the extent to which the child relives and 'outgrows' each of the earlier phases until he reaches the stage appropriate to his current maturational level."[1] It is not unusual for children who are experiencing developmental regression or arrest (with speech or motor development, for example) to move forward after emotional issues are addressed in the play therapy.

While clients grow and change at different rates and in different ways, we can see several identifiable stages in the developmental process of play therapy. Clark Moustakas suggests that emotionally disturbed children in play therapy proceed through the following stages:

1. *Diffuse negative feelings,* expressed everywhere in children's play. Children often enter therapy experiencing negative feelings, but the feelings are unfocused, perhaps because they have not been acknowledged or affirmed.

2. *Ambivalent feelings,* generally anxious or hostile. As children experience the therapeutic environment of play therapy, they discover that their feelings are acceptable, but they do not know what to make of them.

3. *Direct negative feelings,* expressed toward parents, siblings, and others, or in specific forms of regression. As children begin to make sense of the negative feelings, it becomes safe to be direct in the understanding of and expression of these feelings. Regressive behavior may take place.

4. *Ambivalent feelings,* positive or negative, toward parents, siblings,

and others. As children attempt to sort out feelings, ambivalence again becomes an issue.

5. *Clear, distinct, separate, usually realistic positive and negative attitudes,* with positive attitudes predominating in the children's play.[2]

Notice that we are talking almost exclusively about feelings. Even so, we cannot dismiss the importance of behaviors because behavioral difficulties most often prompt the referral to counseling. Behavior is often motivated by emotional needs or at least by the self-perception of these needs. As children feel, so will they behave. This means that children who feel positively about themselves (having a self-concept based on the truth that they are made in the image of God) not only will exhibit positive behavior but also will grow and develop as God intended. Helping children experience this is a goal that extends beyond therapy; it should be a goal for parents, teachers, and all adults who interact with children.

Moustakas also notes that all children, regardless of their level of adjustment, display similar types of negative play.[3] "The difference between well-adjusted and disturbed children lies not primarily in the type of negative attitude they show, but rather in the quantity and intensity of such attitudes."[4] This dynamic can be seen both inside and outside the playroom. The difference between an adjusted child expressing anger and a maladjusted child expressing anger will be the intensity and duration of the aggressive play. Children who are not experiencing difficulties will play with a toy gun in the playroom just as children who are having problems will. This does not mean that children who shoot the therapist with a dart gun have aggressive tendencies. However, the children who engage in hostile and aggressive gunplay for an extended period of time may be processing issues of anger and hostility.

In their play therapy training workshops, Drs. Byron and Carol Norton identify five stages in the therapeutic process of play:

1. *Exploratory stage.* The child assesses both the environment and the therapist.

2. *Limit-setting stage.* The child explores the boundaries and level of safety in the play environment and with the therapist. Establishment of trust is a major aspect of this stage and the previous one.

3. *Dependency stage.* The child further explores the therapeutic relationship and develops some level of dependency on the therapist through the expression of emotional needs.

4. *Therapeutic-growth stage.* The child feels a greater sense of empowerment and mastery over emotional issues, which is evidenced in the play.

5. *Termination and closure stage.* The child's sense of growth and independence becomes internalized, and conclusion of the play therapy relationship becomes appropriate.[5]

Although we will not always be able to fit children's development neatly into these stages, it is helpful to keep them in mind for assessment of therapeutic progress.

ASSESSING PROGRESS

Evaluating children's progress in play therapy must extend beyond the lessening of problem behavior. Some parents quickly terminate therapy when symptoms subside only to find that the symptoms reappear shortly thereafter. Does this mean the therapy was ineffective? Does this show that play therapy fails to produce long-term change? To both of these questions, I would answer no. Symptom reduction is but one indicator of progress. Of course, we would expect some symptom reduction for the acting-out child because the need to express self has an outlet in the play sessions. As a result, the need to express self negatively outside the playroom is diminished. This does not mean the underlying issues have been fully resolved. I usually tell parents that I would like to see their child at least four to five times before I have a clear concept of the underlying issues. I also request that the parents not terminate therapy before discussing the situation with me.

When assessing progress, look for changes in the play patterns. Garry Landreth suggests the importance of identifying "firsts": "That movement in the therapeutic process is indeed occurring can be determined by carefully noting in each session those behaviors that the therapist can recall as having occurred for the first time in the relationship with the child."[6] If Timmy has spent his time in the playroom with his back to the therapist and begins to turn toward the therapist, that's a first. If Susan has been playing next to the therapist during the play sessions and begins to venture out into the playroom, that's a first. If Ken has spent multiple sessions playing in the sandbox, burying and unburying toys, and moves to another type of play, that's a first. Changes in the play indicate changes in the child.

Let me give an example of a "first" I observed in the playroom. I had been seeing nine-year-old Ben for several weeks when his generally aggressive behavior turned toward me. He was enthralled with the handcuffs and finally decided to use them on me. For the next few weeks, Ben shackled me in handcuffs and tied me up with rope. For those readers who are raising their eyebrows and wondering what therapeutic value such activity has, please bear with me. It was, in fact, an empowering experience for Ben to control the session and the therapist in this way. Here was a child who was telling me what had happened to him. Ben had been treated in psychiatric hospitals and residential treatment programs for four and a half years. For half of his life—beginning at age two—he had been receiving some level of inpatient care. Ben had received just about every possible childhood diagnosis, ranging from ADHD to schizophrenia. He had been placed on a wide variety of medications and was taking mood-stabilizing and antipsychotic medications when he began play therapy with me. His experience with me was his first exposure to play therapy.

Ben knew what it was like to be locked up. He had been

physically restrained by hospital staff and confined to various treatment facilities. Handcuffing me in the play sessions was more than just "controlling" me and the playtime; it was a metaphor for what he had experienced. Ben was telling me through his play what he had experienced. It was a first when he began this type of play (about five sessions into the therapeutic process), and it was a first when he discontinued this play (about eight sessions later). Although Ben is still in therapy at the time of this writing (now eleven years old) and will probably require long-term psychiatric intervention, he has made significant progress, and his future looks hopeful.

So what does it mean when children engage in repetitive play? Why is it that some children repeat the same play activity session after session? At least two possibilities exist. First, it may be that the repetitive play is a key issue for certain children and represents a theme that requires an extended time to process. I encourage the counselor to be patient and trust the process; rushing children does not honor them or adequately meet their emotional needs. The repetitive play will change when the children have processed issues and are ready to move on. Traumatized children will often engage in repetitive play.

The second possibility is that the children have been communicating their issues to the play therapist through the play but the therapist has not communicated understanding. The therapist just is not "getting it." The children are not receiving the messages, "I'm here. I hear you. I understand. And I care."[7] So the children feel the need to engage in repetitive play until the therapist truly hears them.

Recognizing play themes in therapy is another important aspect of assessing progress. "A theme is the recurrence of certain events or topics in the child's play either within a session or across several sessions."[8] Ben's play with the handcuffs signaled a theme, and switching to a new play activity indicated that he was emotionally able to address new issues. Once again, I would caution against overemphasizing interpretation of play themes. While interpreting themes is interesting, it tends to shift the focus off children and the process and onto the therapist's interpretive musings.

In an ideal world, we could assess a client's progress and determine readiness for termination through empirical measures. In reality, though, emotional growth and development are not so easily defined. It is not possible to measure progress precisely, even with assessment instruments. Behavioral checklists often indicate a parental perception of behavioral change, but this cannot accurately measure emotional readiness to end therapy. These measures can be one indicator of progress, but they must be accompanied by identifiable changes inside and outside the playroom and by discussion with the parents. It is helpful to videotape play sessions so that you can examine an audiovisual comparison of play themes and behaviors. Haworth suggests a series of questions to assess a child's progress:

- Is the child less dependent on the therapist?
- Is the child less concerned about other children using the room or seeing the therapist?
- Can the child now see and accept both good and bad in the same person?
- Has the child demonstrated changes in attitude toward time, in terms of awareness, interest, or acceptance?
- Has the child changed reactions to cleaning up the room (less concern if the child formerly had been meticulous or interested in cleaning up as contrasted to earlier messiness)?
- Does the child now demonstrate self-acceptance and acceptance of his or her own gender?
- Do you see evidence of insight and self-evaluation? Does the child compare former actions or feelings with present ones?
- Do you see a change in the quality or amount of verbalization?

- Do you see less aggression toward or with toys?
- Does the child accept limits more readily?
- Have the child's forms of art expression changed?
- Does the child show less need to engage in infantile (for example, bottle) or regressive (for example, water) play?
- Does the child engage in less fantasy and symbolic play and more creative-constructive play?
- Have the number and intensity of fears diminished?[9]

These questions are important indicators both inside and outside the playroom. We should expect to see increased levels of independence in therapy and at home and school. We should also anticipate changes that are more global and generalized in the life of the child, including

- Increased ability to solve problems
- Increased verbalization (although this should not be an agenda for the therapist)
- Greater willingness to experiment and explore
- Increased self-worth and self-confidence and corresponding decreased shame and self-deprecation
- Decreased anxiety and depression
- Increased ability to organize and order things and corresponding decreased chaotic thinking and behavior
- Increased ability to express emotions and tolerate other people's expression of emotions
- Decreased aggression
- Decreased fear of confrontation and corresponding increased willingness to negotiate
- Increased willingness to give and receive nurture
- Increased tolerance of frustration
- Increased willingness to seek assistance
- Increased ability to make decisions
- Changes in creative expression, including stories, artwork, etc.

WORKING WITH OTHER PROFESSIONALS

Unfortunately the mental health profession is quite "turf oriented." In many communities, it is often the letters that follow a person's name (Ph.D., M.S.W., M.D., etc.) that bring credibility to his or her work. Clients are the casualties of these turf wars. We professionals should seek to work together for the sake of the children. Since we know that a divided house will not stand, the Christian counseling community should bear the standard for interdisciplinary cooperation.[10]

When I worked in the area of therapeutic foster care, most of my clients had many adults making demands and decisions. The agency I worked with was a private, nonprofit organization that had its own network of foster homes and that received referrals from local child protective service (CPS) agencies and probation departments. Most foster children had a CPS caseworker, a probation officer, an attorney, a court-appointed advocate, an assigned mental health worker, a psychiatrist, and a special education teacher. This cast of characters was in addition to me, the primary therapist. Imagine what this scenario was like for the foster child. How could the child face this myriad of powerful adults who controlled his or her life? It was a very disempowering and out-of-control experience. It was, needless to say, a constant struggle for me to keep the channels of communication open among all these professionals. Working in a collegial and multidisciplinary manner was a challenge at times, but it is vitally important for the welfare of clients.

The counselor who works with children will inevitably interact with the schools, the legal system, and the medical community. Be familiar with these resources, and see them as resources. Kevin O'Connor refers to this network as the child's "ecosystem": "The focus is on the intervention to be carried out with the individual child, but you should not ignore the potential value of intervening or at least facilitating interventions with some of the other individuals or systems that comprise the child's ecosystem."[11] Regular supervision and case consultation (while respecting client confidentiality) with professionals within and outside your own area of expertise are beneficial.

Sometimes it is necessary to refer a child whose case is beyond our ability or experience. Some counselors have the misguided notion that referring a client is evidence that they have failed. Nevertheless, it is imperative to recognize the limits of our own skill and to act in the best interests of the client. Clearly, it is unethical to practice outside the scope of our expertise. Just as members of the body of Christ need each other's different gifts and abilities, so our clients need the variety of resources available in the home, school, church, and community. It is critical, therefore, that we counselors be aware of the resources in our communities and use the resources when a need arises. Always keep parents closely involved in the referral process since they are the ones who will make appointments and follow through with the referral for the child.

GROUP PLAY THERAPY

A powerful therapeutic intervention with children involves the combination of the benefits of play therapy and group counseling. Although very little has been written about the subject in the play therapy literature, the use of group play therapy has developed along with the rest of the field. Children can benefit from the relationships and interactions with other children within the context of a group play setting. In the same way that group counseling works with adults, group play therapy provides for children a psychosocial process through which they grow and learn about themselves and others:

> In group counseling relationships, children experience the therapeutic releasing qualities of discovering that their peers have problems too, and a diminishing of the barriers of feeling all alone. A feeling of belonging develops, and new interpersonal skills are attempted in a "real life" encounter where

children learn more effective ways of relating to people through the process of trial and error. The group then is a microcosm of children's everyday world. In this setting children are afforded the opportunity for immediate reactions from peers as well as the opportunity for vicarious learning. Children also develop a sensitivity to others and receive a tremendous boost to their self-concept through being helpful to someone else. For abused children who have poor self-concepts and a life history of experiencing failure, discovering they can be helpful to someone else may be the most profound therapeutic quality possible. In the counseling group, children also discover they are worthy of respect and that their worth is not dependent on what they do or what they produce but rather on who they are.[12]

Child psychologist Haim Ginott, who wrote the only book about group play therapy, *Group Psychotherapy with Children: The Theory and Practice of Play Therapy*, suggests that group play therapy is based on the assumption that children will modify their behavior in exchange for acceptance.[13] This premise, combined with the capacity and tendency of children to seek out and establish relationships, underlies the therapeutic advantage for using group play therapy.

Before discussing the therapeutic goals of group play therapy as well as some technical considerations, let's look at reasons for placing a child client in a therapeutic play group.

1. Groups may promote spontaneity in children and thus increase their level of participation in the play. The therapist's ability to communicate permissiveness is enhanced by the group dynamics, thus freeing children to risk engagement in various play behaviors.

2. The children's feelings are dealt with at two levels—the intrapsychic issues of individual group members and the interpersonal issues with the therapist and other group members.[14]

3. Vicarious learning and catharsis take place within the group

play setting. Children observe the behavior and emotional expression of the other group members. They learn coping behaviors, problem-solving skills, and alternative avenues of self-expression. As children see other group members engage in activities that they may initially feel cautious or apprehensive about, they gain the courage to explore.

4. Children experience the opportunity for self-exploration and self-growth in group play therapy. This process is facilitated by the responses and reactions of group members to a child's behavioral and affective expression. Children learn to evaluate and reevaluate themselves in light of peer feedback. The opportunity for reflection and action leads to insight about self.[15]

5. Groups provide greater opportunities to anchor children to the world of reality. Limit setting and reality testing occur not only between the individual group member and the therapist but also among the children themselves. Because the group serves as a tangible microcosm of society, the group play therapy experience is tied to reality—"Children compel each other to become aware of their responsibilities in interpersonal relations."[16]

6. Because play groups serve as a microcosm of society, the therapist gains greater insight into the children's presentation in their everyday lives. This "real-life" perspective may be seen in the microcosm evident in the playroom.

7. The group play setting may reduce children's need or tendency to be repetitious and/or to retreat into fantasy play. Although these behaviors may be necessary for some children in the processing of their issues, the group play therapy setting can bring those children "stuck" in repetition or fantasy into the here and now.

8. Children can "practice" for everyday life. The play group provides the opportunity for children to develop interpersonal skills, master new behaviors, give and receive assistance, and experiment with alternative expressions of emotions.

9. The presence of more than one child in the play therapy setting often assists in the development of the therapeutic relationship. As

withdrawn children observe the therapist building trust with other children, they are drawn in. This helps reduce the anxiety of children unsure about the setting and the person of the therapist.

Unlike traditional group therapy, there is no overall goal of group cohesion in group play therapy. The focus of treatment continues to be on each individual child, with the group serving as a unique catalyst for achieving any individual goals. Haim Ginott suggests that the primary goal for group play therapy, like all therapy, is enduring personality change (a strengthened ego and enhanced self-image). To this end, Ginott proposes several questions, from which we can summarize the primary therapeutic goals of group play therapy:

1. Does the method facilitate or hinder the establishment of a therapeutic relationship?
2. Does it accelerate or retard evocation of catharsis?
3. Does it aid or obstruct attainment of insight?
4. Does it augment or diminish opportunities for reality testing?
5. Does it open or block channels for sublimation?[17]

The answers to these questions bring focus to the goals of therapeutic play groups. Group play therapy should facilitate

1. The establishment of a therapeutic relationship
2. The expression of emotions
3. The development of insight
4. Opportunities for reality testing
5. Opportunities for expressing feelings and needs in more acceptable ways

The opportunity for connecting with others in reciprocal ways leads to a greater capacity to "sublimate"—that is, to redirect behaviors into a more self-enhancing and interpersonally appropriate manner. Group play experiences foster insight, which leads to a greater degree of self-control and thus decreases externalizing (acting-out or aggressive) and internalizing (acting-in and regressive) behaviors. Children also have increased opportunities to express feelings, desires, and needs in the group play therapy setting.

Before conducting group play therapy, consider several issues. One of the first considerations should be the facility to be used for the play group. A regular counseling office would probably not be appropriate because of the necessity to set too many limits. If you think that individual play therapy has the potential to be messy, it is nothing compared to the potential of a group play therapy session. The room should also not be too small or too large. The same considerations on room size discussed in chapter 5 apply to work with groups in the playroom. Additionally, a room that is too small can lead to frustration and aggression between group members. A room that is too large not only creates the possibility of uncontrolled behavior but also enables the withdrawn child to avoid interaction. The play materials listed in chapter 5 are adequate to facilitate interaction between group members. It would not be appropriate to provide enough toys of any one type so that each group member can have one; learning to share and resolve conflict would not be facilitated.

The role of the therapist in group play therapy is similar to that in individual play therapy. Obviously, the group play therapist must have a high tolerance for messiness and noise and must be able to handle occasional (sometimes constant) chaos. The therapist must keep responses balanced between group members and must avoid placing all the focus on children who are more active or needy. Be patient. Let the children work things out for themselves (while setting appropriate limits). If this is not possible for you, why have group play therapy?

Therapeutic responses should not be intrusive and should include the child's name. If you make a comment without the child's name, how will the child know you are speaking to him or her? As I mention this, I should also say it is important not to use the third person in your responses. When tracking, do not say, "Geri is playing in the sand" but "Geri, you're playing in the sand."

Limits and limit setting are unique in the therapeutic play group. Group members experience limits set not only by the therapist but also by the other group members. As suggested above, this serves a key function. The group play therapist also must be keen in anticipating limits and resolved to set limits. Clear and total (not conditional) limits are also imperative when working with groups. The rationales for setting limits in individual play therapy (chapter 7) also apply to group play therapy.

Group composition and selection are other important issues in conducting group play therapy. Ginott asserts that the basic requirement for selection to a group is the presence of and capacity for "social hunger."[18] This refers to children's need to be accepted by their peers and a desire to attain and maintain status in the group. Except for special cases, it is generally recommended that group members not know each other before their experience in the group. Sibling group play therapy, except in cases of extreme sibling rivalry, is one exception that has solid potential for therapeutic gain.

I generally like to use individual play therapy as a screening for potential group play therapy members. Even a single play session may reveal the indication or contraindication for inclusion in a group. (I will comment below on children not suitable for group play therapy.)

Group size should be limited. I generally prefer three to four children; five or more seems to be too large. It is difficult to attend to too many children, and most facilities cannot accommodate a large group. Remember that two children make a group, and even this small a group can be very beneficial. It is helpful to keep the group balanced. For example, avoid composing a group of children who have experienced the same trauma. Or if the group has two girls, then balance it out with two boys. If the group has two withdrawn children, balance it with two outgoing or assertive children. The age range of children in group play therapy should generally not exceed twelve months. The difference between a three-year-old and a five-year-old is simply too great. Unless developmental delays are an issue, I stick pretty closely to this rule of thumb. In terms of gender, Landreth suggests that children generally do not need to be separated by gender until age eight or nine.[19]

Some children will not respond well to group play therapy. These children should generally be seen on an individual basis. The following is a brief list of contraindications:

1. Siblings who exhibit intense rivalry
2. Extremely aggressive children
3. Sexually acting-out children
4. Children experiencing difficulty due to poor infant-mother attachment
5. Sociopathic children (intending to inflict harm or revenge)
6. Children with an extremely poor self-image[20]

Although group play therapy has been successfully employed with children with a wide variety of presenting problems, its use has been limited in the treatment of children. Group play therapy blends the benefits of play therapy and group process, and it helps children learn not only about others but also about themselves. Children grow and heal in a process that helps them translate their learning into life outside the play setting. Group play therapy can be a challenge for the play therapist, but it is such an opportunity for hurting children.

USING PRAYER IN COUNSELING

If we are going to call what we do Christian counseling, it makes sense to incorporate prayer into the process. But what is appropriate? How can prayer be included in the therapy process in a way that's helpful and not harmful to clients?

I believe that human beings are composed of a body, soul, and spirit. As 1 Thessalonians 5:23 says, "May your whole spirit, soul and body be kept blameless at the coming of our Lord Jesus Christ." Therefore, counseling interventions should encompass physiological, emotional, and spiritual aspects of our clients. I frequently remind myself that the battle cannot be won merely on the merits of my own skill and expertise. "For our struggle is not against flesh and blood, but against the rulers, against the authorities, against the powers of this dark world and against the spiritual forces of evil in the heavenly realms."[21] Through prayer and intercession, I have access to the Creator of my wounded clients.

We have all heard the saying "Time heals all wounds." This is supposedly a comforting thought for the person in emotional pain. In my opinion, this maxim is not true. Time does not heal all wounds: God heals all wounds. Time puts more distance between a person and a hurtful event, and time gives a person the opportunity to develop more sophisticated coping mechanisms to deal with the pain. Most assuredly, the healing process for any client takes time. But it is not the time that brings healing. Healing is done by the God who is outside time, the Creator of our beings. This principle, therefore, reminds me that while the therapy process may be fast or slow, ultimately it is my responsibility to apply my God-given skills and gifts to all of my clients and to rely heavily on the Spirit of God for the ultimate outcome.

Like many Christian counselors, my practice is comprised of some clients who do not share my faith. In fact, because of the various settings in which I have worked, the majority of my clients have not been Christians. Prayer should, nevertheless, be a priority. As Dr. Gary Collins, president of the American Association of Christian Counselors, asserts: "Before, during, and after counseling, the counselor must seek divine guidance. More than any other form of helping, spiritual counseling can involve us in conflict with satanic forces. This is one major reason why Christian counselors need to pray for special strength, wisdom, and direction. At times you may choose to pray directly with the counselee. Always you should spend at least some time alone in prayer concerning each counselee." [22]

This brings us to an important issue: Should we incorporate prayer into the play therapy process? Some therapists seek to pray with clients as often as possible, while other counselors never pray with clients. My approach is this: It is not my desire to take on a role of teacher, parent, or even pastor for my clients. It is, however, the heart of a pastor that motivates my work with children. I do not want my clients to view me as a spiritual authority any more than I want them to view me as a psychological authority; this will hinder the development of an open and egalitarian relationship. As a result, I will pray with a child in the play therapy room under two conditions: if the child asks me to pray or if the Holy Spirit leads me to pray. I have some hesitancy saying this because I know that some counselors may insist that it is always the Holy Spirit leading them to pray. I would caution against confusing your own need to help (or rescue) with the leading of the Lord. Remember, we must attend to the children's needs, not our own. If I feel compelled to pray with children, however, I do so at the beginning or end of the session to avoid interrupting the flow of play.

I find prayer to be a particularly helpful tool in my work with parents. Often, by the time their child arrives at my office for counseling, the parents are exasperated and desperate. In addition to educating them about the counseling process and discussing background information, it is important to give the parents hope. The apostle Paul tells us: "For everything that was written in the past was written to teach us, so that *through endurance and the encouragement of the Scriptures we might have hope*" (italics added). [23] I certainly do not want the parents to hope in *me,* so I prefer to direct them, through prayer and the Word of God, to the only One who can truly give hope.

Praying with Christian parents is a routine part of my interaction with them (many of my referrals are Christian parents who are reluctant about having their children in counseling). With all of the parents I see—regardless of their spiritual beliefs—I will let them know it is my intention to pray for their child and for their family. With the non-Christian parents I see, this will often open up a dialogue. If I feel led by the Holy Spirit to pray with non-Christian parents, I have no guarantee that they will not be put off. I will, of course, ask their permission (only rarely will someone decline) and then say a simple prayer. I have encountered some parents who have told me flat out that "religion" is not going to help their child. My response is that prayer is one of the counseling tools I have, and I will do everything I can from my training and experience to help their child. My intention is to let them know that I am on their side in seeking to help their child.

Counseling children often focuses on training their parents. Scripture is full of principles and truths about parenting. I will share these principles, whether or not my clients' parents are Christians. It is always possible for me to affect a child with a touch of God's kingdom, but it may be more helpful to impact the parents, through whom the child might experience profound spiritual change.

A final comment on prayer and spiritual issues. While I find that working with children is highly rewarding, I also find that it is quite challenging and draining. Prayer and the spiritual support of family and colleagues are essential. To prevent burnout, we must do more than give out; we must take in. If our emotional and spiritual well runs dry, our clients suffer, our families suffer, and we suffer. So pray for your clients, pray for your families, and pray for yourself. Seek out and accept the support of colleagues and Christian friends.

TERMINATION

At the outset of this section, I must state my dislike for the word *termination.* It sounds so final and foreboding. I am not sure we can find a better word to describe the conclusion of a therapeutic relationship, but *termination* does not describe the process adequately. The growth process is developmental, and as such, the conclusion of therapy means the *beginning* of a new stage or phase rather than the *end* of something. Like emotional development, growth in Christ is a progression, as we see from the words of the apostle Peter: "For this very reason, make every effort to add to your faith goodness; and to goodness, knowledge; and to knowledge, self-control; and to self-control, perseverance; and to perseverance, godliness; and to godliness, brotherly kindness; and to brotherly kindness, love. For if you possess these qualities in increasing measure, they will keep you from being ineffective and unproductive in your knowledge of our Lord Jesus Christ." [24] It is on the foundation of each of these qualities that the next is built. It can likewise be on the foundation of the therapeutic relationship that a child continues the physical, emotional, and spiritual development that God desires.

Focus on this orientation—that therapy is a stepping-stone for further growth experiences—from the beginning of the counseling process. Frederick Allen wrote: "The values of the therapeutic experience in which a child and therapist are engaged, emerge in part around the fact that this relationship is begun with the goal of its eventual termination. From the first hour, this is the basic orientation of the therapist. Each move the therapist makes that helps the child to be a participant in his own change is one that helps that child to assume responsibility for a self which he can accept as uniquely his and which is the very core of his living. With this orientation, the ending phase of therapy becomes a process of affirming or reaffirming the difference a child perceives in himself as he develops within the steady framework of a relationship made possible by a therapist and child together." [25]

Handle the process of termination with as much care as you handle the beginning of the therapeutic relationship. Include the child in the planning for termination, which means together deciding the date for the final session. This will, of course, be partially dependent on the age and developmental level of the child. Landreth notes, "When the therapist determines the child no longer needs the play therapy experience or becomes aware of the child's readiness to discontinue the relationship, this should be responded to in the session with the same degree of sensitivity as would any other feeling or decision by the child."[26] If termination is not undertaken appropriately or if the parent abruptly halts the child's therapy, the client will likely experience feelings of rejection and loss. Although these feelings may occur regardless of how termination proceeds, it is clearly better to address them within the therapeutic process.

Remember the "specialness" of the therapeutic relationship and experience for a child in play therapy. Children need time to grieve the loss of this relationship. As a result, introduce the idea of ending therapy at least two, and preferably three, sessions before the termination date. In addition, it is best to broach the subject at the beginning of the session. This timing allows children to process their feelings about ending the relationship. In the same way children must work through entering therapy, they need to work through the ending of the relationship. I occasionally use storytelling as a technique to introduce termination to clients.

Sometimes it is helpful to taper off therapy sessions so the relationship does not end abruptly. If a client's sessions have been scheduled weekly, consider switching to every other week, then every three weeks, and then once a month until termination. Regardless of the timetable for conclusion, it is important to remind the child *at each session* about the number of remaining sessions. Children have a different concept of time from that of adults; one week is an awfully long time for a child to remember something. It is important to honor them with this reminder.

Children may respond to the process of ending the therapeutic relationship in a number of ways. Frequently, young clients will regress in their play behaviors. It is not uncommon for play themes that emerged at the beginning of therapy to reemerge at this point. For example, it is not uncommon to see themes of aggression that were characteristic of an initial session, such as attacking the bop bag, to recur at the time of termination. In the course of one or two sessions, a child may "reenact" the entire process of therapy. If this happens, do not feel that all therapeutic progress has been lost! This is not the case. It is more likely that this behavior is the child's way of processing old issues and reaffirming the change that has occurred.

This cycle is similar to what often occurs when we move away from a close friend. During the last few get-togethers, we reminisce about the relationship, both the good and the bad. In this way, we savor experiences and memories so that they can be carried into the future. Many relationships experience this dynamic, including the therapist-child relationship.

Another common response for children is to be angry about termination and to send a message of rejection to the therapist. The message may be: "I feel rejected by you, so I am going to reject *you.*" While it is tempting to provide soothing and reassuring messages at this point, I suggest maintaining the same level of acceptance of feelings that has been present throughout the therapeutic process. In other words, remain consistent in your emotional responses. Guard against meeting your own needs in the termination process by giving verbal assurances that everything will be okay or that children can call whenever they wish. Remaining available to continue the therapeutic relationship is one thing, but comforting children with reassuring comments denies children the right to express their feelings about ending a special relationship.

Although I wish I could say that all of my counseling cases have had positive and long-lasting results, that is simply not true. Like most therapists, I work with children who come from extremely dysfunctional and hurtful environments, and they may well return to the pain from which I so desire to deliver them. In situations where treatment has not been as successful as I would like, a few reminders help me keep things in perspective. First, I trust the process—that is, by entering the world of the child and providing some of the unconditional love of the Creator, progress will be made. Similarly, I remind myself that even if my intervention is brief, it can and should be a bright spot for children who may come from lives with few bright spots. I try to rely on prayer, remembering that healing ultimately depends on the Designer of these children, not on me. So even if the process terminates before I would like it to, I hope to have been a taste of the kingdom for the hurting children I see.

Child's play is not mere sport. It is full of meaning and serious impact. Cherish it and encourage it. For to one who has insight into human nature, the trend of the whole future life of the child is revealed in his freely chosen play.

—F. W. FROEBEL

10/ PARENT TRAINING: FILIAL THERAPY

The foundation of a solid relationship with a child is unconditional love. Only that type of love relationship can assure a child's growth to his full and total potential. —DR. ROSS CAMPBELL

Parent training is one of the most powerful tools, if not *the* most powerful tool, in ministering to the needs of children. Whole books have been written for parents and parent trainers on the subject. My strong preference for parenting intervention is filial therapy, which focuses on training parents to build and enhance the parent–child relationship, using skills from the field of play therapy. It goes without saying, then, that a counselor using filial therapy with parents needs to be a trained play therapist. At the University of North Texas, graduate students who want to take the semester-long course in filial therapy must have completed the introductory course in play therapy as a prerequisite. As with other modalities, therapists should be thoroughly educated in filial training before incorporating it into their practice.[1]

One of the most special examples of parents' using play to touch their child involves John and Lori, colleagues of mine, and their son,

Kevin. Out on an errand with his father, three-and-a-half-year-old Kevin ran out into the street and was hit by a car. Kevin sustained trauma to his brain, and after being released from the hospital, he could not walk (although he was not paralyzed). He wore a helmet to protect his head. He slept an inordinate amount of time and slept with his parents. John and Lori were later to be told that Kevin could be expected to have lasting mental and physical difficulties. Although Kevin's higher-level intelligence function was apparently not impaired, he was left with some substantial learning difficulties.

John and Lori were naturally shaken by the trauma, but they were also determined to support Kevin in every way. Both John and Lori are counselors, and Lori is trained in play therapy. As Lori recounted this story to me, she recalled that she had used her play therapy skills in "special playtimes" with her daughters years earlier to deal with the crisis of a family divorce. Although Lori had not yet heard of filial therapy as an intervention, she naturally chose to use her play therapy skills with her children. Kevin was privileged to have a half-hour playtime with his mother almost every night (about four nights a week) after supper.

At one point in these playtimes, Kevin wanted to play out violent scenes, such as cowboys and Indians and cops and robbers, involving blood, death, and "going to the medicine man." Lori resisted as Kevin persisted in wanting to play out multiple similar themes. After experiencing several playtimes with this dynamic occurring, Lori realized that Kevin was needing to work through the accident. She wasn't ready to work it through, but Kevin was! Lori allowed Kevin to go ahead with this play, and he did so for two solid months. The same play ensued—accident scene after accident scene. Sometimes people would die in the imaginary play, and sometimes they would live. Sometimes people would go to the "medicine man." Then, as suddenly as this type of play emerged, it stopped.

Shortly thereafter, during a bath time with his father, Kevin looked up at John and began sobbing. He blurted out, "Daddy, I'm sorry I was a bad boy and ran out in front of a truck!" Kevin was struggling with guilt. He thought he had done something wrong. What a wonderful experience for Kevin to be able to work through these painful emotions with the people whom he loved the most, and who cared for him the most.

Kevin had his difficulties. He entered play therapy at the age of six, often playing out scenes of tornados and storms. Life must certainly have felt like a tornado—raging and out of control. Kevin was sad and angry at being behind in school. Expressions of rage were not uncommon. His parents never wavered in their support.

This isn't just Kevin's story—it is his family's. John and Lori have traveled the journey with him. Lori is convinced that without the regular playtimes with Kevin in the weeks and months after the accident, he would not have progressed as he did. How has Kevin progressed? He is now a teenager who is able to come to his parents when he needs emotional support. And, lest I forget to mention, he is also a starting defensive back on the high school football team and an honors student.

While Kevin's story certainly is dramatic, it illustrates the importance and benefit of the parent-child relationship. The healing power of play within the parent-child relationship works, even in the case of trauma.

Kevin's story illustrates the healing power of play within the parent-child relationship. While most parents are not trained counselors, as Lori and John are, all parents can learn to build safe relationships with their children. Filial therapy gives parents the tools to strengthen their relationships with their children and to create a healing environment.

The word *filial* comes from the Latin words *filius,* meaning "son," or *filia,* meaning "daughter." Surely, it is the Creator's design that relational conflicts be resolved within the family. Filial therapy can help lay the foundation for this: "Through didactic instruction, viewing of videotapes, and role playing, parents' sensitivity to their children is enhanced, and parents learn how to create a non-judgmental, understanding, and accepting environment during which children feel safe enough to explore other parts of themselves as persons and other ways of relating to their parents."[2] Parents can indeed become the primary agents of therapeutic change in the life of their child through this process. Research on the efficacy of filial therapy has shown this parent training to be effective with a wide variety of parent populations, ranging from incarcerated fathers to parents of chronically ill children to single parents.[3]

In his book *Are You Listening to Your Child?* Dr. Arthur Kraft discusses the benefits of "parents as psychotherapists." With a tongue-in-cheek jab at professional psychotherapists, he writes:

> There was a time when it was thought that parents were rather evil people who had done all sorts of terrible things to their kids, and the best thing professionals could do for the child was to let the parents pay the bill and otherwise keep them out of it. I have a suspicion that there was an element of psychologists taking second-hand revenge on their own parents thereby. In any case, this notion has been on its way out for some time now (particularly since I became a parent).
>
> There is a major advantage to the parent being a psychologist for his own child. If a professional psychologist has an effective play session with a child, it is just for an hour a week. If a father or mother has such a session, there is apt to be carryover during the rest of the week. Ultimately, what happens is, although the parents focus on the play session, the generalization of new behavior and awareness to the rest of the week becomes, hopefully, a way of life.[4]

My basic philosophy of training parents is that *rules without relationship equal rebellion*. Mothers and fathers can have the best parenting books and disciplinary tools available, but if the parent-child relationship is poor, misbehavior and rebellion will occur. Ross Campbell, in his excellent book *How to Really Love Your Child,* touches on this in his preface: "The problem, as I see it, usually lies in the parents not having a general, balanced perspective on how to relate to a child. Most parents have the essential information per se, but there is confusion about *when* to apply *which* principle under *what* circumstance. . . . Excellent books and seminars on childhood have addressed the issue of discipline but failed to make clear that discipline is only one way of relating to a child. . . . The problem is not whether to discipline; the problem is how to manifest our love to a child through discipline and when to show it in other, more affectionate, ways."[5]

When I conduct parent training, I am primarily interested in helping parents build their relationships with their children. Just as the therapeutic limit-setting model begins with affirming feelings (thus enhancing the relationship), discipline in the home or at school is far more effective when based on the foundation of a solid relationship. Quite simply, children will accept direction and correction much better from a parent or teacher whom they respect. Children respect those who take the time to cultivate relationships with them.

BACKGROUND AND RATIONALE FOR FILIAL TRAINING

Filial therapy was developed by Bernard and Louise Guerney in the early 1960s as an innovative approach to the treatment of emotionally disturbed children.[6] The premise was to train parents of emotionally disturbed children to conduct play sessions at home and therefore become the primary agent of therapeutic change. The Guerneys believed that if parents could be taught to assume the role of the therapist, they could conceivably be more effective than a professional because parents naturally have more emotional significance in the life of their children.[7] Also, the anxiety symptoms that children had learned in the presence of or under the influence of parents could be more effectively unlearned or extinguished within the parent-child relationship. Another rationale suggests that interpersonal problems caused by a breakdown in communication and expectations could be corrected if parents would clearly delineate what is and is not appropriate behavior according to time, place, and circumstances.

Before the Guerneys' work, some precedent for training parents to be therapeutic change agents in the lives of their children had been set. In the early 1900s, Sigmund Freud used the father of a five-year-old phobic child in the case of "Little Hans."[8] Freud provided instruction to the father for having playtimes at home and would later interpret the play in sessions with the father. In the late 1940s, Dorothy Baruch recommended parent-child play sessions at home for the purpose of enhancing communication and relationships.[9] Natalie Rogers-Fuchs, with the counsel of her father, Carl Rogers, conducted home play sessions based on the writing of Virginia Axline.[10] Rogers-Fuchs reported positive changes in herself and in her daughter, who had been experiencing emotional difficulties related to toilet training. Clark Moustakas's description of home play is one of the earliest: "Play therapy in the home . . . is a way through which the child opens himself to emotional expression and in this process releases tensions and repressed feelings."[11] These early experiences of parent-child play interactions differed from filial therapy in two ways: The parents did not participate in regular training and supervision from a professional, and they did not share their experiences in a support-group format.[12]

Bernard Guerney and Lillian Stover suggested several important advantages to using filial therapy. First, filial therapy has the potential for making better use of the therapist's time. Second, it is possible to avoid the fears and rivalry that may develop in the parents as their children decrease dependency on them and form attachments with the therapist. Third, this approach can reduce the feelings of guilt and helplessness that often arise when parents "turn over" their children to an expert for treatment. And finally, filial therapy helps parents develop appropriate responses to new child-behavior patterns.[13]

An important rationale for using filial therapy is based on the application of a training (educational) and supportive (involvement) treatment to parents who exhibit a need for both. Psychologists, educators, and ministers have developed a variety of parent-education groups, and developmental theorists and counselors have explained the need for parents to learn behaviors and emotional responses in parenting. The *integration* of these two elements, however, has not been widely applied. Parent education and parent involvement are key components to treating and training families: "Separately applied, neither a didactic approach nor one which offers experiential learning opportunities alone is as useful and powerful as both conditions applied together. The two components appear to have a complementary value and the effect of each is enhanced when they are applied in combination."[14]

Psychologist Rise Van Fleet lists several principles central to filial therapy.[15] First, filial therapists must recognize the importance of play in child development. This includes a consideration of play as the primary means by which children communicate. Second, filial therapists must believe that parents are capable of learning the necessary skills to conduct child-centered play sessions with their children. Third, filial therapists must have a preference for educational versus biological models of evaluation and treatment. Dr. Van Fleet summarized the goals of this approach: "Overall, filial therapy aims to (a) eliminate the presenting problems at their source; (b) develop positive interactions between parents and their children; and (c) increase families' communication, coping, and problem-solving skills so they are better able to handle future problems independently and successfully."[16]

PARENTS AND THEIR CHILDREN

Filial therapy is structured to enhance the parent-child relationship. In *Play Therapy: The Art of the Relationship*, filial-training courses are usually referred to as **C**hild-**P**arent **R**elationship Training (**CPR** *for Parents*—indeed some parent-child relationships do need resuscitation).[17] Essentially, I train parents to conduct with their children thirty-minute playtimes during which they employ basic play therapy skills. I do not train parents to be play therapists; I train them to increase their sensitivity to and awareness of their children.

Parents are urged to conduct these playtimes with their child for a half hour once a week, which, in comparison to other training programs, is a minimal time requirement and a relief to busy parents. The fact that filial therapy also includes "supervision" of the parent–child play sessions also sets the process apart from other parent-training formats.

Parents often need guidance in the spiritual training of their children. Christian counselors are in a unique position to help in this area. Sometimes parents need to be reminded that, whether or not they know it, they are teaching their children about religion.

> For a long time parents fooled themselves into thinking they could preserve their children's individuality and responsibility for choice by not identifying their children with any religion. When their children grew up, parents claimed, they would be able to make their own choice of religious faith. That usually meant that the children went unbaptized, attended Sunday school spasmodically, and drifted from church to church, if they went at all, with no basic beliefs about God. Parents thought they were right in not giving their children a religion, and a poor religion at that. Inevitably parents give their children the attitudes, values, and beliefs by which they live, and that is what religion is.
>
> It may be a poor religion, centered on material possessions, and measured by dollar signs, regularly worshipped at the bank and expressed in the faith that money and gadgets will bring peace and happiness. It may be a conceited religion, centered on the individual himself, committed to personal desires, and characterized by scornful indifference to others. It may be an ethical religion, centered on law, both biblical and civil, and expressing itself in personal honesty, individual integrity, and a sense of responsibility. Or it may be the Christian religion,

centered on the love of God, shown in the life, teaching, death, and resurrection of Jesus Christ, expressed in putting the needs of others before one's own, dying to oneself and coming alive to others, and in loving God by loving other people in the everyday contacts of life.

The basic, determining factors in the day-by-day living of parents make up their religion, and it is this that they pass on to their children. Boys and girls can be reared with no more vacuum in their spirits than in their stomachs. So the old idea of "no religion" was ignorance. Inevitably, unconsciously, and without question parents pass on to their children their own God or gods.[18]

It is important to remember that parenting is both a responsibility and a ministry. Scripture is clear that we are to train our children in the way of the Lord, have compassion on them, discipline them in love, not frustrate them, and model for them the character of God.[19] Parenting is not the responsibility of the government, the church, or the Christian school. It is the responsibility of moms and dads. Counselors, at every level, have the opportunity to support parents in this biblical mandate.

I do not believe God calls men and women into ministry without providing the opportunity for training. While anyone can become a parent, not everyone can fulfill parental responsibilities. Training must be part of the process of learning to parent effectively. Filial training provides an opportunity to train parents who may then in turn train their children. The supervision model I discussed in chapter 3 is exemplified in filial-therapy training. Just as Christ *taught* his disciples, *modeled* ministry for them, *released* them to minister, and *supervised* them, so counselors can implement these steps in our work with parents.

CONDUCTING FILIAL TRAINING

My preference is to conduct filial-therapy training in a group format. Although I have trained individuals or couples by themselves, the dynamics of a group approach cannot be duplicated. It is reassuring for parents to know that the other parents in the group struggle with similar issues. The groups are normally limited to six or eight persons, whether eight individual parents, four couples, or a mixture of both individuals and couples. It becomes cumbersome to handle the dynamics of the group and to provide appropriate supervision of parent-child play sessions with more than eight people.

Training benefits all parents, but it is advisable to screen out parents who have significant emotional problems themselves (severe depression, psychosis, etc.). Likewise, filial therapy is appropriate for parents of all children, not just children who are experiencing emotional and behavioral difficulties. I have trained grandparents, parents of teenagers, and first-time pregnant parents in my training, all of whom seemed to benefit from the training.

The groups last for ten weeks and meet weekly for two hours each session. No new participants should be added after the second week. The duration is necessary so that the parents can be trained and supervised adequately and so that proper support can be extended to the parents, who may be dealing with emotionally charged issues with their children. Other parent-training models have different timetables, some longer and some shorter. Ten sessions are a minimum for filial-therapy training, but it is often difficult to hold parents for longer in today's busy lifestyle.

The training process centers on discussion and interaction. I am reluctant to cast myself as the "expert," as this tends to inhibit parents from volunteering their own solutions. As I turn questions back to the group, they generate possible solutions through lively discussion. I give homework assignments each session and review the homework at the beginning of each subsequent meeting. Homework includes worksheets on recognizing their children's feelings; exercises on reflective listening and limit setting; lists for purchasing toys for the filial toy kit; instructions for setting up the playtimes; and instructions for conducting the playtimes. Homework reinforces the training, and reviewing it reinforces the material covered in the assignments. Parents are encouraged to ask questions and take notes. It is not possible to give a step-by-step delineation of each session, but a summary outline of the sessions follows.

The outline comes from the material of Dr. Garry Landreth in his book *Play Therapy: The Art of the Relationship.*[20] Dr. Landreth is in the process of writing a filial-therapy text that will greatly enhance the material offered in his play therapy text. There are other filial-therapy models, which are longer and more involved, but I have found significant success with this model. Considerable research on filial therapy with several different parent and child populations using this model indicates the power and efficacy of this approach. If you choose to use this model of filial therapy, be sure to seek the appropriate training.

Session one: Parents introduce themselves and briefly discuss the child of focus. Parents should be encouraged to conduct the special playtimes with the child that is most in need of a stronger relationship with the parents (this will be, of course, the child exhibiting adjustment difficulties). All play sessions should be conducted by the same parent because alternating between parents sets up potential confusion and conflict. The therapist explains the purpose of the training, conducts some role playing, and gives out homework. The goal of the first session is to sensitize the parent to the child's emotions and to instruct in the use of reflective listening.[21]

Session two: The group reviews the homework and continues in role playing, with the therapist modeling empathic responses. The parents watch a videotape of the therapist conducting play therapy (it is advisable to show a tape of yourself, not another therapist). The therapist gives parents a list of toys to use for the playtimes and demonstrates each toy and discusses how it can be used. The therapist assigns homework, which includes putting together a toy kit and selecting a place for the play session.[22]

Session three: The parents report on toys they collected and the session location they have selected. The parents watch another videotape of the therapist conducting play therapy. The homework assignment is to make a "Do Not Disturb" sign with the child for use during the play session and to conduct the first play session. One parent agrees to videotape his or her play session. The therapist encourages parents to adhere to the following rules during the play times.[23]

Don't
1. Don't criticize any behavior.
2. Don't praise the child.
3. Don't ask leading questions.
4. Don't allow interruptions of the session.
5. Don't offer information or teach.
6. Don't preach.
7. Don't initiate new activities.
8. Don't be passive or quiet.[24]

Do
1. Do set the stage.
2. Do let the child lead.
3. Do track behavior.
4. Do reflect the child's feelings.
5. Do set limits.
6. Do salute the child's power and effort.
7. Do join in the play as a follower.
8. Do be verbally active.[25]

Session four: As parents give reports of the first play session, the therapist supervises and the group gives feedback. The focus is on the parents' feelings about the experience. The group views the videotape of a parent–child play session and gives feedback. Another parent agrees to videotape his or her next session. Every parent should have at least one session videotaped and reviewed by the group.[26]

Sessions five through nine: Following approximately the same format as session four, parents give reports of the play session, the therapist supervises, and the group gives feedback. The therapist gives homework assignments and continues the training and role playing, discussing limit setting in detail. The parents begin to generalize their experiences and skills outside the playtime.[27]

Session ten: Parents report on their play sessions, view a videotape, and review and evaluate the training process. The therapist shares notes from the first session of the parents' description of their children to identify change that has occurred. Parents or children requiring additional intervention are scheduled for further assistance.[28]

I have had success with filial-therapy training in my private practice, in agency work, and at churches. It is not uncommon to hear feedback that parents trained in filial therapy have had success using the techniques in their marital relationships and their jobs as well. Investing in relationships works. Training parents to affirm and empower their children offers an added benefit: It affirms and empowers the parents. Children benefit from association with empowered adults and can be helped toward their own empowerment when they observe their parents' confidence.[29] And, similar to the dynamics in the playroom, filial therapy is also an incredible force in the growth and development of a child's self-concept.

RECOMMENDED READING FOR PARENTS

I do not assign parents additional reading on top of the filial training because I want them to focus on the training materials I give them. I want them to feel fully fed but not choking on too much information. However, ambitious parents often request more reading. While many good books about parenting are available, I prefer to point parents to materials that will further my focus on relationship building, as opposed to discipline or behavior management. I often recommend the following books:

- *How to Really Love Your Child* by Ross Campbell
- *Between Parent and Child* by Haim Ginott
- *How to Talk So Kids Will Listen & Listen So Kids Will Talk* by Adele Faber and Elaine Mazlish
- *Siblings without Rivalry* by Adele Faber and Elaine Mazlish

---

There is little that gives children greater pleasure than when a grown-up lets himself down to their level, renounces his oppressive superiority and plays with them as an equal. —*SIGMUND FREUD*

PART THREE

Treating Children with Distinct Needs

As you move into this third section of the book, you will notice a conceptual shift in focus. The previous chapters have focused on the world of children and making contact with them in that world. The following chapters focus on specific childhood problems or disorders and how play therapy can facilitate the healing process.

I include these chapters with some hesitancy. It is not my intention to focus on children's problems; it is my intention to focus on children. Children experience enough labeling in life without counselors adding to the mire. This book is not about childhood psychopathology; it is a book about reaching children through the world of play.

Nevertheless, the informed counselor makes for a more empathic counselor. The material provided on specific diagnostic categories is intended not to change the manner in which we approach children in the counseling room but to provide some basic information about some childhood issues along with suggestions for treatment approaches.

I believe that a focus on "problems" and "diagnosis" is not only misguided but also can be detrimental to our child clients. If children are viewed as people to be cured or changed, is it not possible that we will lose sight of who the children are as persons? Although I use the word *treatment,* I hesitate to talk about "treatment" issues because the word *treatment* implies the application of specific techniques. This has the potential to take the focus off the relationship, which I feel is the core of healing both in and out of the counseling office.

Recognizing my concerns and the shift in focus of the next several chapters, do not lose sight of the most important element of counseling children: the children themselves. While diagnosis, prognosis, and treatment planning are important, they are not as important as children's natural medium of communication and the therapeutic relationship. In the end, children should be our central focus.

11/ Treating
Traumatized Children

The hearts of small children are delicate organs. A cruel beginning in this
world can twist them into curious shapes . . . hard and pitted as the seed
of a peach. . . . Or again, the heart . . . may fester and swell until it is
. . . easily chafed and hurt by the most ordinary things.

—CARSON McCULLERS

It is a sad fact of today's society that children often experience trauma. "One reality not widely recognized is that children are more prone to victimization than adults are."[1] Victimization not only damages children's bodies and emotions, but it also wounds their souls. Clinical Professor of Psychology at the New York School of Medicine, Dr. Leonard Shengold calls victimization "soul murder."[2] Soul murder is "the dramatic term for circumstances that eventuate in crime—the deliberate attempt to eradicate or compromise the separate identity of another person."[3]

In today's world, abuse claims the lives of millions of children. "Sexual abuse, emotional deprivation, physical and mental torture can eventuate in *soul murder.* . . . Children are the usual victims. For the child's almost complete physical and emotional dependence on adults easily makes for possible tyranny and therefore child abuse."[4]

Scripture tells us that "the thief comes only to steal and kill and destroy."[5] It is the enemy's plan to rob children of their childhood because in doing so the enemy steals from their adulthood and weakens the effectiveness of the church. This should not come as a surprise. Scripture shows us that throughout history, children have been targeted for "murder": In Moses' time newborn boys were ordered slain by the pharaoh, and in Jesus' time Herod gave the same directive.

It is important to recognize that children view trauma differently from the way adults do. Adults generally have greater coping mechanisms (as well as established defense mechanisms) with which to defend against and process traumatizing experiences. The loss of a pet, a routine hospital procedure, or a job-related move may not seem extraordinary in an adult's life, but to a child, these same events may be genuinely traumatizing. Children are no different from adults when it comes to fearing and being adversely affected by what is unknown. The limited understanding and developmental immaturity of a child, however, simply make for a decreased ability to deal with pain and trauma. Understanding the child's world and the child's perspective becomes all the more important when dealing with traumatic issues. Perhaps you have heard the following story, which so vividly illustrates the child's perspective on a potentially traumatizing situation that was so hard for this child to understand.

A little boy was told by his doctor that he could save his sister's life by giving her some blood. The six-year-old girl was near death—a victim of a disease from which the boy had made a marvelous recovery two years earlier. Her only chance for restoration was a blood transfusion from someone who had previously conquered the illness. Since the two children had the same rare blood type, the boy was the ideal donor.

"Johnny, would you like to give your blood for Mary?" the doctor asked.

The boy hesitated. His lower lip started to tremble. Then he smiled, and said, "Sure, Doc, I'll give my blood for my sister."

Soon the two children were wheeled into the operating room—Mary, pale and thin; Johnny, robust and the picture of health. Neither spoke, but when their eyes met, Johnny grinned.

As his blood siphoned into Mary's veins, one could almost see new life come into her tired body. The ordeal was almost over when Johnny's brave little voice broke the silence. "Say, Doc, when do I die?"

It was only then that the doctor realized what the moment of hesitation, that trembling of the lip, meant. Little Johnny actually thought that in giving his blood to his sister, he was giving up his life![6]

It is important to understand how children process the world around them. A detailed explanation of the surgical procedure probably would not have taken away Johnny's anxiety. But a relationship with a person who understands his world would give him a place in which to process it.

WHAT IS TRAUMA?

How do we define *trauma?* A traumatizing event and the results of trauma may run along a continuum. "An event traumatic to one youngster may be just a bad experience to another, or it may be traumatizing at one stage in life and not traumatizing earlier or later."[7] This is important to understand because in treating children, we must neither dismiss nor assume trauma, neither minimize nor magnify the experience. Beverly James, a social worker specializing in treating traumatized and attachment-disordered children, gives a workable definition in her book about traumatized children: "Trauma, to paraphrase *Webster's New Collegiate Dictionary,* is an emotional shock that creates substantial, lasting damage to an individual's psychological development. . . . 'Trauma' also refers to overwhelming, uncontrollable experiences that psychologically impact victims by creating in them feelings of helplessness, vulnerability, loss of safety, and loss of control. Although other emotional reactions may be seen (or may exist and not be seen), these are the states most likely to be present and to be uncovered by the clinician. The child victim may exhibit severe psychiatric symptoms or may superficially appear symptom-free."[8]

In her extensive research on childhood trauma, psychiatrist Lenore Terr suggests that children, regardless of their age, exhibit four primary characteristics following the exposure to trauma: (1) strongly visualized or otherwise repeatedly perceived memories of the trauma; (2) repetitive behaviors; (3) trauma-specific fears; and (4) changed attitudes about people, aspects of life, and the future.[9] Unlike adults, who may reexperience memories of a traumatic event in an abrupt and intrusive manner, children tend to reexperience memories during times of relaxation such as while watching television, before falling asleep, and while playing. The child who experiences posttraumatic visualizations or memories may do so while daydreaming in a class or while playing in the counseling session. Traumatized children generally do not find themselves suddenly interrupted with dysphoric sensorium (unpleasant input to the sensory apparatus) in contrast to adults who experience trauma. Repetitive behaviors usually take the form of either reenactment or posttraumatic play. "Posttraumatic play . . . is a grim, long-lasting, and particularly contagious form of childhood repetitive behavior. . . . Reenactments can occur as single behaviors, repeated behaviors, or bodily responses."[10]

In explaining trauma-specific fears, Dr. Terr gave the example of a dog phobia: "Whereas neurotically or developmentally phobic children may fear *all* dogs, the dog-bitten youngster will fear the German shepherds, the Dobermans, or whatever species actually created the traumatic state."[11] In terms of changed attitudes about people, life, and the future, traumatized children experience a profound limitation of future perspective. These children view the future as uncertain and view themselves and others as quite vulnerable and helpless.

Dr. Terr additionally categorizes trauma conditions of childhood into two categories, either Type I or Type II. *Type I trauma* involves a single, sudden blow—an unexpected stressor—and includes full detailed memories, "omens," and misperceptions. *Type II trauma* involves long-standing or repeated experiences and includes rage, denial, and numbing, as well as self-hypnosis and dissociation.[12] I have found these categorizations to be more helpful in assessment and case conceptualization than in treatment.

Several authors have identified various traumagenic states or conditions in the evaluation and treatment of traumatized children. Prominent researchers in the field of child sexual abuse David Finkelhor and Angela Browne identified four categories of trauma for the sexually abused child.[13] Beverly James has expanded on these to include the effects of any traumatic event on a child. Her categorization of traumagenic states includes: self-blame, powerlessness, loss and betrayal, fragmentation of bodily experience, stigmatization, eroticization, destructiveness, dissociative/multiple personality disorder, and attachment disorder.[14] Grant Martin, in his book *Critical Problems in Children and Youth,* provides an understandable summary chart of James's traumagenic states.[15]

Self-blame is a common characteristic for children who have been traumatized. When children experience victimizing or traumatizing circumstances, their inherent egocentrism leads them to believe that they are to blame. Young children simply tend to believe that the sun rises and sets because of them. So when trauma occurs, they instinctively think that they are the cause. It becomes crucial, therefore, that children believe that the traumatic event is not their fault.

Traumatized children feel a strong sense of *powerlessness.* Although the word *empowerment* is overused in modern psychology and counseling, it is a primary therapeutic goal for children who have been traumatized. They must regain a sense of power and control in their lives. Trauma is overpowering, and the physiological and psychological immaturity of children exacerbates the effect. Many children hold on to the powerlessness they experienced when they were traumatized. As a result, they develop significantly impaired self-images.

Loss and betrayal surround children who have been traumatized. Perhaps the most notable loss is the loss of dignity and a sense of safety. In addition, they may feel the loss of security because people didn't protect them from trauma. The losses that traumatized children experience are tremendous, including such areas as loss of attention; loss of a parent; loss of a home, friends, or school; and loss of bodily parts or function through medical trauma. Betrayal, which is essentially a loss of trust, shakes the very foundation of childhood development. The children who experience betrayal view the world as an unsafe and threatening place and often believe that they do not deserve any better than the traumatizing experience.

The *fragmentation of bodily experience* that Beverly James talks about is a very real experience for trauma victims. Children (and adults) who have experienced some physical trauma appear to have encoded the traumatic event through sensory and muscular memory as well as affective memory. Children who have been traumatized through accidents, sexual or physical abuse, or surgery do not trust, respect, or feel mastery over their bodies. One of the reasons that play therapy is helpful in treating this element of trauma is that in play, children have the opportunity to engage all of the body's senses in the therapeutic process and can express themselves nonverbally and actively.

Stigmatization also marks children who have endured trauma. They feel an internal sense of shame as well as an external categorization and labeling. These children experience pronounced shame and alienation from others because of the traumatizing experience. It is not uncommon to encounter children like Amy, whose story introduced chapter 6. An inordinate portion of her identity was based on a traumatic molestation. Despite their own efforts to compensate, such children are often stuck in a relentless pursuit of acceptance. Group therapy, both for stigmatized children and the parents of these children, can greatly facilitate the abatement of shame and alienation.

Traumatized children may experience *eroticization,* which can be quite disturbing to parents, teachers, and even counselors. Through the experience of molest and rape, children may perceive that their value is centered on being sexual; thus they often become eroticized. The child's entire personality may be wrapped up in the view of being valued only for his or her sexuality. Without a doubt, children who carry these messages into adulthood are at risk of entering inappropriate sexual situations. Since the parents or caretakers of these children are often the most challenged by such behaviors, it is important to provide support and training for them. Social-skills training about appropriate and inappropriate touching may be an important adjunct intervention.

Destructiveness is another hallmark of traumatized children. Many children lose their impulse control, establishing a self-defeating cycle of aggression and destructiveness. This cycle may lead to frightening displays of temper and release of rage. This destructive behavior often causes people to dislike or punish the traumatized child. This can, in turn, cause the hurting child who is acting out to internalize shame and anger even further, which leads to greater displays of destructive behavior. It is important for parents and counselors to work together on behavioral strategies and to provide a play therapy experience for the child. The following chapter will discuss the benefits of play therapy for aggressive behavior.

Dissociative disorders can provide an efficient way for a child to cope with traumatic events. Although defense mechanisms such as denial, repression, and dissociation are seen as dysfunctional, they realistically serve a very valid function for the child experiencing trauma. It may be that the only way for a child to cope with an uncontrollable situation is to dissociate; fragmentation and depersonalization can help protect from overwhelming emotions and traumatizing experiences. The problem is that while these help to defend in the midst of trauma, these defenses do not serve well in terms of daily functioning. Children need to be free to explore all feelings and feeling states in counseling. Although counselors should not reinforce dissociation, they should accept it so that the child may integrate within the counseling process.

Attachment disorders are additional ways children may respond to trauma. Attachment is vital for survival, so it is understandable that threats to attachment are life-and-death issues for children. Children may experience attachment disorders from repeated traumatizing events that prevent a secure attachment from forming or from a single event such as parental abandonment, death of a parent, or removal from the home. The crucially important relationship that is established in play therapy forms a primary foundation for the development of positive attachments.

PLAY THERAPY AND THE TREATMENT OF CHILDHOOD TRAUMA

Children who have been traumatized have a need for a therapeutic experience that is safe and empowering. It needs to touch their senses and provide them with an opportunity to gain the mastery and control that have been stripped away by the traumatizing event. I believe that touching the senses is key here. If you look at the diagnostic criteria for Posttraumatic Stress Disorder in the DSM-IV, many of the diagnostic descriptors are sensory based.[16] This is because trauma is sensory based. Trauma overwhelms the senses, both psychologically and physiologically. It makes sense, therefore, for the treatment to be sensory based. "Talk-based" counseling approaches do not meet this need: "Psychological trauma is an extremely stressful event or happening that is usually atypical in the life experiences of the child and is remarkably distressing to the child to the point of being overwhelming and causing the child to be unable to cope. Young children should not be expected to verbally describe such experiences because they do not have the verbal facility required to do so, and such experiences are usually too threatening for the child to consciously describe. The natural reaction of children is to reenact or play out the traumatic experience in an unconscious effort to comprehend, overcome, develop a sense of control, or assimilate the experience. This repetitive playing out of the experience is the child's natural self-healing process."[17]

Charlie's experience illustrates this dynamic of repetitive playing out of a traumatic experience. Eight-year-old Charlie had been severely sexually abused; the injuries were so severe that Charlie needed corrective surgery. His behavior in the foster home ranged from depression and isolation to aggression and delinquent behavior. His play in the counseling sessions moved from being occasionally controlling to being very aggressive. Charlie began to play "cops and robbers"; he took on both roles. He would give me the play money and then rob me of it; then he would suddenly switch roles and arrest me for robbery. This play moved to a prevalent and repetitive theme. He would stab the bop bag in the lower part of the back and then would attempt to do the same with me. Although I set a limit on this latter activity, Charlie needed to express himself through this play. It was an effort to "comprehend, overcome, develop a sense of control, [and] assimilate" his experience—it was also his way of telling me as his therapist: "This is what I experienced. I want you to know how I was hurt, and I need to know whether or not you will still accept me." As he worked through these issues in the play therapy, Charlie's behavior in the foster home and at school significantly improved. Charlie moved from long-term residential treatment to "adoptable" status. Traumatized children need to have special places like these to play out and process their experiences.

Although I would caution against taking a therapeutic approach that is too directive, which might tend to advance the therapist's agenda at the expense of the child, remember that the following issues are critical to treatment.

1. The child needs to acknowledge and explore his or her pain while in therapy, in order to integrate the experience.

2. A serialized course of treatment is often more successful than one uninterrupted period of therapy. The treatment is sequenced over time so that it is responsive to developmental vulnerabilities that arise from the trauma over time.

3. The needs of the child usually cannot be effectively met by a clinician working alone, without the support of others involved with the child. The caregivers must be considered part of the treatment team, and their active participation is needed.

4. A direct, active treatment approach is needed not only to elicit from the child material that is unlikely to emerge spontaneously but also to demonstrate that the issues need not be shameful and can be dealt with directly.

5. Positive clinical messages have to be intense to be heard and felt through the child's defenses. The genesis and passage of these messages must be fun for both the child and the treatment team in order to balance the hard work being accomplished.

6. The clinical course must include attention to the physical, cognitive, emotional, and spiritual parts of the child since the damage usually affects all these areas.

7. Many of these children engage in behaviors that are secret and dysfunctional and that continue long after the traumatic incident itself. Dissociation and deviant sexualized behaviors, which often develop after traumatizing events, are not likely to be uncovered unless a determined effort is made to discover them by a knowledgeable clinician.

8. Working with traumatized children means dealing with gross, sometimes horrible, situations which may have a

strong personal impact on the therapist; this impact may interfere with treatment.[18]

Play provides children with the opportunity to *abreact*. Abreaction is a process by which "trauma victims resolve the experience. . . . [It is] a mental process in which repressed memories are brought to consciousness and relived with appropriate release of affect."[19] Sigmund Freud noted in 1920 that for children, play offers an abreactive experience for them to work through traumatic events.[20] The abreactive nature of play is additionally facilitated by the therapeutic distance that is part of play therapy. Charles Schaefer suggests several properties that allow play to provide the sense of distance and resultant sense of safety that children experience: (1) *symbolization*—children can used a toy predatory animal to represent an abuser; (2) *"as if" quality*—children can use the pretend quality of play to act out events as if they are not real life; (3) *projection*—children can project intense emotions onto puppets or toy animals, who can then safely act out these feelings; and (4) *displacement*—children can displace negative feelings onto dolls and other toys rather than expressing them toward family members.[21]

Children who have experienced psychic trauma will engage in posttraumatic play. Psychiatrist Lenore Terr suggests eleven characteristics of posttraumatic play:

1. Compulsive repetition
2. Unconscious link between the play and the traumatic event
3. Literalness of play with simple defenses only
4. Failure to relieve anxiety
5. Wide age range
6. Varying lag time prior to its development
7. Carrying power to nontraumatized youngsters
8. Contagion to new generations of children
9. Danger

10. Use of doodling, talking, typing, and audio duplication as modes of repeated play
11. Possibility of therapeutically retracing posttraumatic play to an earlier trauma[22]

I generally do not take any more of a prescriptive approach with traumatized children than I do with any other presenting problem. I may stock the playroom with additional toys that children might relate to their trauma. For instance, I may provide a toy tractor for the child whose father was killed in a farming accident, toy power tools for the child who has lost some fingers in a woodworking accident, hospital toys for the terminally ill child. I will not, however, direct a child to play with any particular toy provided; I will simply make the toys available.

It is difficult to list or categorize types of play to look for with traumatized children. Most of these children will play out the trauma, but the therapist may not always recognize the process. A child who vigorously cleans toys in the sink may be dealing with a sense of being dirty from having experienced sexual trauma, may be acting out life in the home of an obsessive-compulsive parent, or may be dealing with enuresis. Other possibilities may certainly exist as well. The point is that it is more important for children to have the opportunity to express themselves and feel the acceptance and understanding of the therapist than it is for the therapist to be able to interpret the play themes.

I would expect that traumatized children will experience regression and abreaction in the play. The child who was sexually abused at age four and enters therapy at age seven will often regress to age four in the play while acting out the trauma. It is also possible that this child will regress to an age earlier than the age of the trauma in order to experience within the fantasy of the play what life was like before the trauma. It is not uncommon for the traumatized child to regress a little bit in the play to test the therapist's level of acceptance. When children find that it is safe to regress a little bit, they will feel safe to go further and further, until they are able to bring the play back to the trauma itself. Following this regression and abreaction, traumatized children often will further test limits in the play (which, in fact, is testing the relationship) and will be able to gain the impulse control that is a problem for many traumatized children. Often traumatized children will be experiencing some level of developmental arrest. As the children have the opportunity to process the trauma in the play, they will be able to progress to the appropriate developmental level. Quite simply, after the regression comes progression.

Play is children's way of making sense of the traumatic event. In children's efforts to make sense of what happened to them, they often "act out" after a traumatic event. Posttrauma reactions can be seen in their behavior, affect, and certainly through their play. Children's wounds begin to heal as they build a relationship with a counselor who understands and accepts them, as they experience the therapeutic distance of the play therapy setting, and as they process issues in their natural medium of communication. In their book *The Gift of Play,* Maria Piers and Genevieve Landau assert: "Children actually heal themselves of emotional injuries through play, coping with and mastering potentially devastating occurrences. . . . Without the chance to experience the natural healing power of imaginative play, the emotional wounds caused by such events might never close, leaving the child with a lifelong residue of anxiety and insecurity. If children did not play, they could not thrive, and they might not survive."[23]

THE SEXUALLY ABUSED CHILD

Sexual abuse of children has become an epidemic problem in the United States. In 1992 there were 493,000 allegations of sexual abuse, of which 197,000 cases were confirmed.[24] These statistics are misleading, however, because they are reported by local welfare agencies, which deal primarily with sexual abuse within the family. Tragically, the frequency and severity of child sexual abuse is considered as high within the Christian church community as in the general population.[25] Christian counselors working with children can expect to have sexually abused children on their caseload.

Sexual abuse has been defined in a number of ways. One author notes that child sexual abuse is "the sexual exploitation of a child who is not developmentally capable of understanding or resisting the contact or who is psychologically and socially dependent on the abuser."[26] Another posits that sexual abuse is any occurrence in which a child has been "tricked, coerced, forced, or threatened" to have any kind of sexual contact with an adult or other child.[27] The important point is that sexual contact between an adult and a child is by definition exploitative and traumatic. A continuum of sexual activity may be considered abusive, including genital exposure, fondling, masturbation, oral-genital contact, as well as digital, object, or penile penetration of the vagina and anus.

The impact of sexual abuse must also be considered along a continuum. In his book *Psychotherapy of Sexually Abused Children and Their Families,* William Friedrich suggests, "Sexual abuse and its impact should be seen along a continuum ranging from neutral to very negative. Sometimes when we see only one type of child or family, we may believe that abuse is either much more discrete in its impact or primarily very negative. It is important to recognize this variability because it reminds us again of the hopefulness that can be present even in traumatic events and that the possibility for positive change always exists. It also forces us to realize that there are strengths and sources of resilience in the individuals whom we see that exceed any of the curative powers that we might be able to bring to these dysfunctional systems."[28]

Several experts in the field of treating sexually abused children have developed lists of specific behaviors that are exhibited by these children. One widely used list has been developed by Dr. Suzanne Sgroi in her text *Handbook of Clinical Intervention in Child Sexual Abuse:*

- Overly compliant behavior
- Acting-out, aggressive behavior

- Pseudo–mature behavior
- Sexual behavior
- Persistent and inappropriate sexual play with peers, toys, or self; sexual aggression with others
- Detailed and age-inappropriate understanding of sexual behavior
- Arriving early at school and leaving late with few, if any, absences
- Poor peer relationships or inability to make friends
- Lack of trust, particularly with significant others
- Nonparticipation in school and social activities
- Inability to concentrate in school
- Sudden drop in grades
- Extraordinary fear of males (in cases of male perpetrator)
- Running away from home
- Sleep disturbances
- Regressive behavior
- Withdrawal
- Clinical depression
- Suicidal feelings[29]

It is important to note that the existence of any one or even a combination of several of these behaviors does not necessarily mean that a child has been sexually abused. While this statement may seem obvious, let me give an example that may be easily misinterpreted. If a five-year-old girl is found to be chronically masturbating in her kindergarten class, it is likely that the teacher will assume some type of inappropriate sexual activity has occurred. And why not? This is not typical behavior for most kindergarten girls. It is certainly a possibility that the child has been exposed to some type of sexual trauma. Another possibility may also exist. Suppose this girl had recently had a rash in her vaginal area (it is possible for a child that young to have a yeast infection). It is only natural that she would scratch where it itches. The child might discover that scratching and rubbing in that area is pleasurable, and the masturbation then becomes a habit. The problem is that public masturbation is definitely not socially acceptable, even if the child's motivation is no different from another child's habit. Obviously, some intervention is necessary—but not calling out the cavalry.

In their book *Treating Sexually Abused Children and Their Families,* Beverly James and Maria Nasjleti suggest twelve possible indicators of child sexual abuse. They also caution that none of these behaviors alone necessarily means that sexual abuse has occurred, but a combination of these behaviors indicates that further evaluation is necessary.

1. Excessive masturbation
2. Excessive sexual acting-out toward adults
3. Simulation of sophisticated sexual activity with younger children
4. Fear of being alone with an adult, either male or female
5. Violence against younger children
6. Self-mutilation
7. Bruises and hickeys or both in the face or neck area or around the groin, buttocks, and inner thighs
8. Fear of bathrooms and showers
9. Knowledge of sexual matters and details of adult sexual activity inappropriate to age or developmental level
10. Combination of violence and sexuality in artwork, written schoolwork, language, and play
11. Extreme fear or repulsion when touched by an adult of either sex
12. Refusal to undress for physical education class at school[30]

I should probably make a point about investigations for child sexual abuse. Although people in the field disagree on this subject, I generally believe that it is not appropriate for a therapist to be a sexual abuse investigator. I am principally a therapist with children, and even after a disclosure once therapy begins, I prefer not to take on an investigative role. The potential for damaging the therapeutic relationship is too great. I will make the required child-abuse report and will cooperate with an investigation, but I will not begin interrogating the child for purposes of investigation or prosecution. It may be beneficial for an investigator to take on a child's case therapeutically in some situations, but I would be quite reticent about going back to investigating once therapy has begun. If it is handled well, the investigation process can be therapeutic, but it can also retraumatize the child. A colleague of mine has developed a sexual-abuse interviewing protocol that incorporates play therapy techniques within the investigation process. That protocol will be published within the next year.[31]

I believe that a play-based approach to treating child sexual abuse is most beneficial. The child who has experienced this devastating trauma has internalized a variety of negative messages about self, others, and the world. Play provides an opportunity to process and externalize these messages. Children, through the fantasy of the play, manage the clearly unmanageable—the abuse itself. In *Play Therapy Interventions with Children's Problems,* the authors assert the following:

> The emotional dynamics resulting from abuse must be matched by an equally dynamic therapeutic process as is found in the play therapy relationship. Children who have been abused cannot be expected to verbally describe their experience and their reaction because they lack the cognitive-verbal ability to do so. Abused children come from inconsistent environments. The play therapy relationship provides children with an absolutely consistent environment, for without such the child cannot feel safe, and it is this dimension of predictable safety that allows children to express, explore, and resolve through play deep-seated emotional pain. Abuse and neglect cause serious inner conflicts and relationship problems for children, and play therapy provides the modality necessary for

children to develop adaptive and coping mechanisms on their own terms and at their own emotional pace.[32]

In her book *The Healing Power of Play: Working with Abused Children,* Eliana Gil suggests several crucial variables to be considered in the play-based treatment of abused children:

- "Because abuse is interactional and usually occurs within the framework of a family, the child can profit from an opportunity to experience a safe, appropriate, and rewarding interaction with a trusted other."[33]

- "Because physical and sexual abuse are intrusive acts, the clinician's interventions should be nonintrusive, allowing the child ample physical and emotional space."[34]

- "Probably in no other kind of therapy is an ongoing assessment so necessary. Children may unfold during therapy, sharing their emotions and feelings as they begin to trust. They are also in a state of continuous developmental change with accompanying personality transfigurations."[35]

- "Because abused, neglected, or emotionally abused children are frequently under- or overstimulated, they lack the ability to explore, experiment, and even play. The clinician must facilitate these natural, now constricted or disorganized tendencies."[36]

- "Because abused children are frequently forced or threatened to keep the abuse secret or somehow sense that the abuse cannot be disclosed, efforts must be made to invite and promote self-expression." [37]

- "Abused or traumatized children may also have a tendency to try to suppress frightening or painful memories or thoughts and in some cases may use denial and avoidance fully."[38]

- "Because posttraumatic play often occurs in secret, the therapeutic environment must create a climate for this type of play."[39]

- "All abused children can benefit from learning skills to employ in difficult, frightening, or abusive situations. Allowing the child to anticipate and plan for crises is useful."[40]

TRAUMATIC GRIEF

Grief and loss are typical issues in the developmental cycles of life. They are, however, perhaps more challenging to deal with in children because children lack the abstract thinking skills and formal operations to process loss as adults do. This is combined with children's egocentric nature, as discussed earlier. These factors make grief and loss for children a traumatic occurrence.

Loss is, at the least, very confusing for children. Ponder the case of four-year-old Kevin, who has just had one of his pet goldfish die. This is not a great loss, granted, but Kevin doesn't understand it. He could be wondering, *What's wrong with the goldfish? Did I do something wrong?* Kevin's parents may decide to give the goldfish a burial at sea—they flush the fish down the toilet. Now how does Kevin perceive this? He still has not grasped the finality of death, but he has witnessed his parents' response. Remember that Kevin is four, and toilet training was a fairly recent accomplishment. Could it be possible that he will connect the flushing of the goldfish (which he still does not understand) with the flushing of the toilet following toileting, which contains a part of him? Although this is not a traumatic loss, it could be a formative experience for children before they experience significant grief and loss.

In his book *Children Mourning, Mourning Children,* Kenneth Doka suggests several considerations in dealing with children and loss: First, children are always developing; therefore, their understandings of death and their reactions to illness and loss are also undergoing change. Second, children grieve in ways that are both different from and similar to the way adults do. Third, children need significant support as they deal with loss.[41] These issues are important in the evaluation and treatment of grief and loss with children. Therapists must consider more than at what age children can cognitively understand death. Therapists must also consider children's physical, emotional, and spiritual development as well as the fluidity of the developmental phases. In some ways, children grieve similarly to adults. Both children and adults are affected by the depth of a relationship, the prevailing circumstances at the time of a loss, the support or lack of support available, varying levels of coping skills, as well as differences of gender, culture, and religion. However, children *process* grief differently from the way adults do. Thus the need for expressive and projective interventions such as play therapy becomes important. Finally, children need significant support during times of loss. This may sound obvious, but when children are experiencing significant loss, the adults in their lives may also be grieving. In the adults' attempts to process their own grief, they may minimize or dismiss the need for the children to process the same loss.

From their work in the area of children and death, Mark Speece and Sandor Brent identified five principal subconcepts involved in children's concepts of death.[42] *Universality* refers to children's recognition that all living things must eventually die. *Irreversibility* refers to children's comprehension that once the physical body has died, it can never be alive again. *Nonfunctionality* refers to children's understanding that once a living thing has died, all of its functional capacities cease. Irreversibility and nonfunctionality are what is meant by the "finality" of death.[43] *Causality* refers to children's attempt to figure out what brings about death. *Life after death* refers to children's understanding of some type of continued life-form; children will understand these concepts to varying degrees, depending on developmental level and the level of trauma resulting from the severity of the loss.

An additional issue to consider when working with children and loss is children's concept of time. A week may seem like a year to a toddler. Think about the three-year-old child whose parents have recently been divorced. The mother has primary physical custody, but the father, who has moved away, gets to have the child for the summer as part of the custody arrangement. Three months for a three-year-old is fully one-twelfth of that child's life. You can assume that the child's loss of a two-parent family at home will be compounded by the loss and confusion involved in the custody arrangement. Children's concept of space and time will affect their perception of loss and also the corresponding grief issues.

As discussed in previous chapters, play and play therapy enable children to make sense of what is for them a nonsensical situation. Managing the unmanageable, which can and does occur in the fantasy of the play, is crucial for the grieving child. The authors of *Play Therapy Interventions with Children's Problems* discuss the importance of play for grieving children:

> Contrary to what many adults think, very young children do experience grief. Even infants have been shown to experience sadness. The experience of grief is not dependent on a person's mental facility or ability to understand but rather on the person's capacity to feel and ability to experience. Therefore, all children can be assumed to grieve and should be dealt with accordingly, that is, through their most natural medium of expression and communication, play. Separation can be considered loss for very young children. Loss of an object of love precipitates the experience of grief, which should be considered to be a process rather than a specific emotion, and can be expressed in a variety of ways, often hidden from the awareness of significant adults in their lives since children express grief differently than adults. Children do not generally experience long periods of acute pain but rather deal with the pain in short bursts, almost as though they have a short attention span for pain. Children deal with their feelings through play, often in a form of symbolic distancing which allows the child to feel safe in the midst of acting out the experience.[44]

Children process grief in play therapy in a variety of ways. They may play out a funeral using toy animals, paint morose pictures in dark colors, or bury and unbury items in the sand. Regardless of the play materials utilized, children will often replay the loss experience, although it will be couched in symbolic play. To be able to do this in the process of the play therapy relationship is a healing process for grieving children. I like to use storytelling as an adjunct intervention (see chapter 8) and would recommend composing a story to fit the child's situation. Bookstores offer a wide variety of children's books about grief issues, but I prefer to compose a personal story for children if the situation arises.

I have found that it is especially important to work with the parents of grieving children. In addition to encouraging them to seek counseling themselves for the grief issues, helping the parents to help the child is critical. When children are experiencing loss, parents are often at a loss for what to do. They often need to be educated about grief and children. Training can cover issues as basic as what to say to children. Many parents don't realize that if they tell their children that "Grandpa has gone to sleep" when their grandfather has died, the children may end up having sleep disturbances. What children would want to go to sleep if it meant that they might never wake up?

Beverly James discusses the need for children who are removed from their parents to mourn their loss, which seems to apply to grieving and loss in general: "Children need to mourn their losses, and they need adult help to do so. They are not able to let go of a wounded bond, no matter how dysfunctional, unless they have something with which to replace it, something to hang onto. But they cannot find something else to hang onto as long as their emotional focus and energy are on maintaining ties to the attachment. Asking these children to let go of this tie is like asking ship wreck victims in the middle of a storm-tossed ocean to let go of the piece of wood they are clinging desperately to. They see we have a rope, but are compelled to hang onto what they have."[45]

Grief and loss, therefore, involve more than processing what has been lost. They move children toward new things as well. As play therapy gives children the opportunity to face pain and act out their loss, it also provides a place for them to experience new understandings.

We cannot force children who are experiencing grief and loss to grab the life preserver that we have to throw to them. We can, however, help to calm the storm by providing children with a safe place to process their pain. Before Christ calmed the sea when he was crossing the lake with his disciples, he had told them: "Let us go over to the other side."[46] He had not said how they were going to get there, only that they would get there. In treating children who have experienced loss, abuse, and trauma, the ultimate calming of the storm comes from the Lord. I find it reassuring to hold on to the promise that we *will get there*.

Play transforms reality by assimilation of reality to the needs of the self.   —*JEAN PIAGET*

12/ TREATING DISRUPTIVE BEHAVIOR PROBLEMS

Even a minor event in the life of a child is an event of that child's world and thus a world event.   —GASTON BACHELARD

Bruce was referred to my office for acting-out behaviors. His parents were frustrated, and his teachers were worn-out. From the description that Bruce's parents gave of him during the intake session, I was beginning to get a little worried about the integrity of my playroom, not to mention my own personal safety. He sounded out of control. He had been alternately labeled as defiant, disruptive, lazy, and uncooperative. Bruce's parents had received suggestions ranging from medication to residential-treatment care to the idea that perhaps they were not providing him with enough love and attention. They were exhausted and were looking for an instant miracle cure.

Unfortunately, we have no instant miracle cure for disruptive behavior problems. The etiology of behavior difficulties can be widespread. The good news for Bruce's parents, however, was that they were not alone in their struggle and that interventions for the situation were available.

It is obvious that many children are referred to counselors for the issues of disruptive behavior and noncompliance. The children referred are simply not doing what they are expected to do:

> While these children may receive various diagnoses of oppositional disorder, conduct disorders, attention deficit disorders, adjustment reactions, and so forth, a major concern of the parents or teachers referring such a child is his or her inability to comply with directions, commands, rules, or codes of social conduct appropriate to the child's age group. Parents may complain that the child fails to listen, throws temper tantrums, is aggressive or destructive, is verbally oppositional or resistant to authority, fails to do homework, does not adequately perform chores, cannot play appropriately with neighborhood children, lies or steals frequently, or behaves inappropriately in other ways. However, all of these behaviors are violations of commands, directions, or rules that were either previously stated to the child or are directly stated in the particular situation. Hence, noncompliance, broadly defined, encompasses the majority of acting out, externalizing, or conduct problem forms of behavior.[1]

The difficulties associated with disruptive behavior problems are multifaceted, and the treatment approach must be as well. Play therapy is not a panacea approach for these problems any more than medication is. Before I discuss specific issues such as ADHD, conduct problems, and aggression, I would like to discuss some general principles in working not only with children with disruptive behavior problems but also with their parents.

I have found that parent training and support are two of the most important aspects of any intervention with disruptive children. By the time most parents seek the help of a counselor, they are like Bruce's parents, exasperated and devoid of hope. When many parents arrive at the counseling office, they are in crisis. It helps to remember those basic crisis-counseling skills. Your initial goal is to educate and support the parents in their time of crisis.

As I have mentioned previously, I begin my counseling with children by meeting with the parents in the first session. If it is indeed my sense that the parents are feeling in crisis and overwhelmed, I will spend much of the first session giving them support and making a few suggestions. I may give them a parent-training suggestion out of the filial-therapy model (chapter 10) or explore alternate methods of discipline. I may make an immediate referral for psychiatric intervention if that is warranted. I will often use some of the assessment instruments that I discussed in chapter 4. The assessment not only will give me a clearer picture of the child but also will help in diagnosis (if needed for insurance reimbursement purposes) and the need for a medication evaluation referral.

One small intervention that I will try to make is to have the parents contract with me to do at least one thing for themselves over the next week. Most parents of disruptive children expend much of their energy on handling the challenging behaviors. They find little energy left for life. Their emotional well is running or already has run dry. I briefly brainstorm with parents about something that they might do for themselves during the next week—going to a movie, playing a game of tennis or a round of golf, spending time with friends, or getting their hair done. I have noticed in the course of these discussions that many parents have given up hobbies and pastimes because of the challenges of everyday life. By making the effort to resurrect lost interests and care for themselves, many parents will feel more energized and better equipped to face the demands of a disruptive child.

Children misbehave for a variety of reasons. Drs. Walter Byrd and Paul Warren, in their book *Counseling and Children,* suggest several goals of misbehavior. These include:

Goal 1—Attention Seeking. The child may have sought proofs of acceptance, approval, and significance from parents by demanding inordinate amounts of attention. If the parent supplies attention to the child when he or she is not making a bid for it, then the child will usually reduce his or her need to compete for it.

Goal 2—Control of Power. In some family systems, maintaining and controlling power are the means by which the family parcels out worth and significance. The child struggling to gain control will give the parents the message "You don't love me" if the child can't have his or her own way. The child will feel that only when one is in control—even if that control occurs through manipulating the parent—can one be sure of worth and value.

Goal 3—Animosity of Revenge. Sometimes a child's goal is to misbehave in order to intimidate or pay back others for perceived injustices. The child in this situation has felt wronged or mistreated and thinks the only way to be significant or to see real hope in the situation is to retaliate. This child seeks to hurt others in order to offset feeling hurt.

Goal 4—Reflection of Inadequacy. Sometimes, oppositional behavior is the child's statement that he or she feels inadequate and wants to be left alone. It's a way of driving people away from what is perceived as a hopeless situation. The child doesn't want others to see how inadequate, stupid, or "damaged" he or she is.[2]

While recognizing these goals generally will not change my therapeutic approach to the child, it is very helpful for parents to recognize some of the possible motivations behind their children's behavior. I have already discussed in previous chapters that I believe it is the underlying emotions that need intervention. This is certainly the case for children with disruptive behavior problems.

I believe play therapy addresses all of the goals Byrd and Warren mention. Children in play therapy have the opportunity to receive attention and acceptance, be in the lead and learn self-control, express feelings of anger and animosity without fearing retaliation, and process feelings of inadequacy in the play and build a positive self-concept.

Behavioral interventions are also important when working with children who exhibit disruptive behavior. Education of parents should focus on building relationships and fostering communication skills, but it may be equally important to discuss issues of rules and discipline. I often work with parents on anger management because any discipline rendered in anger—whether verbal or non-verbal, time-out or spanking—is potentially, and probably, abusive.

One behavioral intervention that has proven effective with non-compliant children is the token economy. Many children seem to need a systematic reward system. While some counselors suggest a star chart to monitor behavioral compliance (giving or withholding rewards depending on the child's behavior), I prefer a chip and point system. While a star chart may visually appeal to the child, a tangible token can be both visually and kinesthetically satisfying. I will suggest to parents that they use play coins or poker chips to set up a "token economy" at home. Children can earn chips for chores or compliant behavior and can then exchange their chips for various rewards or privileges. Generally, I suggest with a family of more than one child that all children be on the system, with older children having the option of a point system if they are resistant to the tokens.

Internationally recognized as an authority on Attention-Deficit Hyperactivity Disorder, Dr. Russell Barkley, author of *Defiant Children: A Clinician's Manual for Parent Training,* lists several advantages of the chip/point system, illustrating the effectiveness of this behavioral intervention for noncompliant children:

1. Token systems permit parents to manage child behavior by drawing on rewards more powerful than mere social praise and attention.
2. Token systems are highly convenient reward systems. Chips and points can be taken anywhere, dispensed any-

time, and used to earn virtually any form of privilege or tangible incentive.

3. Token rewards are likely to retain their value or effectiveness throughout the day across situations. In contrast, children often satiate quickly with food rewards, stickers, or other tangible reinforcers.

4. Token systems permit a more organized, systematic, and fair approach to managing children's behavior.

5. Token systems result in increased parental attention to appropriate child behavior and compliance. Because parents must dispense the tokens, they must attend and respond more often to child behaviors they might otherwise have overlooked.

6. Token systems teach a fundamental concept of society, that privileges and rewards as well as most of the things we desire in life must be earned by the way we behave.[3]

Any behavioral interventions that counselors suggest or implement in a family system should be based on sound rationale and theory. The goal should encompass more than the extinction of undesirable behaviors but also the development of the parent-child relationship and the biblical pattern of family structure.

ATTENTION-DEFICIT HYPERACTIVITY DISORDER

Attention-deficit hyperactivity disorder (ADHD) is one of the most referred for and heavily studied psychological disorders of childhood.[4] It is estimated that some 3 percent to 5 percent of school-age children have ADHD and that boys with ADHD outnumber girls by a 6 to 1 margin.[5] Grant Martin notes that this means that, on average, every classroom will have at least one ADHD child.[6] Throughout the history of psychology and psychiatry, professionals have used many terms to describe or label ADHD, ranging from brain damage to hyperactive child syndrome to ADHD. Future name changes will no doubt be proposed.

The hallmark characteristics of ADHD are inattention, impulsivity, and overactivity. One of the leading experts in the field, Dr. Russell Barkley, offers the following "consensus" definition: "Attention-Deficit Hyperactivity Disorder is a developmental disorder characterized by developmentally inappropriate degrees of inattention, overactivity, and impulsivity. These often arise in early childhood; are relatively chronic in nature; and are not readily accounted for on the basis of gross neurological, sensory, language, or motor impairment, mental retardation, or severe emotional disturbance. These difficulties are typically associated with deficits in rule-governed behavior and in maintaining a consistent pattern of work performance over time."[7]

Several broad characteristics describe children with ADHD. The first is *inattention*. Children with ADHD experience difficulty staying on task, focusing attention, and maintaining concentration as compared to other children their age. *Distractibility* is another common characteristic. Whereas most children seem to be able to filter out distractions, ADHD children have difficulty concentrating on the task at hand because they are distracted by external surroundings or internal stimuli. Another characteristic is *impulsivity*. These children tend to act without thinking. Although they may be aware of the consequences of their actions, they do not take the time to consider them. This is what Barkley referred to above as problems with "rule-governed" behavior. *Overactivity* is also a problem. ADHD children are easily aroused and typically restless. Their emotions are usually expressed with greater intensity than other children's. These children also tend to have a *poor social sensitivity*. They may misread or miss altogether common verbal or nonverbal cues regarding appropriate behavior. These children may talk too loudly and often talk out of place, blurting things out at the wrong time. Finally, *delaying gratification* is very difficult for ADHD children.

Working toward delayed rewards is extremely challenging for the ADHD child.

Although ADHD has been so heavily researched, the precise causes of the disorder are not known. "A wide variety of causative factors have been proposed to underlie ADHD, yet no single variable has been found to account for its genesis fully. . . . The major causal variables that have been identified can be categorized as neurological factors, toxic reactions, genetic linkage, and environmental factors."[8] Despite publicity that a poor diet or excessive sugar is a cause for ADHD symptoms, no clear clinical evidence supports this belief.[9] However, if parents notice that their children's behavior changes after the children have eaten certain foods, they should modify their children's diet. A chaotic home environment does not appear to cause ADHD, but it seems obvious that such a home has considerable potential to exacerbate symptoms. The leading factors in determining the etiology of ADHD are the hereditary and neurological issues. Researchers are finding an increased incidence of ADHD among the biological parents and siblings of children with ADHD.[10] There is also increasing evidence that "neurological dysfunction, perhaps related to neurotransmitter imbalances, is associated with ADHD."[11]

Assessment of ADHD is not a simple task. It must involve observations from parents and teachers, a complete developmental history, diagnostic testing, and a physical exam by a physician. A complete evaluation is expensive, and counselors need to be sensitive to balance the need to be thorough with the parents' ability to handle the expense. Martin comments about this sensitivity:

> Always remember the anxiety and concern a family brings to your office. You may have seen hundreds of children, but all the family is concerned about is how you are going to help them deal with their child. You need to be professional and objective in your efforts, letting the love of God radiate through you in the process. The family needs to be treated humanely, diplo-

matically, sensitively, and compassionately. Be patient and understanding of their pain. Give an overview of the process and tell them specifically what the evaluation will involve, how long it will last, and what it will cost. Keep them informed, and don't drag out the evaluation. Let the family know your faith is important in dealing with difficult assessments like ADHD, and don't be afraid to acknowledge the limits of your knowledge and that of the profession.[12]

A number of useful assessment instruments help counselors evaluate children and ADHD. I have not always been a big fan of psychological testing, although I recognize the benefits for diagnostic purposes. What I have come to realize, however, is that testing of children is not as much for the sake of the children as it is for the parents. The parents have a genuine *need to know*—what is going on with their child, what they can do, and what they may have done wrong. For these reasons, assessment tools provide genuine benefit. Diagnosing ADHD should involve specific assessment because the primary treatment focus will be pharmacological.

Barkley has developed a clinical interview specifically tailored for interviewing parents of ADHD children. It is available in his *Attention-Deficit Hyperactivity Disorder: A Clinical Workbook.*[13] Some instruments that I have used include the Child Behavior Checklist (parent and teacher report forms), the Conners Rating Scales (for both parents and teachers), the Attention-Deficit Disorders Evaluation Scale (home and school versions), and the ADD-H Comprehensive Teacher Rating Scale.[14] It also may be helpful to have the parents fill out some self-evaluation forms to further assess the home environment. I have used the Family Environment Scale, the Parenting Stress Index, and the Locke-Wallace Marital Adjustment Test.[15] The overall goal of all of these assessment instruments is to provide a broad and clear clinical picture of the child and the family.

Assessment of ADHD can be a challenge for the individual clinician and the physician. The hallmark symptoms of ADHD may not manifest themselves in the office of the evaluator. It is important to consider various factors that may affect the severity of the symptoms. For example, ADHD symptoms seem to manifest themselves more in a group setting than in a one-on-one situation. This is why the classroom is such a challenge for these children and why an individual interview may yield minimal results. Also, as noted above, delayed gratification is difficult for ADHD children and may exacerbate symptoms. This is usually not a factor in an individual evaluation because the feedback is immediate rather than delayed. ADHD children are also bored easily. Familiarity and routines may lead to a greater degree of symptoms. A one-on-one interview, however, is novel. Have you ever wondered why an ADHD child can have such difficulty sitting still for one minute in a classroom but can sit for hours and play video games? Video games provide a one-on-one activity, give immediate feedback, and have a greater degree of novelty. These issues and others will affect the evaluation process.

Treatment of ADHD needs to be multifaceted. A recent book chapter about ADHD suggests that "the interventions that have shown the greatest effectiveness with ADHD children are pharmacotherapy, parent counseling and training in child-management skills, and classroom behavior-modification techniques."[16] I would agree that these interventions are necessary. I would also, however, strongly recommend individual counseling for the child.

It is important to understand that treatment of ADHD is based on management as opposed to cure. It is probably inappropriate to proceed with any one of the above mentioned interventions alone. Medications are indicated in most cases of ADHD (discussed in chapter 15). Obviously, the nonmedical psychotherapists should refer these children for a medical evaluation and be supportive of any prescribed interventions. Parents need to know that medications for ADHD are appropriate and safe. Using medication is not a sign that the parents have somehow failed.

Parent counseling and training should be both educational and supportive. Parents need to learn to view the world through the eyes of their children. A number of good programs train parents; I am, of course, biased toward a filial-therapy approach (discussed in chapter 10). I have also found that the limit-setting model that is proposed in chapter 7 is very effective with ADHD children. Parents often need to learn about the basics of giving commands to their children (e.g., making eye contact, giving only one command at a time, and reducing distractions like the television). Parent training in a group format is very helpful because parents learn that they are not the only ones in their struggle. Marital therapy may also be appropriate.

Many therapists who work with ADHD children advocate social-skills training that focuses on the development of self-control. I endorse this. I recommend, however, that this be done through parent counseling and through a play therapy approach to individual child counseling. Children should be learning social skills at home, and if there is a deficit there, I would like to intervene with the parents. Behavior-management programs are necessary and appropriate and should be tailored for the needs of the child. A simple star chart can be so helpful for ADHD children, as long as the rewards or consequences are not long delayed.

Barkley has a behaviorally based parent-training program described in his book *Defiant Children: A Clinician's Manual for Parent Training.*[17] I have also found Michael Gordon's book *ADHD/Hyperactivity: A Consumer's Guide* to be a helpful resource.[18] For Christian parents, I would recommend Grant Martin's book *The Hyperactive Child,* which is comprehensive, informative, and practical.[19]

Although I have heard some presenters discount play therapy and any other individual child treatments for ADHD, I am convinced that play therapy is helpful and needed. If for no other reason, the child who has been labeled ADHD most certainly has issues of low self-esteem, anger, and depression. These children have often been singled out by teachers, ostracized by peers, and perhaps excessively punished by parents. Medication does not address these issues. In play therapy, a child can address these issues as well as learn self-control. Dr. Louise Guerney, in a book chapter about play therapy with learning disabled and attention-deficit children, asserts the following:

> The use of play therapy with learning disabled children does not require the clinician to take a position on the primacy of medical intervention or on the etiology of the problems presented. The play therapist can proceed to undertake therapy because of the developmental value of the play therapy experience for the child. Play in a special and interpersonal environment can permit learning disabled children to succeed and develop a feeling of satisfaction with themselves and their competencies. The world of learning disabled children typically provides limited or at least very selective positive feedback as a result of the children's incompetence in important task areas. They may stop trying since they feel they have little effect. Permitting the child to master situations that are labeled "play" as opposed to "real" should make the threat of evaluation less heavy.[20]

Dr. Heidi Kaduson has adapted a list from Michael Gordon to come up with some ideal characteristics of a play therapist working with an ADHD child.

CHARACTERISTICS OF THERAPISTS EFFECTIVE WITH ADHD CHILDREN

1. Thoroughly knowledgeable about ADHD and accepts the legitimacy of the disorder
2. Tough as nails about rules but always calm and positive
3. Ingenious about modifying therapy strategies and materials

4. Tailors therapy strategies to meet child's needs
5. Mixes high- and low-interest tasks in tune with child's predilections
6. Knows to back off when child's level of frustration begins to peak
7. Knows to back off when therapist's level of frustration begins to peak
8. Speaks clearly in brief, understandable sentences
9. Looks the child straight in the eye when communicating
10. Has a very predictable and organized playroom
11. Provides immediate and consistent feedback (consequences) regarding behavior
12. Controls the playroom without being controlling—is willing to share control of the playroom with the child
13. Develops a private signal system with child to gently notify him when he's acting inappropriately
14. Maintains close physical proximity without being intrusive
15. Ignores minor disruptions—knows how to choose battles
16. Has no problem acting as an "Auxiliary Organizer" when appropriate and necessary—helps make sure child is organized for homework, parents are involved in play therapy process, etc.
17. Maintains interest in the child as a person with interests, fears, and joys—even after a trying session
18. Willing to consult with parents frequently about parenting, personal problems, their own problems with attention, etc.
19. Has a great sense of humor[21]

It may also be helpful to work with the school of the ADHD child. This should obviously be done with respect for the school's domain—remember not to be involved in a "turf" battle. Teachers and other school personnel will be less threatened by a counselor who takes the role of a consultant rather than of the child-therapy expert. Classroom-management techniques can obviously be helpful in handling the ADHD child. The ideal situation is one in which the child counselor is asked to conduct in-service training for a school district. One suggestion that may be important for the school is to give the ADHD child assignments in smaller increments. If a fourth grader has the attention span of a first grader, teachers should give the child fourth-grade work in first-grade increments.

CONDUCT PROBLEMS AND AGGRESSION

"Acting out" is a normal part of childhood. When the acting-out behaviors intrude on the rights of others and impair the normal functioning of families, classrooms, and other social settings, an intervention of some sort becomes necessary. These behaviors may range from minor (yet challenging) issues, such as whining, yelling, refusal to follow directions, and temper tantrums, to more serious issues, such as stealing, vandalism, and physical aggression. Child and adolescent researchers Karen Wells and Rex Forehand noted in their review of various studies that anywhere from 33 percent to 75 percent of child referrals to mental health clinics were for conduct-disorder problems.[22] As many as 4 percent to 10 percent of all children exhibit conduct problems serious enough to warrant intervention.[23] Conduct problems are roughly three times more likely to occur with boys than with girls.[24]

Conduct problems may range on a continuum from exhibiting a poor attitude to criminal behavior. Authors of *Fundamentals of Child and Adolescent Psychopathology,* psychiatrists Syed Husain and Dennis Cantwell summarize the clinical picture. Conduct problems may be manifested as

1. physical violence (bullying, cruelty toward peers, assault, and/or mugging)
2. behaviors directed particularly toward adults (hostility, verbal abuse, impatience, defiance, and negativism)

3. destructiveness and stealing (vandalism, setting fires, and breaking and entering)
4. behaviors outside the home involving confrontation with a victim (extortion, purse snatching, and armed robbery)[25]

Other problems may include academic problems, sexual acting out, truancy, running away, anger, depression, and low self-esteem.

A number of issues surround the child who is acting out and aggressive. Antisocial and aggressive behaviors tend to run in families.[26] Violent and aggressive parents simply tend to have violent and aggressive children. The genetic-versus-learned (nature-versus-nurture) question is not as great a concern when it comes to treatment. Spiritually, it should not be a surprise that conduct problems run in families. In 1 Samuel, we see the sons of Eli running amok, and Eli is chastised. We know that sin and the effects of sin are generational—"Yet he does not leave the guilty unpunished; he punishes the children for the sin of the fathers to the third and fourth generation."[27] Behavior problems run in families, whether we call it generational or genetic. Thankfully, through the love and mercy of God through Christ, we can find healing through redemption.

Related to this, conduct-disordered children have often experienced in their early life disruptions that interfered with the development of attachment.[28] When I was working with adolescents who were on probation, I never encountered a juvenile gang member who had come from a home with a father. Clearly, we are seeing the effects of a fatherless generation in our society.

Research reveals also some compelling biological theories for the development of aggressive behavior. These include chromosome abnormalities and unusual levels of testosterone.[29] It may also be important to consider contributory factors such as child temperament, school performance, family size, socioeconomic levels, birth order, marital stress, and general parenting practices.

As I mentioned in chapter 9, I believe that much of a child's behavior is an expression of an emotional need. To reiterate, when a child's feeling of empowerment and control are in line, the behavior should be in line. Traumatized, abused, neglected, or emotionally starving children will often express their needs in the best (and perhaps only) way they know how. Unfortunately, their expression may be inappropriate and disturbing.

Treatment of conduct and aggressive problems should, therefore, look to meet the underlying need as well as to manage behavior. Behavior modification by itself is inadequate. Most people's behavior can be modified, even if by coercive means. But if the underlying physical, emotional, and spiritual needs are not being met, the long-term effectiveness of a purely behavioral intervention is compromised.

Parent training and family therapy are important interventions for the acting-out child. Systemically, the child's acting-out behavior may well be a symptom of the family's dysfunction; for example, a noncompliant and defiant child may reflect marital discord and deflect the parents' attention off each other and onto the child. An appropriate intake evaluation will often reveal this behavior, and if not, the child will exhibit this dynamic in the individual therapy. A family intervention to accompany individual treatment is appropriate. Possible interventions include family sculpting, family puppet play, sandplay, or art intervention. I prefer using projective techniques like those discussed in chapter 8 because I find that families (particularly parents) are less resistant to processing family dynamics when they are not verbally confronted. As the family rules and patterns become evident through one of these expressive approaches, I am able to comment on them, which opens a dialogue on possible ways to change these patterns.

Parent training should involve development of the parent–child relationship and the teaching of parent skills. The filial-therapy approach discussed in chapter 10 is very effective. A parent-training program that simply teaches behavior management and offers new disciplinary tools is inadequate. If the parent–child relationship is poor, the greatest behavior-management techniques in the world will not work. The relationship is foundational.

Medications may be indicated in some cases of conduct-disordered behavior. If the underlying cause is ADHD, then stimulant medication may be indicated. If the underlying cause is depression, then antidepressant medication may be indicated. Some medications have been demonstrated to be effective with aggressive behavior as well. Chapter 15 will address children and medications in greater detail.

Play therapy has been demonstrated to be effective with aggression and acting-out behaviors. An environment that allows children to express negative feelings in their own language, that allows them to experience nonpunitive and consistent limits, and that allows them to process intrapsychic pain is an environment that addresses many of the underlying issues.

> Unlike the typical response to aggression and acting out behavior by parents, teachers, and adults in authority positions, the objective in play therapy is not to stop the behavior but rather to understand the child and provide an acceptable avenue for the child to express unfulfilled feelings, wants, and needs. Many play therapists have a very difficult time trying to respond appropriately to acts of aggression because such acts in the playroom are often directed at the therapist. In such cases, the play therapist may react emotionally as though the act were a personal attack, thus shifting the focus to an issue of transference which must be worked through by the therapist . . . parents and therapists can successfully use play to help children effectively release aggressive feelings and in the process significantly improve their attitudes and behavior outside the playroom. Once the feelings and needs behind aggressive acts have been accepted and allowed to be expressed, children are able to go on to explore more positive behaviors.[30]

Working with externalizing disorders such as disruptive behavior problems can be a significant challenge for the child counselor. These problems often call for a multimodal and often multidisciplinary approach to treatment. Always keep the best interests of the child paramount in the treatment process, but also include the parents, family, and school. Be willing to make appropriate referrals when necessary.

Disruptive behaviors are unfortunately a part of childhood culture in today's society. While society does not generally condone these behaviors, society ironically encourages them. Narcissism seems to be favored over altruism, selfishness over selflessness, division over unity, prejudice over acceptance, competition over cooperation, and pride over humility. Sometimes it feels as if the church is not much better. The ultimate intervention, of course, would be for us all to become more Christlike. When we encounter these problems in our counseling offices, however, perhaps we can extend a bit of God's love and acceptance to the hurting child behind the unacceptable behavior.

In our play, we reveal what kind of people we are.   —OVID

13/ Treating Anxious *and* Depressed Children

Fears never spring from a base of logic. And fears never, ever respond to logic.   —PAUL WARREN AND FRANK MINIRTH

Children should not have to experience anxiety and depression. I would like for my own children not to have to feel worried, scared, or sad. It just does not seem fair that children, who should be busy with the business of just growing up, should have their emotional lives invaded with weighty concerns. But children do experience disruption and distress in their lives, and they need to have their emotional responses recognized and validated. Parents and child counselors must address the reality of childhood anxiety and depression.

CHILDHOOD FEARS AND ANXIETY

The fear and anxiety children feel can be a response to a specific stressor, or anxiety may be a childhood personality characteristic. Syed Husain and Dennis Cantwell distinguish between anxiety traits and states: "As a trait, anxiety is defined as an enduring characteristic of one's personality and is independent of circumstances; as a state, on the other hand, it is a transient phenomenon occurring in association with an environmental or life event."[1] Childhood fears are a natural part of growing up and often can be handled by parents. The determination of the necessity for therapeutic intervention is not clear cut, but generally, "it can be said that fears which consistently inhibit normal daily activities are those that require intervention by a counselor."[2] Some of the childhood symptoms of anxiety and excessive fears include hyperactivity and agitation, irritability, crying, sleep disturbances, nightmares, hyperventilation or other breathing difficulties, excessive perspiration, appetite disturbances, enuresis, obsessive thinking, nausea or other gastrointestinal problems, tics, and other psychosomatic responses.

The prevalence of childhood fears and anxiety has been documented. Researchers R. Lapouse and M. Monk investigated children's fears and reported that 43 percent of children between the ages of six and twelve experienced seven or more fears.[3] Walter Byrd and Paul Warren noted that a more recent study of a thousand children found that approximately 90 percent of children between the ages of two and fourteen have a specific phobia or fear.[4] Additionally, research indicates that children's fears are quite stable in terms of type and quantity, with one study reporting 83 percent of identified childhood fears still present after one year.[5] Other studies appear to demonstrate a relationship between childhood anxiety and fear and adult anxiety disorders.[6]

An important consideration in the diagnosis and treatment of childhood fears and anxieties is an understanding of what normal fears are for the average child. Editors of the book *The Practice of Child Therapy*, Richard Morris and Thomas Kratochwill, list several common fears for the developing child:

- *0- to 6-month-olds* fear a loss of support and loud noises
- *7- to 12-month-olds* fear strangers and sudden, unexpected objects

- *1-year-olds* fear toileting, strangers, and separation from parents
- *2-year-olds* fear loud noises, dark rooms, large objects or machines, and separation from parents
- *3-year-olds* fear masks, the dark, animals, and separation from parents
- *4-year-olds* fear noises, the dark, animals, and separation from parents
- *5-year-olds* fear the dark, animals, "bad" people, separation from parents, and injury
- *6-year-olds* fear supernatural beings, injury, thunder/lightning, being alone, and separation from parents
- *7- to 8-year-olds* fear supernatural beings, the dark, fears based on media events, being alone, and injury
- *9- to 12-year-olds* fear tests in school, school performance, injury, physical appearance, thunder/lightning, and death[7]

These fears and anxieties are "normal." It may be important to educate parents about these as well as other basic developmental milestones. When these types of fears become pervasive and intrude on daily functioning, however, some manner of therapeutic intervention becomes appropriate.

In trying to differentiate between fears that are normal and those that are not, it is helpful to distinguish between the terms *fear* and *phobia*. Isaac Marks, author of *Fears, Phobias, and Rituals,* suggested that a phobia is a specific category of fear. A phobia is a fear that (1) is out of proportion to the demands of the situation; (2) cannot be explained or reasoned away; (3) is beyond voluntary control; and (4) leads to the avoidance of the feared situation.[8] Others have proposed additional criteria, suggesting that a phobia is a fear that persists over an extended period of time, that is nonadaptive, and that is not "age or stage" specific.[9]

The DSM-IV has a number of specific diagnoses that could be identified here.[10] I am more comfortable, however, following the

simplified classifications used by Byrd and Warren in their text.[11]
They discuss fears and anxiety in seven categories:

1. *Simple fear or phobia,* which normally arises in childhood
   and does not need special attention unless it persists or
   causes adaptation difficulties
2. *Separation anxiety,* which essentially involves a child's significant fear of separation from parent(s) or significant
   others
3. *School refusal,* which involves a child's very real fear of going to school, as opposed to truancy
4. *Avoidant disorder of childhood,* which generally involves a
   child moving beyond excessive shyness to going to great
   lengths to avoid contact with unfamiliar people
5. *Overanxious disorder,* sometimes called generalized anxiety
   disorder, which involves excessive anxiety not related to
   a single event and is often found in children living with
   high performance expectations
6. *Obsessive-compulsive disorder,* which involves symptoms of
   repetitive thoughts and compulsive actions designed to
   relieve a perceived and irrational fear
7. *Posttraumatic stress disorder,* which involves children developing specific fears and unnamed anxieties after facing a
   substantial stressful event or circumstance

A number of therapeutic interventions have been used with
children experiencing fears and anxiety. Systematic desensitization
involves a gradual exposure to the anxiety-producing stimulus
while the child is engaged in an activity that is antagonistic to the
anxiety, such as a form of relaxation training. Behavioral approaches
focus on the importance of the causal relationship between behavior and stimuli and use methods such as positive reinforcement,
shaping, and extinction. Still other therapies include cognitive-
behavioral approaches and relaxation-training methods, including

biofeedback and hypnosis. Pharmacological intervention may be appropriate (see discussion in chapter 15).

These approaches to treating childhood fears and anxiety have been well researched and documented. I am concerned, however, that these interventions may not address the child's underlying issues. Recognizing that behaviors (including fear and anxiety) are an expression of emotional needs, it would seem that providing a therapeutic experience that touches these needs might be helpful as well. We must remember the truth expressed in the quotation that begins this chapter: Fears do not spring from a base of logic, and they do not respond to logic. Treatment should respect the "non-logical" condition of childhood. Play therapy has been demonstrated to be an effective intervention for children experiencing anxiety and fear.[12] This alternative to cognitive verbalization and/or direct confrontation of the feared stimulus can be a welcome experience for the child bound by fear.

The issue of safety is a concern for any child who enters counseling, especially if the presenting problem is related to fear or anxiety. The therapeutic distance that is created through metaphor and fantasy provides this safety. Play therapy provides an accepting and nonthreatening environment in which children are able to express their fears and anxieties through the safety of symbolic play. The fearful and anxious feelings that simply cannot be talked out can be played out in a manner that allows children to move at their own pace as their level of comfort dictates. Feeling afraid means being out of control. In the process of playing out frightening experiences, children experience being in control of the frightening experience because they are in control of the play and can thus determine the outcome.[13]

Anxious children in counseling will often express themselves either in overly active play or in a refusal to engage. Overly active play can be an avoidance mechanism for children, protecting them from the strange therapist. Children with separation anxiety will not want to leave their parent in the waiting room and may be slow to connect with the playroom and therapist. *Actively* communicating understanding and acceptance is vital. Remember, children will not play where they do not feel safe. Overanxious children are often overwhelmed by the playroom, just as they are overwhelmed by their world. Anxious children are often perfectionistic; as a result they constantly seek the approval and leading of the therapist. These children need to know that they are playing "properly." It is important for the therapist to communicate acceptance and encouragement but to avoid praise and approval, which will perpetuate the pattern of perfectionism.

Often, play therapy must be accompanied by other therapeutic interventions. Family and behavior-therapy interventions in combination with the individual work with the children may be indicated. Family therapy may be appropriate when parents or other family members either consciously or unconsciously reinforce the children's anxiety through dependence and isolation.[14] Behavioral approaches, such as positive reinforcement and modeling, become more effective and less controlling and intrusive in follow-up to, and in combination with, play therapy. Antianxiety medications may be appropriate in some cases. Parent training is a very important adjunct to any of these combinations.

Byrd and Warren suggest the "E.A.R.S. for Fears" acrostic in dealing with childhood fears and anxieties. This is a helpful tool for parents to use in conjunction with play therapy and in place of counseling if the issue does not warrant such intervention.[15] The components consist of

E—*Earnestly listen,* which is a key in reducing anxiety

A—*Accept the child's story,* even if the story doesn't make any sense

R—*Reassure* because children need to know that you take them seriously and that you will "be there"

S—*Suggest* so that children may consider various solution options and have support and encouragement in the attempt to resolve the issue

CHILDHOOD DEPRESSION

Only in the last twenty years has the professional mental health community recognized that children can become depressed.[16] In diagnostic terms, childhood depression is seen as essentially similar to depression in adults; the DSM-IV does not have a separate diagnostic category for mood disorders in children.[17] The current consensus is that depression in childhood is indeed its own "distinct clinical entity whose defining characteristics are isomorphic with its adult counterpart."[18]

The prevalence of childhood depression has been well researched and documented, although the statistics vary, depending on the population being studied and the diagnostic criteria used. One study found that 13.7 percent of 400 children referred to a psychiatric setting showed depressive conditions.[19] Another study found that 53 percent of 141 children in a psychiatric inpatient setting were depressed.[20] Approximately the same high incidence of depression was reported by another study of nonhospitalized children referred to an educational diagnostic center.[21] Using a depression-screening inventory with first, fourth, and eighth graders, another study reported over 21 percent met the criteria for mild depression.[22] Suicide in young children is on the rise, though not as rapidly as with adolescents. In 1982, 200 children between the ages of five and fourteen committed suicide in the United States.[23] Dr. Alan Bergman, of the American Association of Suicidology, notes that the youngest reported case of suicide, with suicidal intent, is four years old.[24]

Depression in children should be considered from a developmental perspective. Professors of psychology Drs. Nadine Kaslow and Lynn Rehm assert: "Depression should be evaluated in relation to what is 'normal' for a particular stage of development. Developmentally oriented writers have expressed concerns about adopting the adult, essentially unmodified DSM-II-R criteria for children because these criteria do not account for age-related differences in the defining attributes or manifest expressions of childhood depression and because developmental advances in cognitive structures and functioning influence the manner in which children experience, interpret, and express emotions at different ages."[25] Simply put, depression looks different with different stages of child development.

In infancy, depression is primarily related to children's loss of bonding and attachment with their mothers. These infants are unresponsive and listless, have appetite and sleep disturbances, and often present with a sad face. They have been described as having anaclitic depression or may be diagnosed as "failure to thrive." As children enter the toddler and preschool years, depression becomes more difficult to identify. Children experience the frustration of struggling for autonomy, which is compounded by their knowing what they want but not having the cognitive or verbal sophistication to articulate it. Moods change rapidly with this age group, and children begin to build defenses against negative emotions.

The middle childhood years, from ages six to nine years, bring many changes to children's lives. The beginning of school brings new pressures to children. Since children's thinking is more intuitive than logical at this stage, emotions are more concrete and immediate. They are not able to look beyond the immediate situation; consequently, adult explanations are usually futile. Social withdrawal, aggression, and sleep and appetite disturbance are common symptoms. A positive parental response to the child's emotional presentation is vital.

At ages nine and ten, children begin more solidly to develop an awareness of self. How they view themselves and how they believe they are perceived by peers become increasingly important. Because of this evaluation of self and others, "A dysphoric or depressed response follows trauma or crises in the environment. By now, this response includes a sense of personal failure or perhaps disappointment with others, and the child begins to verbalize a sense of worthlessness or even guilt as part of the depressed-symptom picture." [26] As children move toward adolescence and become more autonomous, the access to and involvement with dangerous activities increase, thus making suicide assessment an increasingly crucial intervention.

Assessment of childhood depression should begin with a complete physical examination to rule out medical problems that contribute to depression. These include such diagnoses as endocrinological, cardiological, and neurological disorders. Getting a complete family and developmental history is also important. Information on infant-mother attachment, developmental milestones (speech, motor), relationships (with parents, siblings, and peers), school history, and family history of emotional disorders can be vital in assessment and treatment planning. Children with a clinically depressed parent are at a significant risk of developing depression themselves.[27]

Assessment of depression in children should always include an evaluation of suicide risk. Suicidal ideation and behavior must always be taken seriously and considered a psychiatric emergency requiring immediate intervention. Children do not developmentally comprehend the irreversibility of death and may accidentally hurt or kill themselves in a cry for help. I encourage parents to "keep up their antennae" when they suspect the potential for self-harm, to increase their level of supervision, and to watch for any unusual behavior. A child who is throwing away or giving away toys and is also depressed may be a child contemplating suicide.

Treatment of childhood depression should be multimodal. Individual counseling is crucial; obviously I endorse a play therapy experience. Play therapy may be the only place children can build an empathic and trusting relationship as well as the only place to "talk" about emotional pain. In play, children are able to express negative feelings: "Being able to vent worries, fears, sadness, anger, hopelessness, and conflict in a safe environment and within a safe relationship helps externalize these feelings. This allows for emotional growth."[28] Themes of sadness, hopelessness, grief, and loss may be evident in the play. Children who are suicidal may also throw objects away and exhibit themes of death. It is not unusual for depressed children to exhibit aggressive and destructive behaviors at home and school. These behaviors will often manifest themselves in the play before children are able to address underlying issues of depression.

The play therapist may have a difficult time establishing a therapeutic relationship with the depressed child. While children who are depressed have strong needs for acceptance and attachment, their very emotional neediness may prevent them from reaching out. The counselor's expression of acceptance will enable children to accept themselves. The play therapist will need to be patient. I try to avoid coaxing depressed children out of their shell, confident that as we establish a relationship, the issues will emerge.

I have found that group play therapy often works well with depressed children. Having several children in the playroom can assist in the development of the relationship between the depressed child and the play therapist. It is also generally less threatening to engage in play and experience new things in the presence of several children. The activity of the group seems to assist individual children in their awareness of the acceptance and permissiveness of the play experience. Depressed children often have limited peer interactions and social skills, which are easily addressed in a group play setting.

Family therapy and parent training and therapy are also appropriate interventions for depressed children. Certainly children's depression will have an effect on the family system, and the depression may well result from difficulties within the family. It is common for children to manifest the symptoms of a family's dysfunction. A primary goal of family therapy would be not only to remove the "problem" label from the child of focus but also to provide opportunity to help the family to acknowledge and process the emotions the children have expressed in the individual play counseling.

Parent training may be an adjunct intervention that will help parents learn to build the parent–child relationship as well as to recognize and affirm the child's expression of emotional self. Since depressed children often have a depressed parent, therapy for the parent(s) is often a crucial component in the healing process for the family.

Medical interventions may also be appropriate. Although pharmacological treatment should not be the only intervention for the child who is depressed, it can be a key part of the treatment regimen. Chapter 15 will focus on the use of medication with children. The depressed child who cannot function and/or who may be suicidal should be considered for hospitalization.

Working with anxious and depressed children can be anxiety-provoking and depressing. It takes a lot of work. It is important to remain upbeat and animated, not to the point of leading children or being intrusive but rather to provide a positive picture of acceptance, which the children probably have not seen in their families for a while. With anxious children, do not let the children struggle alone with their feelings of anxiety; be actively involved in the children's struggle to express self. Children dealing with these issues are not seen as "normal" and will not feel very "normal" themselves. A positive counseling experience helps them to normalize, which provides a foundation on which they may process the pain and turmoil inside.

Play provides a courage all its own.   —JEROME BRUNER

14/ TREATING OTHER COMMON CHILDHOOD PROBLEMS

*One of the most obvious facts about grown-ups, to a child, is that
they have forgotten what it is like to be a child.*   —R. JARRELL

Eight-year-old Monica's case was referred to me by her biological
mother and stepfather. She was a precocious girl who loved gym-
nastics and made the best of the challenging visitation arrangement
between her two parents. Monica's primary presenting problems
were wetting the bed and pulling out her eyelashes. The diagnoses
of *enuresis, nocturnal only* and *trichotillomania,* however, did not describe Monica. She exhibited a zest for life that was tempered by
her confusion and sadness over her parents' situation. Monica's
treatment plan included play therapy, medication for the enuresis, a
behavioral-management program for the hair pulling, and parent
training. Significant improvement occurred in all areas.

Child counselors will meet with a wide variety of presenting
problems in the course of their work, including such disorders as
trichotillomania and pica (eating nonnutritive substances). The
diagnosis, while important, does not assist in establishing a thera-

peutic relationship. As I suggested in the introduction to this book, understanding children's world and understanding how to make contact with children is more important than knowing everything there is to know about etiology and technique. It is not my intention to cover every childhood disorder in the pages of this book. I would like to comment, however, about sleep difficulties, enuresis and encopresis, and tic disorders.

SLEEP DIFFICULTIES

Children need adequate sleep for their physiological and psychological well-being. If you are a parent, you are well aware that if your children do not get adequate sleep, you will know it. For that matter, you will probably not get adequate sleep yourself! Mild sleep disturbances are very common in childhood, especially for children who are between the ages of two and five years. These are normal reactions and are generally expressions of the anxieties and insecurities of growing up. Disturbing dreams and restlessness in sleep are the two most common sources of sleep disturbance.[1] The underlying causes of sleep disturbances include anxiety, internal conflicts, physiological disorders, overstimulation, fear of the dark, and family or situational stress.[2]

In their book *Counseling and Children,* Walter Byrd and Paul Warren summarize sleep research that has been done with children:

> Recent sleep research has established that sleep is cyclical in nature. During sleep time, the child goes in and out of four different stages of sleep. After emerging from the deepest sleep stage, rapid eye movements (REM) sleep usually occurs, during which time vivid dream activity happens. Studies of sleepwalking, sleeptalking, night terrors, and bedwetting show these disturbances often occur during sudden and intense arousal from deep sleep stages and are not related to REM sleep. The disorders just mentioned are actually called disorders of sleep arousal.

Narcolepsy, or excessive sleepiness, on the other hand, is associated with the abnormal occurrence of REM sleep. Disorders of
arousal of sleep are most often associated with signs of neurological
immaturity. Furthermore, sleep arousal disorders rarely occur in a
family pattern. Before sleep research and sleep studies in children
became highly sophisticated, these arousal disturbances were commonly considered to be caused by bad dreams. The specific and
actual causes, however, of these sleep arousal disorders are still poorly
understood.[3]

Nightmares affect about 5 percent of the population.[4] Nightmares primarily result from underlying fears that are expressed in
sleep and frequently are precipitated by stressful events. The fear and
anxiety children experience through nightmares are very real and
need to be affirmed by parents and the child counselor. Nightmares
occur during REM sleep and "represent the child's anxieties and
conflicts in relation to earlier developmental issues that gain access
to consciousness during sleep."[5]

Sleep terrors, as opposed to nightmares, occur from a sudden
awakening from REM sleep with an accompanying expression of
intense panic and anxiety as well as physiological arousal. Sleep
terrors usually occur in children who are between the ages of five
and seven. Studies estimate that approximately one percent to 4
percent of all children experience sleep terrors at some time.[6] When
children who are experiencing sleep terrors are awakened, they
often have no memory of any dream; they often become calm and
want to return to sleep. The onset of sleep terrors is often associated
with emotional stress or trauma, although it is not specifically
related to other childhood pathology.[7]

Sleepwalking, or somnambulism, usually occurs in the first several hours of sleep and is most common with children who are
between the ages of six and twelve years.[8] Sleepwalking children
will be difficult to arouse and will appear to have low levels of
awareness. Their eyes will be open but glassy, and their expression
generally flat. Despite popular opinion, sleepwalkers are not consid-

ered to be acting out a dream. Some evidence suggests that sleep-walking may be associated with central nervous system functioning, but, again, there is no evidence that it is related with other psycho-pathology.[9] Increased stress may make the occurrence of sleepwalking episodes more frequent.

Counseling interventions for children with sleep disorders will vary. In some cases, pharmacological interventions are appropriate (see chapter 15). Often the most appropriate treatment is counseling for the parents. For example, parents often assist and perpetuate childhood sleeplessness. Parents who have established a pattern of allowing young children to sleep with them or who have rocked and walked with an infant for hours (which may be necessary for the child with colic) often find it difficult to break this pattern. It is not unusual to discover that parents have been struggling with their children's sleep difficulties for years.

Play therapy may be an effective avenue through which children can express their nightmares and fears as well as their frustration with the fatigue resulting from poor sleep patterns. My therapeutic approach to sleep concerns will not vary from my normal approach in the playroom. Some children will play with the dolls and doll bed when the presenting problem is a sleep disturbance, and others will not. When children express their intrapsychic issues through play and when they gain mastery over the play and related metaphors, their sleep problems often dissipate.

Sometimes the interventions can be very simple. Children who are having difficulties going to sleep may be afraid of a shadow on the wall caused by a stuffed animal next to the night-light. The intervention may be as simple as rearranging the children's rooms. I will often begin my interview of the parents with some questions about the physical arrangement of their children's bedrooms and what is on the walls.

Although cultures vary on the issue, having children sleep with their parents is generally not a good idea. Parents need and deserve privacy, and children need to learn to be independent of their parents at night. Although an occasional incident of sleeping with parents is perfectly acceptable, using this as a regular intervention may teach children that some nighttime difficulties are so real and frightening that they are not able to cope with them on their own. Parents may even be unintentionally reinforcing their children's fears. Byrd and Warren appropriately summarize that "the parent who deals with the young child's fears should approach the child with reassurance, firmness, and protectiveness. Attempts to uncover the subconscious origins of the child's fear generally fail."[10]

Most sleeping difficulties will lessen without the need for a counseling intervention. You can help parents to be attentive, supportive, yet firm in their interventions. For children whose sleep difficulties stem from trauma or family stress, individual and/or family counseling will be indicated. If unconscious issues surface during the child's sleep (when conscious defense mechanisms are not readily available to protect), counseling should provide the opportunity for the child to process the underlying issues. Parents' verbal assurances, while they may be helpful, will not impact the underlying anxiety the child feels. In the same way, a verbally based therapy will be inadequate, and the child counselor should seek to reach the child through expressive and projective means. For serious sleep disorders, counselors may need to refer parents to a sleep-disorder clinic.

ENURESIS AND ENCOPRESIS

"Elimination disorders," as they are called, seem to have more serious social and psychological implications than physiological ones. Children who are experiencing one or both of these difficulties will simultaneously be experiencing the embarrassment, depression, and anxiety that accompany socially unacceptable behaviors.

Enuresis is a "persistent, involuntary passing of urine in times and places not culturally appropriate."[11] Functional enuresis is defined as urinary incontinence that is not attributable to an organic condition and that occurs at least two times a month for children who are between the ages of five and six and at least once a month for children over the age of six.[12] Functional enuresis is a chronic condition with an excellent long-term prognosis but a poor short-term one.[13]

Primary enuresis describes the situation of the child who has never experienced an extended period of dryness; *secondary enuresis* describes the situation of the child who has experienced urinary continence for an extended period and then begins to wet again. Frequently, secondary enuresis will occur for a child following a stressful event such as the birth of a sibling, parental divorce, starting school, physical or sexual abuse, or some other trauma. Children who are sexually abused sometimes develop enuresis as a conscious or unconscious mechanism to make themselves uninviting to the perpetrator. Secondary enuresis is generally seen as having psychological precursors, while primary enuresis is considered more neurological, relating to immature bladder control.

Enuresis is more common in boys than in girls, although 80 percent of all children are dry by the time they reach age five.[14] Enuresis is nocturnal (nighttime) for 80 percent of enuretic children, diurnal (daytime) for 5 percent, and both nocturnal and diurnal for 15 percent of the children.[15]

The evaluation of enuresis should begin with a complete medical examination, which includes a thorough history, a careful physical exam, and selected lab tests to evaluate the genitourinary system. The history should determine the frequency of the enuresis, the family history of enuresis, and the possible existence of stressors or crises in the life of the child and family.

Treatment of enuresis generally involves behavior management, the use of conditioning devices, and pharmacotherapy. Individual counseling alone will not treat primary enuresis, but it can help to deal with the comorbid symptoms of anxiety, depression, and poor self-esteem. Secondary enuresis may well respond to individual therapy, particularly if the child is responding to a stressor with incidents of incontinence.

Generally, it is appropriate to begin treatment with behavioral approaches. Parents should be encouraged to limit nighttime liquid intake, wake the child at night to use the bathroom, and use a reward system, such as a star chart, for dry nights. I discourage parents from punishing their child for wetting because it rarely has any positive effect. If the parents want the children to wash the bedding and pajamas as a natural consequence, I will not suggest otherwise, except to discourage doing this in a punitive manner.

The behavioral intervention of using conditioning devices like bed alarms can be effective. Sensors are placed on the child's bed or in the child's clothing, and when the child urinates in bed, an alarm goes off. This takes an effort on the part of the child and the parents, who may be awakened by the alarm when the deep-sleeping child is not. This intervention, which operates on a classical learning basis, has been successful for many children.

While medications are also available for the treatment of enuresis (see chapter 15), many children have relapse after discontinuing the prescription. Some physicians advise using the medication only in cases of vacations or spending the night at a friend's house.

Encopresis involves the voluntary or involuntary passage of feces in culturally inappropriate times and places. Prevalence studies are rare, but a 1982 study reported that 1.5 percent of second graders were found to be encopretic.[16] While the psychological effects of enuresis are distressing, the emotional symptoms that accompany encopresis can be much worse. Children who soil can experience extreme frustration, rejection, and physical pain, and the emotional results can endure for a longer time.

Like enuresis, encopresis can be primary or secondary. *Primary encopresis* involves a child continuing to have fecal incontinence after the age of four, with no extended period of bowel control. *Secondary encopresis* occurs when the bowel control is lost after an extended period of continence.

The causes of encopresis are not fully understood. Some clinicians consider poor or harsh toilet training to be a cause of encopresis. It is certainly possible that toilet training that is undertaken too early or that is too demanding could cause children significant anxiety about passing feces. It is also possible that children could develop encopretic symptoms following a trauma or other stressful event. For example, children at the foster agency for which I worked often developed encopresis after the occurrence of sexual abuse.

Encopresis commonly occurs because of children's chronic retention of fecal material. Whether because of the pain of bowel movements, abusive toilet training, passive and/or aggressive parent-child problems, trauma, or any other precursor, constipation and impaction of fecal material can lead to the encopresis. What happens is that the functioning of the child's colon is disrupted by the fecal mass, and the child leaks a liquid stool in his or her clothing.

The treatment for this situation must begin medically, by emptying the colon of the impacted feces. This may be accomplished by a stool softener, suppositories, or a series of enemas. The treatment itself can be traumatizing. The bowel must then be retrained. This should involve a specific behavior-management program using a token system such as a star chart. Parents should not punish children for soiling incidents, but it is appropriate for them to have the children clean up themselves as well as their clothing following soiling.

Family counseling and individual counseling may be indicated for the encopretic child. The soiling will undoubtedly increase tension in the family. Parent and family support are important in the identification of problem areas and for support during the treatment phase. Parents may feel responsible for the encopresis, and children may feel considerable shame and self-deprecation. The interpersonal conflicts and power struggles that may be factors in the encopresis need to be addressed in family counseling.

Although play therapy is not generally appropriate as the only intervention with enuretic or encopretic children, it offers considerable benefit potential for children who are processing a wide variety of related issues. "Enuresis and encopresis problems may not occur in the presence of other children, but are usually known by other children by smell and because such information readily passes from one child to another as interesting information. Consequently, the resulting peer difficulties may have drastic consequences on the child's self-esteem and other psychological problems secondary to the wetting or soiling problem may develop. Play therapy provides children with a safe place to act out the accompanying frustration, anger, and helplessness and to restore a sense of personhood."[17]

TIC DISORDERS

The DSM-IV defines a tic as a "sudden, rapid, recurrent, nonrhythmic, stereotyped motor movement or vocalization."[18] Common tics may be eye blinking, facial twitches, and shoulder shrugging. Vocal tics are repeated noises or phrases. Tics appear to be exacerbated by stress and alleviated by relaxation and sleep.

Surveys on the prevalence of tics in children note that some 12 percent to 24 percent of school-age children have a history of some type of tic.[19] These are transient and tend to remit over time. The persistence of the tics for longer than a year would move the diagnosis to chronic motor disorder or vocal tic disorder. Various causes have been proposed for the development of tics in children, including a normal developmental phenomenon, a physical (motor) manifestation of stress, a learned behavior pattern, a delay in biological maturation, previous hyperkinesis or impulsiveness, a secondary symptom of an organic disorder, and familial history of tics.[20]

The treatment of tics should include individual and family counseling. Anxiety reduction should be a focus of the individual child counseling. Family counseling should focus not only on helping the family identify anxiety-producing situations but also on planning for reframing or decreasing them. Parents should be advised not to reinforce the tic behavior by calling attention to it.

The persistence of tics for more than two weeks should be evaluated by a child psychiatrist. Tourette's syndrome is a tic disorder that should be evaluated and treated by a physician, although the child counselor should remain involved after the referral. Tourette's syndrome is a neurological disorder that consists of the following symptoms: "The tics in Tourette's disorder frequently involve the head, torso, and upper and lower limbs. The vocal tics are presented in the form of grunting, barking, and sniffing sounds. One-third of the tics present coprolalia, which includes the sputtering of curse words. Often complex motor tics such as touching, squatting, retracing steps, and twirling are also present. . . . In half the cases the first symptoms to appear are bouts of single tics such as eye blinking, tongue protrusion, sniffing, throat clearing, uttering sounds or words, and coprolalia."[21]

Treatment of Tourette's syndrome most often includes psychiatric medication (see chapter 15). This should be accompanied by individual counseling and parent training. The child with Tourette's syndrome is likely to be dealing with anger, embarrassment, and low self-esteem. Play therapy gives these children the opportunity to gain some mastery and control when this disorder seems so unmanageable. Counselors can teach parents about Tourette's syndrome and can help them to recognize and work with their child's emotional issues surrounding the disorder. Local support groups may be available for the parents of children with Tourette's syndrome.

Many parents bring their children into counseling so that their children can be "fixed." It is not my agenda, however, to fix children. While symptom abatement is desirable, it should not be the focus of the therapeutic process. It should be the by-product of healing on the inside. Discussing specific disorders has value, but the most important focus is the person of the child.

Most of us are unaware that neuroses flourish when children feel unsafe.
—DOROTHY BRIGGS

15/ CHILDREN
and
PSYCHOPHARMACOLOGY
written with Ross Tatum, M.D.*

Since many psychological problems have biological components and since the Lord usually works by natural means, I believe God is in agreement with the major asset that drugs have contributed to psychiatric therapy. —FRANK MINIRTH AND WALTER BYRD

It may become necessary in the treatment of children to refer them for psychopharmacological therapy. The responsible child counselor should have at least a rudimentary knowledge of psychopharmacology and should be willing to make an appropriate psychiatric referral when necessary. Unfortunately, this often does not happen. This oversight is sometimes compounded by Christian parents' belief that medication amounts to an admission of parental failure and is not scriptural. While respecting the beliefs and convictions of clients' parents, counselors should educate parents about appropriate use of medications and help them understand that psychopharmacology may be a necessary part of the overall treatment program.

*This chapter is adapted from "Play Therapy and Psychopharmacology: What the Play Therapist Needs to Know." Copyright Association for Play Therapy. Used by permission.

We do not wish to undertake a detailed apologetic for the use of medications in working with children. Suffice it to say that pharmacologic interventions are necessary for some child clients. Denying medications to children who need them may be worse than prescribing drugs as a quick fix for children who do not. Withholding medications from any client out of fear or ignorance not only is unethical but also limits God by not taking advantage of modern psychiatry's increasing knowledge about the neurobiology of God's creation, human beings. It is therefore our contention and recommendation that Christian counselors working with children recognize the benefits and limitations of medications as an adjunct treatment tool: "Psychotropic medications have tremendous potential to assist Christians having emotional difficulties. It is important to recognize the limitations of medication. These drugs are useful for the control of symptoms and the correction of certain biological problems in some patients. The drugs do not affect basic personality organization, character style, cognitive modes, or conscious and unconscious psychological conflicts. This material is all left for the therapist to work through with the patient."[1]

GENERAL CONCERNS

Mental health providers face increased pressure from managed health care to provide brief therapy interventions with all clients. The swift symptom reduction that pharmacologic treatment provides is attractive to insurance companies and third-party-payment providers. While this may be acceptable for the executive of a managed-care organization, it fails to recognize that children process psychological issues on their own terms and in their own language (play). Symptom reduction, while important, cannot be the primary focus of child therapy. It probably will be the by-product of an encompassing treatment plan. Although it is not our intention to address the political issues of managed health care, we do want to remind Christian child counselors to stay alert about these issues.

According to the membership rolls of the American Association of Christian Counselors, the vast majority of counselors have a master's degree in some area of the mental health field.[2] Due to a variety of limitations, psychopharmacology is not included in the curriculum requirements for all accredited master's degree programs in counseling, psychology, and marriage and family therapy.[3] Although many doctoral-level training programs offer pharmacology courses, few require them. An unfortunate result of this trend is that students of counseling and psychotherapy often ignore the treatment possibilities of medications or the negative side effects that medications might bring.[4]

Our belief is that the possession of even a cursory knowledge about psychopharmacology places the Christian counselor in a better position to provide quality treatment. Gaining an understanding of the clients' medical records and assessing the need for a psychiatric referral are imperative in planning and implementing treatment. In order to meet the needs of the child client most effectively, counselors must become knowledgeable about psychopharmacology and must overcome issues of power, control, and "turf" through education and awareness.

PSYCHOPHARMACOLOGY WITH CHILDREN

To date, the majority of the research and investigation in the field of psychopharmacology has been with an adult population. Unfortunately, minimal empirical study of the efficacy and safety of psychotropic medication with children is available.[5] Psychopharmacologic treatment of children has not generally been addressed by the Food and Drug Administration (FDA). It should be noted, however, that FDA approval is not meant to direct prescribing habits but rather to limit pharmaceutical company advertising. An additional area of concern is that an increasing number of nonpsychiatric physicians—including pediatricians, family doctors, and neurologists—are prescribing psychotropics for children.

Despite these concerns, the use of psychotropic medications for treating children has increased dramatically beyond the common use of stimulants for ADHD. These medications include antidepressants (old and new) for major depression, anxiety disorders, and ADHD; lithium for bipolar disorders; neuroleptics for psychotic disorders; and some antihypertensive agents for dyscontrol.[6] The discovery of new pharmacological treatments and the evaluation of psychotropic uses for nonpsychiatric drugs have led to a significant increase in the pharmacologic treatment of childhood mental health issues.

Nonmedical therapists must recognize the existence of physiological roots in the etiology of psychiatric disorders in children. Researcher at the University of Pittsburgh School of Medicine Dr. Oscar Bukstein noted: "For prepubertal children, biochemical and neurophysiological correlates exist for several disorders. Research has implicated neurotransmitter dysfunction in a variety of psychopathologic behaviors and disorders."[7] Whereas play therapy may address core issues of some disorders and arguably peripheral symptoms in most disorders, neurobiological contributions to childhood psychopathology must be addressed medically.

While pharmacological treatment is primarily the concern of the prescribing physician, therapists treating children must understand the multiple pretreatment and treatment considerations. First, note that several medications may be prescribed for a variety of symptoms or diagnoses. Specific psychotropics may be effective for dissimilar disorders because of their influence on neurotransmitters and psychoendocrine events in the brain along common routes.[8]

Second, consider the developmental issues of childhood and adolescence. From a biological standpoint, children are immature and growing organisms; they metabolize chemical agents differently from the way adults do. Children may respond differently to psychotropic medication taken by the similarly diagnosed adult.[9] Issues of absorption and disposition are primary concerns, and the prescribing physician may look to adjust dosage strength and frequency to achieve the maximum therapeutic effect of a medication. Blood levels may be closely monitored.

Third, a complete physiologic and psychiatric assessment must be done before prescribing psychotropics to children. Drs. Joseph Biederman and Ronald Steingard state the primary goal of such an assessment: "Psychopharmacologic evaluation of the child should address the basic question of whether the patient has a psychiatric disorder (or disorders) that may respond to psychotropics."[10] If this inquiry is answered affirmatively, a complete physical examination (sometimes including laboratory tests), psychosocial history, and baseline behavioral assessment must be conducted. The valuable contribution of the play therapist to this process will be commented on later.

Finally, consider the alternative and/or concurrent treatment approaches in psychiatric intervention with children. "Treatment with psychotropic drugs should always be part of a more comprehensive treatment regimen and is rarely, if ever, appropriate as the sole treatment modality for a child or adolescent."[11] When examining the efficacy of psychopharmacology, consider the effects of concurrent treatment interventions and environmental influences.[12]

GENERAL MEDICATION PRINCIPLES

Therapists treating children should be aware of several rules of thumb for prescribing psychiatric medications for children.

A primary goal in treating children with psychotropics is to achieve the maximum therapeutic response with the least amount of risk to the child. It is important to remember that all medications, including over-the-counter medications, carry some risk, which makes appropriate compliance and careful monitoring of therapeutic and side effects essential. Within this primary goal, therefore, is another principle: no medications are better than some medications; a little medication is better than a lot of medication; and one medication is better than two or more. Having said this, however, we should note that some children may require more than one medication because of the complicated constellation of psychiatric symptoms.

If the symptoms persist after treatment with medication, it is generally considered most appropriate to complete a medication trial before switching medications. This is assuming that no disruptive side effects or other contraindications have developed with the child patient. In most cases, the course of treatment should include periodic attempts to discontinue the medication.

Children metabolize ingested substances differently from the way adults do. Children may require relatively higher doses of a psychotropic medication. Doses are prescribed by weight (mg/kg) and may vary according to metabolic rate.

Noncompliance—which generally means patients do not take their medication or fail to follow prescription instructions—is a treatment issue regardless of client age or treatment modality. Noncompliance with psychiatric treatment clearly makes for a poor treatment outcome and creates considerable difficulty in measuring treatment response. Counselors are often in a position to encourage medication compliance as part of the therapy process.

PHARMACOLOGIC TREATMENT OF CHILDHOOD DISORDERS

Although children are brought in for psychiatric evaluation primarily to address unwanted symptoms, treatment planning generally occurs according to diagnostic category. Discussion of treatment will follow along diagnostic lines. For the sake of brevity, diagnostic definitions are not given. The following table provides a summary of DSM-IV diagnoses and psychotropic medications that may be indicated.[13]

Childhood DSM-IV Diagnoses and Psychotropic Medications That May Be Indicated

DSM-IV Diagnosis	Medications Used
Attention-Deficit Hyperactivity Disorder	*Stimulants, Tricyclic Antidepressants, Clonidine, Wellbutrin*
Major Depression	*Tricyclic Antidepressants, Fluoxetine, Lithium (for tricyclic augmentation)*
Mania (acute and for maintenance)	*Lithium, Anticonvulsants, Antipsychotics, Benzodiazepines*

Mental Retardation (with severe aggression or self-injurious behavior)	*Antipsychotics, Lithium, Propranolol, Naltrexone*
Pervasive Developmental Disorder	*Antipsychotics, Naltrexone*
Conduct Disorder (severe, aggressive)	*Antipsychotics, Lithium, Propranolol, Carbamazepine*
Anxiety Disorders Generalized Anxiety Disorder	*Tricyclic Antidepressants, Benzodiazepines, Antihistamines, Beta-adrenergic blockers (Propranolol), Clonidine*
Separation Anxiety Disorder	*Tricyclic Antidepressants, Benzodiazepines*
Obsessive-Compulsive Disorder	*Clomipramine, Fluoxetine*
Posttraumatic Stress Disorder	*Propranolol, Clonidine*
Panic Disorder	*Tricyclic Antidepressants, Benzodiazepines*
Schizophrenia	*Antipsychotics*
Intermittent Explosive Disorder	*Propranolol, Lithium*
Sleep Disorders	*Tricyclic Antidepressants, Benzodiazepines, Antihistamines*
Enuresis (not due to medical disorder)	*Tricyclic Antidepressants, DDAVP*
Tourette's Disorder	*Haloperidol, Pimozide, Clonidine*

Attention-Deficit Hyperactivity Disorder

The category that has been most researched in the psychopharmacological treatment of children is ADHD. The most commonly prescribed medications for this disorder are the stimulants methylphenidate (Ritalin), dextroamphetamine (Dexedrine), and pemoline (Cylert). Tricyclic antidepressants—imipramine (Tofranil), nortriptyline (Pamelor), and desipramine (Norpramin)—have also been used successfully. While desipramine has been used safely with many children, four cases of sudden death associated with desipramine use have been reported over the last several years. Clonidine (Catapres) has been used to augment partial responses to stimulants and has been used alone to treat hyperactivity. The antidepressant bupropion (Wellbutrin) is also used as an alternative treatment for ADHD.

Affective Disorders

Although the existence of childhood depression is no longer clinically questioned, the efficacy of the commonly prescribed tricyclics has not been established. The tricyclics commonly prescribed include imipramine, amitriptyline (Elavil), desipramine, and nortriptyline. The use of fluoxetine and other specific serotonin reuptake inhibitors in children with depression is increasing. Monoamine oxidase inhibitors (MAOIs) have been used but are generally not recommended secondary to potential problems with dietary restrictions. Lithium is sometimes used to augment a partial response to tricyclics and is also used as the treatment of choice for children with bipolar disorder. Anticonvulsants, such as carbamazepine (Tegretol), have also been used. Neuroleptics (also known as antipsychotics) and benzodiazepines can be used to treat the acute agitation of mania. Long-term use of neuroleptics for the treatment of bipolar disorder is not recommended because of the risk of tardive dyskinesia, which is a syndrome of involuntary movements that can result from use of neuroleptics.

Anxiety Disorders

Medications most often used in the treatment of anxiety problems in children have been tricyclic antidepressants, beta–blockers, antihistamines, benzodiazepines, and clonidine. However, except for school refusal (separation anxiety) and obsessive-compulsive disorder, research on the psychopharmacologic treatment of childhood anxiety is quite limited.[14] Imipramine and alprazolam (Xanax) have been prescribed with minimal success for school phobia and overanxious and/or avoidant disorder. The benzodiazepines, widely used with adults, are used sparingly with children. Obsessive-compulsive disorder has been shown to respond to clomipramine (Anafranil) and to fluoxetine. Psychopharmacologic treatment of posttraumatic stress disorder (PTSD) is generally based on the treatment of comorbid anxiety or mood disorders. Propranolol and clonidine have been reported to be useful in children with PTSD. According to clinical reports, both antidepressants and benzodiazepines may be helpful in treating children with panic disorder.[15]

Schizophrenia

Onset of schizophrenia in prepubertal children is rare, as is psychopharmacologic research among this population. Antipsychotics are prescribed. High-potency neuroleptics such as haloperidol (Haldol) and thiothixene (Navane) likely cause fewer learning problems (but more problems with stiffness) than low-potency neuroleptics such as thioridazine (Mellaril) and chlorpromazine (Thorazine), which are more sedating.[16] Clozapine (Clozaril), which has been used in adults who respond poorly to traditional neuroleptics, has seen some use in adolescents but has not been studied with children.

Enuresis

The initial approach to enuresis should involve behavioral methods or a bed alarm. If these approaches fail, medication can be used. Tricyclics are the drugs of choice. The antidiuretic hormone desmopressin (DDAVP) has also been used and is administered intranasally. Relapse following discontinuation of medication is common.

Sleep Disorders

Although sleep disorders in children are not commonly prescribed for, they do respond to specific medications. Diphenhydramine (Benadryl) has been prescribed for children and adolescents experiencing difficulty falling asleep and frequent night awakenings.

Some benzodiazepines, such as diazepam (Valium) and tricyclics, have been prescribed for night terrors and sleepwalking.

Tourette's Syndrome

Haloperidol and pimozide (Orap) have been used effectively to reduce tic behavior. The tics may also respond to clonidine. Though less effective than haloperidol, clonidine has fewer serious side effects.

Aggression

While not a diagnostic category itself, aggression is a common complaint encountered by those working with children. The symptom of aggression fits into many diagnostic categories. Successful intervention takes into account comorbid symptoms that can be treated, such as problems with impulsivity, depression, bipolar disorder, and psychosis. Antipsychotics have been shown to reduce aggressive behavior in hyperactive and conduct-disordered children as well as children with mental retardation and autism. Because of the risks associated with these medications, they should be used long term only after other options have failed. Lithium and propranolol (Inderal) have also been used to treat aggression.

Other Concerns

The diagnosis of an eating disorder does not call for the use of pharmacotherapy. Severe anxiety, obsessive-compulsive symptoms, or psychosis that may accompany the eating-disorder symptoms may be treated with appropriate medications. Likewise, severe depression may be treated with an appropriate antidepressant. Studies with adults have noted that antidepressants can decrease the severity of binge eating.[17]

In general, developmental disorders are treated according to specific indications. Neuroleptics, such as haloperidol and naltrexone (Trexan), an opiate antagonist, have been used with positive results in children with autism. Again, children on neuroleptics must be monitored closely for the development of movement disorders. Comorbid symptoms associated with developmental disorders such as anxiety, depressive, obsessive-compulsive, and hyperactivity may be treated accordingly.

THERAPEUTIC AND SIDE EFFECTS OF PSYCHOTROPICS

In addition to knowing about the basic psychiatric medications prescribed for childhood disorders, therapists should also be aware of the primary therapeutic effects and potential side effects of psychotropics.

Antidepressants

Enuresis and ADHD are the only established indications for the tricyclics, although they are also prescribed for depression. They may have the possible side effects of dry mouth, constipation, blurred vision, weight change, and decreased blood pressure. Treatment requires electrocardiographic monitoring and recommends the monitoring of blood serum levels. Tricyclics are the most lethal of the psychotropics in an overdose. Specific serotonin reuptake inhibitors may have the side effects of behavioral agitation, sedation, gastrointestinal upset, headache, and weight loss. The rarely prescribed MAOIs require severe dietary restrictions and may have the side effects of hypotension, hypertension, weight gain, drowsiness, and insomnia.

Psychostimulants

The stimulant medications commonly used with ADHD children have been extensively researched and are considered safe and effective. Common side effects include insomnia, decreased appetite, and headache. Less frequently, they may cause agitation, enuresis, and depression. Rarely, tics and psychotic symptoms may occur. Use of pemoline requires lab monitoring of liver function.

Antipsychotics

The neuroleptic medications are used with a variety of symptoms and disorders. These include psychosis, bipolar disorders, aggression, and

254 / **Counseling Children through the World of Play**

tic disorders. Common side effects include dry mouth, constipation, blurred vision, sedation, stiffness, and, in some cases of chronic administration, tardive dyskinesia. Benzotropine (Cogentin) and diphenhydramine are anticholinergic medications commonly used to treat stiffness caused by the neuroleptics.

Lithium

Lithium is used as a treatment for childhood bipolar disorder, schizoaffective disorder, and aggression. Common side effects include polyuria, polydipsia, gastrointestinal upset, tremor, nausea, diarrhea, weight gain, acne, and possible thyroid and renal effects with chronic administration. Treatment requires monitoring blood serum levels and thyroid and kidney tests.

Antianxiety

The benzodiazepines, although used sparingly with children, have been administered effectively with sleep disorders and in overanxious and avoidant children. Possible side effects are drowsiness, disinhibition, agitation, confusion, and depression.

Other

Clonidine, although indicated as a treatment for hypertension, has been used with some success for Tourette's syndrome, ADHD, and aggression. Possible side effects include sedation, hypotension, dry mouth, confusion, and depression. Propranolol, a beta-adrenergic receptor blocker, has been administered for anxiety disorders, aggression, and self-abusive behaviors. The potential side effects are essentially similar to clonidine. Its use is contraindicated in the presence of diabetes or asthma. Carbamazepine (Tegretol) and valproic acid (Depakote) are anticonvulsants that have been used with bipolar disorder. Possible side effects include bone marrow suppression, dizziness, sedation, rashes, nausea, and liver dysfunction. They require blood serum monitoring.

HOW COUNSELORS CAN HELP CHILDREN

Clearly, child counselors who are knowledgeable about the basics of child psychopharmacology are better advocates for their clients, both in the counseling room and in the psychiatrist's office. Several considerations about psychopharmacological issues may help address this dynamic.

Used concurrently, pharmacotherapy and psychotherapy could very well provide the ideal treatment for a child. If medications offer a child a better chance of benefiting from counseling but are not prescribed, the potential efficacy of therapy is diminished. Some authors suggest that concurrent psychosocial interventions are crucial to the lasting therapeutic effects of psychoactive agents.[18]

Counselors can help children deal with the psychosocial effects of taking medication. Taking medications, particularly for an extended period of time, may affect children's or adolescents' self-concept. This could begin a process of chronic self-esteem difficulties. Children who are medicated may identify themselves as having or being a "problem" and may perceive the medication as a mechanism of control. Child counseling, particularly a play therapy approach, provides children with an opportunity to learn self-control, to respect themselves, to make choices, and to accept themselves.[19] Psychologist Douglas Golden noted that in his play therapy work with hospitalized children, a child, through play, can restore a sense of mastery when being medically treated: "The goal of the play therapist is to help the child become involved in his or her own treatment (even if only in some small way) and to help the child retain a sense of competence."[20]

Counseling can help children process situations in which medications might be used as a coercive form of behavioral control rather than as an adjunct to therapy.[21] Although we would hope that medications are not used this way often, sometimes parents, teachers, and therapists can press for medication use because they have a need for an instant panacea. The child in this case has not only lost a sense of power and control but also has been manipulated and disturbed. Counseling should offer this child the opportunity to process these issues. Through play, children can manage an unmanageable situation. They can begin to make sense and bring organization to their confusing world. They can express the grief and anger that often result from being "controlled."

Therapists treating children can make valuable contributions to the psychiatric assessment. With the proper authorization to release information, the child therapist is in a unique position to provide both initial input and ongoing evaluation for the prescribing physician. The assessment necessary to initiate pharmacotherapy is often inadequate if the psychiatrist must rely solely on parental reports and observation of a child in an office. The child therapist will often have greater insight into the child's basic mental status. Providing this input not only is an ethical obligation but also is clearly in the best interests of the child client.

Therapists need to be aware that behaviors of children who should be on medication can be misinterpreted in the counseling session. For example, a child's agitated shifting from one play activity to another may be an indication of personal anxiety due to the new experience of being in the playroom, getting closer to intrapsychic issues, and so forth. Or it may be that the child is an undiagnosed ADHD client who would appropriately respond to stimulant medication.

An inverse situation should also be noted. It is possible that a child may be psychiatrically medicated for what are viewed as biologically based symptoms when in fact the child is behaviorally responding to an emotional trauma or inappropriate parenting. For example, a child who has experienced severe physical or sexual abuse may respond by enacting bizarre defense mechanisms to protect against further adult intrusion. These bizarre behaviors may be interpreted as some level of psychosis, which would appear to indicate the need for neuroleptic medication. These behaviors may well ameliorate in the child-therapy room, where the safety of boundaries and the therapeutic relationship make processing of emotional pain possible.

Therapists can also help children who are uncooperative with psychiatric treatment. It is not uncommon to work with children who are noncompliant with respect to taking medications. In addition to helping children process anger, frustration, and fear in their own language, the play therapist has the opportunity to use directive techniques if deemed appropriate. Structured doll play, artwork, games, storytelling, or other play techniques may be helpful in this situation.

PARENTAL CONCERNS

Parents of children for whom medication has been recommended often have questions about the process and about specific issues. Although nonmedical psychotherapists should defer to a qualified psychiatrist on medication questions, they should have the ability to respond to some of these basic concerns.

Many parents fear that their children will have to remain on medications indefinitely. This is not often the case, but it could happen, depending on the type and severity of the presenting problems. Although studies vary, it has been suggested that upwards of 50 percent of children with ADHD continue to have symptoms into young adulthood. These may require a continuation of medication.

Since the most commonly prescribed psychiatric medications are for children with ADHD, a number of parental concerns center on the stimulant medications. It is important to note that these stimulants are not addictive, and although stimulants have been abused, this is not normally a problem with the child population. Children who take stimulant medication for ADHD are not more prone to adolescent or adult drug abuse. Some parents are concerned about their children being "doped up" on medications, but stimulants do not impair children's sensory perceptions; in fact, they improve concentration and attention. Another concern is that methylphenidate or dextroamphetamine will stunt children's growth. Although growth may be slowed while children are on the medication, it is generally believed that children's long-term height is compromised little. "Drug holidays" (removing the client from medications for a period of time), which have previously been suggested, are not obligatory. If children require the medication in order to have a good weekend or summer, there is no reason to discontinue it. If children's problems are primarily focusing on schoolwork and if they can function well without medication when school is out, it does not hurt to stop it.

Other medications should not be intermittently stopped or discontinued without the consultation of the prescribing psychiatrist. Because of differences in the rates of onset and metabolism, most psychotropic medications should be taken on a regular basis. Unfortunately, many parents are not aware of the therapeutic and side effects of their children's medication. The child counselor should encourage parents to communicate regularly with the prescribing psychiatrist.

CONCLUDING THOUGHTS

Therapists who work with children have an obligation to be educated about issues of psychopharmacology for the sake of their clients, their clients' parents, and the counseling profession at large. Joseph Biederman noted that the long-term outlook for pediatric psychopharmacology is dependent on research to balance the potential risks with the real benefits to suffering children.[22] Non-medical psychotherapists must be a part of this process, which will certainly progress with or without input from child counselors.

An element of this process must involve a willingness to interact and cooperate with the medical profession. In the same way that child counselors need education about psychiatric matters, psychiatrists need education about the world of child counseling. As we have suggested, multidisciplinary cooperation advances the best interests of the children and the profession. One therapist noted a common frustration and a compelling view of medication: "There used to be a sense of shame when you put clients on medication. It was like an admission of failure that therapy wasn't working and that you, the therapist, had to get help."[23] The real failure and shame would be to remain ignorant. For the sake of children, we must learn about these matters.

Of all the needs (there are none imaginary) a lonely child has, the one that must be satisfied if there is going to be hope and a hope of wholeness, is the unshakable need for an unshakable God.   —*MAYA ANGELOU*

Appendix A

ASSESSMENT INSTRUMENTS

Several psychosocial assessment instruments have been mentioned through the course of the book. I have also included some others that I occasionally use in the course of evaluating and treating children. Many of these require the user to meet established qualification criteria prior to administering the instruments. Below is a listing of the titles and publishers of these tests. Several of these tests are available from more than one publisher.

Family Environment Scale
Consulting Psychologist Press, Inc.
3803 East Bayshore Road
P.O. Box 10096
Palo Alto, California 94303
(800) 624-1765
(415) 969-8901

Attention-Deficit Disorders Evaluation Scale
Hawthorne Educational Services, Inc.
800 Gray Oak Drive
Columbia, Missouri 65201
(800) 542-1673 [orders]
(314) 874-1710 [information]

Conners Rating Scales
Psychological Assessment Resources, Inc.
P.O. Box 998
Odessa, Florida 33556
(800) 331-TEST
(800) 727-9329 [fax]

Parenting Stress Index
Psychological Assessment Resources, Inc.
P.O. Box 998
Odessa, Florida 33556
(800) 331-TEST
(800) 727-9329 [fax]

Child Behavior Checklist
University Associates in Psychiatry
One South Prospect Street, Room 6433
Burlington, Vermont 05401
(802) 656-8313

ADD-H Comprehensive Teacher Rating Scale
Psychological Assessment Resources, Inc.
P.O. Box 998
Odessa, Florida 33556
(800) 331-TEST
(800) 727-9329 [fax]

Coopersmith Self-Esteem Inventories
Consulting Psychologist Press, Inc.
3803 East Bayshore Road
P.O. Box 10096
Palo Alto, California 94303
(800) 624-1765
(415) 969-8901

Reynolds Child-Depression Scale
Psychological Assessment Resources, Inc.
P.O. Box 998
Odessa, Florida 33556
(800) 331-TEST
(800) 727-9329 [fax]

Joseph Pre-School and Primary Self-Concept Screening Test
Stoelting Co.
620 Wheat Lane
Wood Dale, Illinois 60191
(708) 860-9700
(708) 860-9775 [fax]

Piers-Harris Children's Self-Concept Scale
Western Psychological Services
12031 Wilshire Boulevard
Los Angeles, California 90025-1251
(800) 648-8857
(310) 478-7838 [fax]

APPENDIX B

INFORMED CONSENT FOR COUNSELING

It is always advisable to have some form of informed consent documentation when providing counseling for a client of any age. The specific issues covered in an informed consent form will vary according to your counseling practice, the mental health licensing laws of your state, and the ethical standards of your professional organizations. Below is one sample of an informed consent that I have used.

DANIEL S. SWEENEY, PH.D.

Welcome! This is a counseling practice deeply committed to quality care. It is my intent to provide quality professional counseling services, combined with biblical and Spirit-empowered healing. It is my hope and prayer that the issues that have brought you into counseling may be resolved as we work together.

Daniel Sweeney is a professional counselor licensed by the state of Texas. His undergraduate degrees are in Pre-Law and in Bible and Theology; graduate degree in Marital and Family Therapy, and doctoral degree in Counselor Education. Daniel's experience includes private practice, pastoral counseling, child play therapy, and community mental health work.

Length of sessions: Counseling sessions last approximately 50 minutes (45 minutes for play therapy sessions).

Payment for service: The fee is _____, payable at the beginning of each session. For clients having insurance, I will provide information forms for insurance reimbursement, but it is the client's responsibility to seek payment from the insurance company.

Cancellation: Since the scheduling of an appointment involves the reservation of time specifically for you, a minimum of 24 hours' notice is requested for cancellation. Sessions that are missed without this advance cancellation must be billed at the full charge.

Confidentiality: All information disclosed within sessions is confidential and may not be revealed to anyone without your written permission except where disclosure is required by law. Disclosure may be required under the following circumstances: Where there is reasonable suspicion of child or elder abuse; where there is reasonable suspicion that the client presents a danger of violence to others; where the client is likely to harm himself or herself unless protective measures are taken; or where the client discloses sexual contact with a mental health professional. Disclosure may also be required pursuant to a legal proceeding.

Additional charges: Other financial considerations may arise in the counseling experience. At times, books will be recommended to save the client time and expense. Testing, which assists with diagnosis and treatment planning, may also be done. Your counselor will discuss these tests and the associated costs with you.

Video/Audio Recording: I [give / do not give _____ (circle one and initial)] my permission for Dr. Daniel Sweeney to videotape sessions for his review. However, he will not publish, communicate, or otherwise disclose, without written consent, any such information, which, if disclosed, would injure me in any way.

Informed Consent: I affirm that prior to becoming a client of Dr. Daniel Sweeney, Dr. Sweeney gave me sufficient information to understand the nature of counseling. The information included the nature of the agency, Dr. Sweeney's professional identity, possible risks and benefits of counseling, nature of confidentiality including legal and ethical limits, and alternative treatments available. My signature affirms my informed, voluntary consent to receive counseling.

Minor client: I affirm that I am the legal guardian of _____ _____. With an understanding of the above requirements, I do grant permission for my child to participate in counseling.

It is my desire that your time spent in counseling and healing will be instructive, profitable, and life changing. It will be my pleasure to assist you through this rewarding and fulfilling process.

With an understanding of the above requirements and conditions, I agree to participate in counseling and release the counselor from any liability.

_____   _____
Client's Signature   Date

_____   _____
Counselor's Signature   Date

Appendix C

PROFESSIONAL DISCLOSURE STATEMENT

In most professional settings, it is advisable to have a professional disclosure statement for liability protection. There are many ways in which to set one up. Below you will find a sample of one of the statements that I have used.

PROFESSIONAL DISCLOSURE STATEMENT

Daniel S. Sweeney, Ph.D. is a Licensed Professional Counselor (LPC) in the State of Texas, a Licensed Marriage, Family and Child Counselor (MFCC) in the State of California, and a Registered Play Therapist-Supervisor (RPT-S) with the Association for Play Therapy. He has undergraduate degrees in Pre-Law (San Jose State University) and in Bible & Theology (San Jose Bible College), a Master's degree in Marital and Family Therapy (Azusa Pacific University), and a doctoral degree in Counselor Education (University of North Texas). Daniel has had experience and has provided counseling, supervision, and training in the following settings: private practice, community mental health (forensic counseling), therapeutic foster care, pastoral counseling, and human service agencies. He primarily works with couples, families, and children.

The phone numbers and addresses of the licensing agencies are as follows:

Texas State Board of Examiners of
Professional Counselors
1100 West 49th Street
Austin, TX 78756-3183
512/834-6658

Board of Behavioral Science
State of California
400 R Street, Suite 3150
Sacramento, CA 95814
916/445-4933

My focus in counseling begins with the development of an egalitarian relationship with my client, including the cooperative development of goals at the outset of treatment. What this means is that I do not consider myself an expert who can direct or advise clients but rather a trained counselor who may facilitate change. My role as a counselor is, therefore, as a facilitator as opposed to a director. I look to explore and evaluate the client's lifestyle, choices, and goals with the objective of identifying possible mistaken beliefs, and to assist the client to reevaluate and develop insight. This will include a greater degree of self-understanding by the client and lead to the desired behavior change.

As a Christian counselor, I also believe that people are made up of body, soul, and spirit. As such, I take a holistic approach by keeping in mind issues of physiology, psychology, and spirituality. It is my desire to provide qualified professional psycho-

---

therapy as well as sound biblical counsel, and I will discuss spiritual matters when appropriate, but also with the full consent and knowledge of my clients.

It is my goal and desire to provide for each client a caring, trusting, and understanding environment. I will discuss with each client my basic philosophy and counseling techniques, as well as my ethical and moral obligations to the client and the profession. This is my responsibility. It is the client's responsibility to make and carry out lifestyle changes. As much as I would like to, I am not able (or willing) to change any person.

Confidentiality is a key part of the counseling relationship. It is not, however, absolute. I will discuss the ethical and legal limits of confidentiality. Some of these limits include (1) determination that the client is a danger to self or others; (2) disclosure of abuse or criminal activity; (3) an order by the court to disclose information; and (4) if I am otherwise required by law to disclose information. If I intend to use any part of the case record for supervision, training, or research purposes, I will discuss this with my client and obtain written release to do so.

The counseling relationship is a professional relationship. It should not, therefore, become a social or business relationship at any time. This would be detrimental to the purposes of counseling and would contaminate the process. As such, I request that my clients do not invite me to social events or solicit me for business. I will do the same. If I encounter clients outside of the counseling setting, I will not acknowledge the existence of any relationship.

Should the client and/or I believe that a referral would be appropriate during the course of the counseling relationship, I will take the responsibility of identifying referral services and assist in making the referral. Referrals may be made for a number of reasons, including the client's or my identifying any source of conflict in the relationship, a client need requiring a greater degree of expertise or a different area of counseling specialization, or a need for medical or psychiatric attention. Referrals will be discussed openly and the transfer completed to the best of my ability.

If a conflict arises in the course of the counseling relationship, it is my desire to discuss this with the client as a part of the open and egalitarian relationship. It is my desire to provide services in a professional manner consistent with accepted legal and ethical standards. If the client is dissatisfied or has a complaint, I would request that he/she discuss the issue with me. If I am not able to resolve your concerns, you have the right to contact either of the licensing agencies noted above.

I look forward to providing my professional counseling services. As a Christian and licensed counselor, I enter each counseling relationship prayerfully and professionally. By the signature(s) below, the client is indicating that he/she has read and understood this statement and that any questions regarding the above information have been answered satisfactorily. The client will receive a copy of this statement. My signature indicates that I verify the accuracy of this statement and that I commit to upholding its specifications.

_____   _____
Client's Signature   Date

_____   _____
Counselor's Signature   Date

APPENDIX D

AUTHORIZATION TO VIDEOTAPE FOR EDUCATIONAL AND TRAINING PURPOSES

It is appropriate to have a specific additional permission form signed by parents if you have any intent to use videotape of their child for training purposes. Below is a sample of what I often use.

PERMISSION TO USE COUNSELING VIDEOTAPE FOR EDUCATIONAL PURPOSES

I give my permission for my child, _____, to participate in videotaped play therapy sessions with Dr. Daniel Sweeney for the purpose of creating a videotape for training purposes. I understand that videotapes of my child's counseling sessions have value as educational tools for counselors-in-training in university-level counseling classes and professional counselors who attend training workshops. I understand that any student or professional who sees a videotape will be reminded of rules of confidentiality that prohibit the discussion of the videotape except for professional training purposes.

I also understand that the confidentiality of my child will be protected and that only my child's first name may be stated in the tape and no other identifying information will be available to those viewing the tape for educational purposes.

My signature below affirms that my child's participation in the videotaping is entirely voluntary.

I affirm that I am the legal guardian of _____
and that I understand the above conditions. I release Dr. Daniel Sweeney from any liability associated with the videotaping or viewing of the counseling sessions.

_____   _____
Parent's (Guardian's) Signature   Date

APPENDIX E

WHERE TO LOOK FOR PLAY THERAPY TOYS

Many play therapy and sandplay toys may be purchased from mainstream stores. I have also found the following companies, several of whom specialize in play therapy equipment, to be quite helpful.

Constructive Playthings (Toys/playroom furniture)
1227 East 119th Street
Grandview, Missouri 64030
(800) 448-4115
(816) 761-9295

Lakeshore Learning Materials (Toys/playroom furniture)
2695 E. Dominguez Street
P.O. Box 6261
Carson, California 90749
(800) 421-5354
(310) 537-5403 [fax]

Rose Travel Kits (Toys/sandplay tools)
102 Foster Ranch Road
Trinidad, Texas 75163
(800) 713-2252
(903) 778-2808 [fax]

Childswork/Childsplay (Games/activities)
The Center for Applied Psychology
P.O. Box 61586
King of Prussia, Pennsylvania 19406
(800) 962-1141
(610) 277-4556 [fax]

WPS Creative Therapy Store (Toys/games/activities)
Western Psychological Services
12031 Wilshire Boulevard
Los Angeles, California 90025-1251
(800) 648-8857
(310) 478-7838

Oak Hill Specialties (Sandplay furniture)
P.O. Box 152
Cloverdale, California 95425
(800) 615-4155

Playrooms (Sandplay miniatures)
P.O. Box 2660
Petaluma, California 94953
(800) 667-2470
(707) 763-8353 [fax]

ENDNOTES

Chapter 1: The Child's World

1. Charles L. Thompson and Linda B. Rudolph, *Counseling Children* (Monterey, Calif.: Brooks/Cole Publishing Company, 1983), 5.
2. Herbert Hoover, "Children," *1000 Tips and Quips for Speeches and Toastmasters,* ed. Herbert V. Prochnow (Grand Rapids: Baker, 1962), 40.
3. William L. Hendricks, *A Theology for Children* (Nashville, Tenn.: Broadman Press, 1980), 247.
4. Robert Coles, *The Spiritual Life of Children* (Boston: Houghton Mifflin, 1990), 108.
5. Hendricks, *A Theology for Children,* 237.
6. Psalm 127:3.
7. Matthew 19:14.
8. Matthew 18:3.
9. Matthew 18:1-4; Mark 10:15; 1 Corinthians 14:20; Ephesians 5:8; 1 Peter 2:2.
10. Coles, *The Spiritual Life of Children,* 127–128.
11. Cited by Laura Myers, "Poll Finds That Children Are Afraid of the Future," in *Dallas Morning News,* 17 May 1995.
12. Sally Wendkos Olds and Diane E. Papalia, "Are Kids Growing Up Too Fast?" *Redbook* 174, no. 5 (March 1990): 91.
13. Cited by Katherine and Richard Greene, "The Shocking Statistics," *Redbook* 174, no. 5 (March 1990): 95.
14. Olds and Papalia, "Are Kids Growing Up Too Fast?" *Redbook,* 92.
15. Ibid., 94.
16. Ibid.
17. Greene, "The Shocking Statistics," *Redbook,* 95–96.
18. David Finkelhor and Jennifer Dzuiba-Leatherman, "Victimization of Children," *American Psychologist* 49 (March 1994): 173–183.
19. U.S. Congress, Office of Technology Assessment, *Children's Mental Health: Problems and Services—A Background Paper* (Washington, D.C.: U.S. GPO, 1986).
20. June M. Tuma, "Mental Health Services for Children: The State of the Art," *American Psychologist* 44 (February 1989): 188–199.

21. Cited by Tuma, "Mental Health Services for Children," *American Psychologist,* 188.

22. U.S. Congress, Office of Technology Assessment, *Children's Mental Health: Problems and Services.*

23. Gwendolyn Zahner et al., "Children's Mental Health Service Needs and Utilization Patterns in an Urban Community: An Epidemiological Assessment," *Journal of the American Academy of Child and Adolescent Psychiatry* 31 (September 1992): 951–960.

24. Cited by Tuma, "Mental Health Services for Children," *American Psychologist,* 192.

25. June M. Tuma, "Specialty Training for Psychologist Service Providers to Children?" *American Psychologist* 38, no. 3 (March 1983): 340–342.

26. Grant L. Martin, "Guest Editor's Page," *Journal of Psychology and Christianity* 12 (winter 1993): 299.

27. Peter Tanguay et al., "Commentary On: 'What Is the Outcome for Children's Mental Health Needs in National Health Care Reform?'" *Journal of the Academy of Child and Adolescent Psychiatry* 33 (November/December 1994): 1221–1222.

28. Romans 8:28.

Chapter 2: Children Communicate through Play

1. Zechariah 8:5.

2. Garry L. Landreth, *Play Therapy: The Art of the Relationship* (Muncie, Ind.: Accelerated Development, Inc., Publishers, 1991), 10.

3. Nancy E. Curry and Sara H. Arnaud, "Personality Difficulties in Preschool Children As Revealed through Play Themes and Styles," *Young Children* 50, no. 4 (May 1995): 4–9.

4. Charles E. Schaefer and Kevin J. O'Connor, eds., *Handbook of Play Therapy* (New York: John Wiley & Sons, 1983), 2–3.

5. Frank Caplan and Theresa Caplan, *The Power of Play* (New York: Anchor Books, 1974), xii–xvii.

6. George Hackett, "A Brave Little Girl," *Newsweek* 110, no. 17 (26 October 1987): 41.

7. Yisrael Gutman and Michael Barenbaum, *Anatomy of the Auschwitz Death Camp* (Bloomington, Ind.: Indiana University Press, 1994), 415, 418; Flora Hogman, "Displaced Jewish Children during World War II: How They Coped," *Journal of Humanistic Psychology* 23 (winter 1983): 51–66.

8. Lenore Terr, *Too Scared to Cry: Psychic Trauma in Childhood* (New York: Basic Books, 1990), 321; Kevin J. O'Connor, *The Play Therapy Primer: An Integration of Theories and Techniques* (New York: John Wiley & Sons, 1991), 9.

9. Erik H. Erikson, "Studies in the Interpretation of Play," *Genetic Psychology Monographs* 22 (1940): 561.

10. Denise C. Weston and Mark S. Weston, *Playful Parenting: Turning the Dilemma of Discipline into Fun and Games* (New York: G. P. Putnam's Sons, 1993), 8.

11. Virginia Axline's book *Dibs in Search of Self* (New York: Ballantine Books, 1964) is a classic in the field of play therapy. I heartily recommend it to all counselors who work with children.

12. Matthew 18:3.

13. 1 Corinthians 9:22.

14. Garry L. Landreth and Daniel S. Sweeney, "Child-Centered Play Therapy," *Play Theory and Applications: A Comparative Casebook,* ed. Kevin J. O'Connor and Lisa Mages (New York: John Wiley & Sons, 1997).

15. Philippians 2:5-7.

16. Jurgen Moltmann, *Theology of Play* (New York: Harper & Row, 1972), 15.

17. Genesis 1:1.

18. Moltmann, *Theology of Play,* 17.

19. Genesis 1:26-27.

20. Moltmann, *Theology of Play,* 18.

21. Robert E. Neale, *In Praise of Play: Toward a Psychology of Religion* (New York: Harper & Row, 1969), 174.

22. 1 Corinthians 13:11.

23. Charles E. Schaefer, *Therapeutic Use of Child's Play* (Northvale, N.J.: Jason Aronson, Inc., 1979), 16.

24. Jean Piaget, *Play, Dreams, and Imitation in Childhood* (New York: Rutledge, 1962), 154.

25. Maria Piers and Genevieve Landau, *The Gift of Play* (New York: Walker and Company, 1980), 33.

26. Piaget, *Play, Dreams, and Imitation in Childhood,* 105.

27. Virginia Axline, *Play Therapy* (New York: Ballantine Books, 1969), 127.

28. Matthew 13:13.

29. Kevin J. O'Connor, *The Play Therapy Primer: An Integration of Theories and Techniques* (New York: John Wiley & Sons, 1991), 7–8.

30. Lawrence K. Frank, "Play in Personality Development," *American Journal of Orthopsychiatry* 25 (1955): 576–590.

31. Landreth, *Play Therapy,* 8.

32. Piaget, *Play, Dreams, and Imitation in Childhood,* 8.

33. Hebrews 11:1.

34. James Fowler, *Stages of Faith: The Psychology of Human Development and the Quest for Meaning* (San Francisco: Harper & Row, 1981), 133.

35. Ibid., 149.

36. Matthew 18:1-4; Mark 10:15; 1 Corinthians 14:20; Ephesians 5:8; 1 Peter 2:2.

37. Harry A. Van Belle, "Adulthood and the Development of Lived Religion," *Christian Perspectives on Human Development,* ed. Leroy Aden, David G. Benner, and J. Harold Ellens (Grand Rapids: Baker, 1992), 53–64.

Chapter 3: Play Therapy As a Foundational Treatment

1. Garry Landreth, *Play Therapy: The Art of the Relationship* (Muncie, Ind.: Accelerated Development, Inc., Publishers, 1991), 14.
2. Walter Byrd and Paul Warren, *Counseling and Children* (Dallas: Word, Inc., 1989), 153.
3. For information about training opportunities in the field of play therapy, contact the Center for Play Therapy, University of North Texas, P.O. Box 13857, Denton, TX 76203. The Center for Play Therapy is the largest play therapy training center in the nation, with eight fully equipped playrooms (including one-way mirrors and videotaping equipment). There are more courses offered in play therapy at the University of North Texas than at any other university in North America. Dr. Garry Landreth, regents professor, is the director of the center.
4. Landreth, *Play Therapy,* 116–117.
5. Romans 1:20.
6. Landreth, *Play Therapy,* 182.
7. Ibid., 14.
8. John 8:43.
9. Haim Ginott, *Group Psychotherapy with Children: The Theory and Practice of Play Therapy* (New York: McGraw-Hill, 1961), 126.
10. Sigmund Freud, *Analysis of a Phobia in a Five-Year-Old Boy* (London: Hogarth Press, 1909).
11. Hermine Hug-Hellmuth, "On the Technique of Child-Analysis," *International Journal of Psycho-Analysis* 2 (1921): 287–305.
12. Landreth, *Play Therapy,* 27.
13. Anna Freud, *The Psycho-Analytic Treatment of Children* (New York: International Universities Press, 1965).
14. Melanie Klein, *The Psycho-Analysis of Children* (London: Hogarth Press, 1932).
15. David Levy, "Release Therapy," *Psychiatry* 1 (1938): 387–389.
16. Kevin J. O'Connor, *The Play Therapy Primer: An Integration of Theories and Techniques* (New York: John Wiley & Sons, 1991), 10.
17. Gove Hambidge, "Structured Play Therapy," *American Journal of Orthopsychiatry* 25 (1955): 601–617; O'Connor, *The Play Therapy Primer,* 11.
18. Jesse Taft, *The Dynamics of Therapy in a Controlled Relationship* (New York: Macmillan, 1933); Frederick Allen, *Psychotherapy with Children* (New York: Norton, 1942); Clark Moustakas, *Psychotherapy with Children: The Living Relationship* (New York: Harper & Row, 1959); Otto Rank, *Will Therapy* (New York: Knopf, 1936).

19. O'Connor, *The Play Therapy Primer*, 12.
20. Virginia Axline, *Play Therapy: The Inner Dynamics of Childhood* (Boston: Houghton Mifflin, 1947).
21. Virginia Axline, "Entering the Child's World via Play Experiences," *Progressive Education* 27 (1950): 68.
22. The leading proponent of child-centered play therapy currently is Dr. Garry Landreth, who has written *Play Therapy: The Art of the Relationship*. Ecosystemic play therapy has been developed and described by Dr. Kevin J. O'Connor, who has written *The Play Therapy Primer*. The leading proponent of Adlerian play therapy currently is Dr. Terry Kottman, who has written *Partners in Play: An Adlerian Approach to Play Therapy* (Alexandria, Va.: American Counseling Association, 1995). Cognitive-behavioral theory has been applied to play therapy by Dr. Susan Knell, whose concepts are outlined in her book *Cognitive-Behavioral Play Therapy* (Northvale, N.J.: Jason Aronson, Inc., 1993). The current leading proponent of a Jungian approach to play therapy is British Columbia's Dr. John Allan, who has written *Inscapes of the Child's World: Jungian Counseling in Schools and Clinics* (Dallas: Spring Publications, 1988). Developmental play therapy was developed by Dr. Viola Brody, who has written *The Dialogue of Touch: Developmental Play Therapy* (Treasure Island, Fla.: Developmental Play Therapy Associates, 1993).
23. Landreth, *Play Therapy*, 42.
24. For information on materials available from the Center for Play Therapy, write: Center for Play Therapy, University of North Texas, P.O. Box 13857, Denton, TX 76203.
25. Garry Landreth, Linda Homeyer, Geri Glover, and Daniel Sweeney, *Play Therapy Interventions with Children's Problems* (Northvale, N.J.: Jason Aronson, Inc., 1996).
26. Aaron H. Esman, "Psychoanalytic Play Therapy," *Handbook of Play Therapy*, ed. Charles E. Schaefer and Kevin J. O'Connor (New York: John Wiley & Sons, 1983), 11.
27. Ibid.
28. Yoram Kaufman, "Analytical Psychotherapy," *Current Psychotherapies*, 4th ed., ed. Raymond J. Corsini and Danny Wedding (Itasca, Ill.: F. E. Peacock Publishers, Inc., 1989).
29. John Allan, *Inscapes of the Child's World: Jungian Counseling in Schools and Clinics* (Dallas: Spring Publications, 1988), 7.
30. John Allan and Keith Brown, "Jungian Play Therapy in Elementary Schools," *Elementary School Guidance and Counseling* 28, no. 1 (October 1993): 30–41.
31. Ibid.
32. Axline, *Play Therapy*.

33. Ibid.
34. Garry Landreth, "Child-Centered Play Therapy," *Elementary School Guidance and Counseling* 28, no. 1 (October 1993): 17–29.
35. Garry Landreth and Daniel Sweeney, "Child-Centered Play Therapy," *Play Theory and Applications: A Comparative Casebook,* ed. Kevin J. O'Connor and Lisa Mages (New York: John Wiley & Sons, 1997).
36. Charles E. Schaefer, *The Therapeutic Powers of Play* (Northvale, N.J.: Jason Aronson, Inc., 1992), 3.
37. Ibid.
38. Landreth, *Play Therapy,* 80.
39. Ibid., 79.
40. Clark Moustakas, *Psychotherapy with Children: The Living Relationship* (New York: Harper & Row, 1959), 69.

Chapter 4: Working with Parents
1. Terry Kottman, *Partners in Play: An Adlerian Approach to Play Therapy* (Alexandria, Va.: American Counseling Association, 1995), 33.
2. Garry Landreth, *Play Therapy: The Art of the Relationship* (Muncie, Ind.: Accelerated Development, Inc., Publishers, 1991), 132–133.
3. For ordering information for these assessment tools, see appendix A. Thomas M. Achenbach and Craig Edelbrook, *Child Behavior Checklist;* Richard R. Abidin, *Parenting Stress Index;* Ellen Piers and Dale Harris, *The Piers-Harris Children's Self-Concept Scale;* Jack Joseph, *Joseph Pre-School and Primary Self-Concept Screening Test.*
4. For ordering information for some of these assessment tools, see appendix A. Rudolph Moos, *Family Environment Scale;* Blaine Porter, "Measurement of Parental Acceptance of Children," *Journal of Home Economics* 46 (1954): 176–182.
5. Shirley Cooper and Leon Wanerman, *Children in Treatment: A Primer for Beginning Psychotherapists* (New York: Brunner/Mazel, 1977), 185.
6. Landreth, *Play Therapy,* 148.
7. Kevin J. O'Connor, *The Play Therapy Primer: An Integration of Theories and Techniques* (New York: John Wiley & Sons, 1991), 287.
8. Landreth, *Play Therapy,* 148–50.
9. Ibid.
10. Marc Nemiroff and Jane Annunziata, *A Child's First Book about Play Therapy* (Washington, D.C.: American Psychiatric Association, 1990).
11. O'Connor, *The Play Therapy Primer,* 283.
12. Landreth, *Play Therapy,* 135.
13. Ibid., 147.
14. O'Connor, *The Play Therapy Primer,* 287.
15. Haim Ginott, *Between Parent and Child* (New York: Avon Books, 1956), 234–241.

Chapter 5: The Playroom and Materials

1. Garry Landreth, *Play Therapy: The Art of the Relationship* (Muncie, Ind.: Accelerated Development, Inc., Publishers, 1991), 111.
2. Ibid., 117.
3. The popularity of Mighty Morphin Power Rangers is not surprising. They are action figures with a great deal of power, and children in today's society feel quite powerless. The violence of the show, however, is excessive. In an article in the *Boston Globe* ("Beware, Work with Power Rangers' Mixed Messages," 2 January 1995), it was noted that the average hour of Power Rangers' programming includes 211 acts of violence.
4. Landreth, *Play Therapy*, 117–120.
5. Ibid.

Chapter 6: Conducting a Child Play Therapy Session

1. Garry Landreth and Daniel Sweeney, "Child-Centered Play Therapy," *Play Theory and Applications: A Comparative Casebook,* ed. Kevin J. O'Connor and Lisa Mages (New York: John Wiley & Sons, 1997).
2. N. Blurton-Jones, as cited in William C. McGrew, *An Ethological Study of Children's Behavior* (New York: Academic Press, 1972), 59.
3. E. Goffman, "Gender Advertisements," *Studies in the Anthropology of Visual Communication* 3 (1976): 2.
4. Garry Landreth, *Play Therapy: The Art of the Relationship* (Muncie, Ind.: Accelerated Development, Inc., Publishers, 1991), 159.
5. Ibid.
6. Ibid., 163.
7. Ibid., 255.
8. Haim Ginott, *Group Psychotherapy with Children: The Theory and Practice of Play Therapy* (New York: McGraw-Hill, 1961), 90.
9. Landreth, *Play Therapy*, 183–184.
10. Ibid.
11. Proverbs 4:23.
12. Thomas Gordon, *P.E. T.: Parent Effectiveness Training* (New York: New American Library, 1975).
13. Garry Landreth tells this in his Introduction to Play Therapy class at the University of North Texas.
14. Daniel Sweeney and Garry Landreth, "Healing a Child's Spirit Through Play Therapy: A Scriptural Approach to Treating Children," *Journal of Psychology and Christianity* 12 (1993): 351–356.
15. Landreth, *Play Therapy*, 239.
16. Landreth and Sweeney, "Child-Centered Play Therapy," *Play Theory and Applications: A Comparative Casebook.*
17. Landreth, *Play Therapy*, 208.
18. Ibid., 251.

Chapter 7: Therapeutic Limit Setting

1. Ray Bixler, "Limits Are Therapy," *Journal of Consulting Psychology* 13 (1949): 1–11.
2. Galatians 3:24.
3. Joachim Guhrt, "Covenant," *The New International Dictionary of New Testament Theology,* vol. 1, ed. Colin Brown (Grand Rapids: Zondervan Publishing House, 1975), 367.
4. Garry Landreth, *Play Therapy: The Art of the Relationship* (Muncie, Ind.: Accelerated Development, Inc., Publishers, 1991), 209.
5. Clark Moustakas, *Psychotherapy with Children: The Living Relationship* (New York: Harper & Row, 1959), 7.
6. Landreth, *Play Therapy,* 217.
7. Haim Ginott, *Group Psychotherapy with Children: The Theory and Practice of Play Therapy* (New York: McGraw-Hill, 1961), 103–104.
8. Landreth, *Play Therapy,* 216.
9. Ginott, *Group Psychotherapy with Children,* 103.
10. Virginia Axline, *Play Therapy: The Inner Dynamics of Childhood* (Boston: Houghton Mifflin, 1947), 128.
11. Bixler, "Limits Are Therapy," *Journal of Consulting Psychology,* 3.
12. Ibid.
13. Terry Kottman, *Partners in Play: An Adlerian Approach to Play Therapy* (Alexandria, Va.: American Counseling Association, 1995), 96–97.
14. Bixler, "Limits Are Therapy," *Journal of Consulting Psychology,* 2.
15. Landreth, *Play Therapy,* 222–223.
16. Ibid.
17. Ibid.
18. Don Dinkmeyer Sr. and Gary D. McKay, *The Parent's Handbook: Systematic Training for Effective Parenting [STEP]* (Circle Pines, Minn.: American Guidance Service, 1989).
19. Deuteronomy 30:19-20.

Chapter 8: Using Stories, Sandplay, and Art in Play Therapy

1. Psalm 78:1-4.
2. Deuteronomy 6:6-9.
3. Joyce Mills and Richard Crowley, *Therapeutic Metaphors for Children and the Child Within* (New York: Brunner/Mazel, 1986), xviii.
4. Ibid.
5. Doris Brett, *More Annie Stories: Therapeutic Storytelling Techniques* (New York: Magination Press, 1992), 5–6.
6. Violet Oaklander, *Windows to Our Children: A Gestalt Therapy Approach to Children and Adolescents* (Highland, N.Y.: The Center for Gestalt Development, 1988), 85.

7. Richard Gardner, *Storytelling in Psychotherapy with Children* (Northvale, N.J.: Jason Aronson, Inc., 1993), 5.

8. John Allan, *Inscapes of the Child's World: Jungian Counseling in Schools and Clinics* (Dallas: Spring Publications, 1988), 200–201.

9. Mills and Crowley, *Therapeutic Metaphors for Children and the Child Within,* 65–66.

10. Karen Lanners and Ken Schwartzenberger, *Therapeutic Stories for Children in Foster Care* (Avila Beach, Calif.: Renderings, 1995).

11. Ibid., ix.

12. Allan, *Inscapes of the Child's World,* 212.

13. Margaret Lowenfeld, *The World Technique,* 2d ed. (London: Allan & Urwin, 1979).

14. H. G. Wells, *Floor Games* (New York: Arno Press, 1975).

15. Lowenfeld, *The World Technique.*

16. Dora Kalff, *Sandplay,* 2d ed. (Santa Monica, Calif.: Sigo Press, 1980).

17. Allan, *Inscapes of the Child's World,* 213.

18. Lois Carey, "Sandplay Therapy with a Troubled Child," *The Arts in Psychotherapy* 17 (1990): 197–209.

19. Kalff, *Sandplay.*

20. Allan, *Inscapes of the Child's World,* 221.

21. Ibid.

22. R. C. Burns and S. H. Kaufman, *Kinetic Family Drawing (K-F-D): Research and Application* (New York: Brunner/Mazel, 1970).

23. Gerald Oster and Patricia Gould, *Using Drawings in Assessment and Therapy: A Guide for Mental Health Professionals* (New York: Brunner/Mazel, 1987), 10.

24. Mills and Crowley, *Therapeutic Metaphors for Children and the Child Within,* 174.

25. Ibid., 179.

26. Allan, *Inscapes of the Child's World.*

27. Ibid., 21–22.

28. Virginia Satir, *Conjoint Family Therapy* (Palo Alto, Calif.: Science and Behavior Books, 1967).

29. Helen Landgarten, "Family Art Psychotherapy," *Family Play Therapy,* ed. Charles E. Schaefer and Lois Carey (Northvale, N.J.: Jason Aronson, Inc., 1994), 221–233.

Chapter 9: Issues in Counseling Children through Play

1. Mary Haworth, ed., *Child Psychotherapy: Practice and Theory* (Northvale, N.J.: Jason Aronson, Inc., 1994), 167–168.

2. Clark Moustakas, "Emotional Adjustment and the Play Therapy Process," *Journal of Genetic Psychology* 86 (1955): 84.

3. Clark Moustakas, *Psychotherapy with Children: The Living Relationship* (New York: Harper & Row, 1959), 18.

4. Ibid.
5. Leaders in the field of play therapy, Byron and Carol Norton have presented numerous workshops on working with children. This material comes from one of their workshops entitled "Reaching Children through Play Therapy," sponsored by their organization, Family Psychological Consultants.
6. Garry Landreth, *Play Therapy: The Art of the Relationship* (Muncie, Ind.: Accelerated Development, Inc., Publishers, 1991), 323.
7. Ibid., 182.
8. Ibid., 324.
9. Haworth, *Child Psychotherapy,* 416.
10. Luke 11:17.
11. Kevin J. O'Connor, *The Play Therapy Primer: An Integration of Theories and Techniques* (New York: John Wiley & Sons, 1991), 282.
12. Robert Berg and Garry Landreth, *Group Counseling and Procedures,* 2d ed. (Muncie, Ind.: Accelerated Development, Inc., Publishers, 1990).
13. Haim Ginott, "Group Play Therapy with Children," *Basic Approaches to Group Psychotherapy and Group Counseling,* ed. George Gazda (Springfield, Ill.: Charles C. Thomas, 1975).
14. Louise Guerney, "Client-Centered (Nondirective) Play Therapy," *Handbook of Play Therapy,* ed. Charles E. Schaefer and Kevin J. O'Connor (New York: John Wiley & Sons, 1983).
15. Haim Ginott, "Group Play Therapy with Children," *Basic Approaches to Group Psychotherapy and Group Counseling.*
16. Ibid., 11.
17. Haim Ginott, *Group Psychotherapy with Children: The Theory and Practice of Play Therapy* (New York: McGraw-Hill, 1961), 2.
18. Ibid., 17.
19. Landreth, *Play Therapy,* 315.
20. This list comes from the writings of Dr. Haim Ginott and workshop materials of Drs. Garry Landreth and Sue Bratton.
21. Ephesians 6:12.
22. Gary R. Collins, *Christian Counseling: A Comprehensive Guide* (Dallas: Word, Inc., 1988), 567.
23. Romans 15:4.
24. 2 Peter 1:5-8.
25. Frederick H. Allen, *Psychotherapy with Children* (New York: Norton, 1942).
26. Landreth, *Play Therapy,* 329.

Chapter 10: Parent Training: Filial Therapy

1. Training in filial therapy may be obtained through university courses and workshops. The Center for Play Therapy at the University of North Texas offers both. Write or call: P.O. Box 13857, Denton, TX 76203; (817) 565-3864. Also, Dr. Louise Guerney, one of the developers of filial

therapy, offers workshops through the National Institute of Relationship Enhancement. Write or call: 4400 East-West Highway, Suite 28, Bethesda, MD 20814; (301) 986-1479.

2. Garry Landreth, *Play Therapy: The Art of the Relationship* (Muncie, Ind.: Accelerated Development, Inc., Publishers, 1991), 339.

3. Alan Lobaugh, "Filial Therapy with Incarcerated Parents" (Ph.D. diss., University of North Texas, 1991); Hilda Glazer-Waldman, Judith Zimmerman, Garry Landreth, and Doug Norton, "Filial Therapy: An Intervention for Parents of Children with Chronic Illness," *International Journal of Play Therapy* 1 (1992): 31–42; Sue Bratton and Garry Landreth, "Filial Therapy with Single Parents: Effects on Parental Acceptance, Empathy, and Stress," *International Journal of Play Therapy* 4 (1995): 61–80.

4. Arthur Kraft, *Are You Listening to Your Child?* (New York: Walker and Company, 1973), 133.

5. Ross Campbell, *How to Really Love Your Child* (Wheaton, Ill.: Victor Books, 1992), 9–10.

6. Bernard Guerney, "Filial Therapy: Description and Rationale," *Journal of Consulting Psychology* 28 (1964): 304–360.

7. Lillian Stover and Bernard Guerney, "The Efficacy of Training Procedures for Mothers in Filial Therapy," *Psychotherapy: Theory, Research, and Practice* 4 (1967): 110–115.

8. Sigmund Freud, "Analysis of a Phobia in a Five-Year-Old Boy," *Collected Papers* (New York: Basic Books, 1959).

9. Dorothy Baruch, *New Ways in Discipline* (New York: McGraw-Hill, 1949).

10. Natalie Rogers-Fuchs, "Play Therapy at Home," *Merrill-Palmer Quarterly* 3 (1957): 89–95.

11. Clark Moustakas, *Psychotherapy with Children: The Living Relationship* (New York: Harper & Row, 1959).

12. Landreth, *Play Therapy.*

13. Stover and Guerney, "The Efficacy of Training Procedures for Mothers in Filial Therapy," *Psychotherapy,* 110–115.

14. P. Carlo, "Parent Education vs. Parent Involvement: Which Type of Efforts Work Best to Reunify Families?" *Journal of Social Services Research* 17 (1993): 135–150.

15. Rise Van Fleet, *Filial Therapy: Strengthening Parent-Child Relationships through Play* (Sarasota, Fla: Professional Resource Press, 1994).

16. Ibid.

17. Landreth, *Play Therapy.*

18. G. Raymond Campbell, "The Responsibility of Parents," *Treasury of Inspiration,* ed. Herbert Prochnow (Grand Rapids: Baker, 1958).

19. Deuteronomy 6:6-9; Psalm 103:13; Proverbs 22:6; Ephesians 6:4.

20. Landreth, *Play Therapy,* 344–348.

21. Ibid., 345.
22. Ibid.
23. Ibid., 346.
24. The first seven items are taken from Louise Guerney, *Play Therapy: A Training Manual for Parents* (1972, mimeographed).
25. Landreth, *Play Therapy,* 346–347.
26. Ibid., 347–348.
27. Ibid., 348.
28. Ibid.
29. R. L. Hegar, "Empowerment-Based Practice with Children," *Social Science Review* 63 (1989): 372–383.

Chapter 11: Treating Traumatized Children

1. David Finkelhor and Jennifer Dzuiba-Leatherman, "Victimization of Children," *American Psychologist* 49 (March 1994): 173.
2. Leonard Shengold, *Soul Murder: The Effects of Childhood Abuse and Deprivation* (New Haven: Yale University Press, 1989), 2.
3. Ibid.
4. Ibid.
5. John 10:10.
6. Robert Coleman, *Written in Blood: A Devotional Bible Study of the Blood of Christ* (Old Tappan, N.J.: Fleming H. Revell Co., 1972), 35–36.
7. Beverly James, *Treating Traumatized Children: New Insights and Creative Interventions* (Lexington, Mass.: Lexington Books, 1989), 1.
8. Ibid.
9. Lenore C. Terr, "Childhood Trauma: An Outline and Overview," *American Journal of Psychiatry* 148 (January 1991): 10–20.
10. Ibid.
11. Ibid.
12. Ibid.
13. David Finkelhor and Angela Browne, "Initial and Long-Term Effects: A Conceptual Framework," *A Sourcebook on Child Sexual Abuse,* ed. David Finkelhor (Newbury Park, Calif.: Sage Publications, 1986).
14. James, *Treating Traumatized Children,* 21–37.
15. Grant L. Martin, *Critical Problems in Children and Youth* (Dallas: Word, Inc., 1992), 138–142.
16. American Psychiatric Association, *Diagnostic and Statistical Manual of Mental Disorders,* 4th ed. (Washington, D.C.: American Psychiatric Association, 1994).
17. Garry Landreth et al., *Play Therapy Interventions with Children's Problems* (Northvale, N.J.: Jason Aronson, Inc., 1996).
18. James, *Treating Traumatized Children,* 3–4.

19. Charles E. Schaefer, "Play Therapy for Psychic Trauma in Children," *Handbook of Play Therapy,* vol. 2, *Advances and Innovations,* ed. Kevin J. O'Connor and Charles E. Schaefer (New York: John Wiley & Sons, 1994), 301.

20. Sigmund Freud, "Beyond the Pleasure Principle," *The Standard Edition of the Complete Psychological Work of Sigmund Freud* vol. 18, ed. James Strachey (London: Hogarth Press, 1920).

21. Schaefer, "Play Therapy for Psychic Trauma in Children," *Handbook of Play Therapy,* vol. 2, 302.

22. Lenore C. Terr, "Play Therapy and Psychic Trauma: A Preliminary Report," *Handbook of Play Therapy,* ed. Charles E. Schaefer and Kevin J. O'Connor (New York: John Wiley & Sons, 1983), 308.

23. Maria Piers and Genevieve Landau, *The Gift of Play* (New York: Walker and Company, 1980), 16.

24. National Committee for Prevention of Child Abuse, *Child Abuse and Neglect Statistics* (working paper, April 1993).

25. Martin, *Critical Problems in Children and Youth,* 96.

26. Ibid., 97.

27. Eliana Gil, *Outgrowing the Pain: A Book for and about Adults Abused as Children* (New York: Dell, 1983).

28. William Friedrich, *Psychotherapy of Sexually Abused Children and Their Families* (New York: Norton, 1990), 102.

29. Suzanne Sgroi, *Handbook of Clinical Intervention in Child Sexual Abuse* (Lexington, Mass.: Lexington Books, 1982), 40–41.

30. Beverly James and Maria Nasjleti, *Treating Sexually Abused Children and Their Families* (Palo Alto, Calif.: Davies-Black Publishing, 1983).

31. Sexual abuse investigations can be delicate matters because of the prevalent potential to lead the child to disclose. Dr. Linda Homeyer, assistant professor at Southwest Texas State University, has developed the Tri-Modal Sexual Abuse Interview Protocol, which is based on incorporating child-centered play therapy techniques into the interview process so as not to lead or coerce a child into disclosure. She has presented her work at several conferences and will be publishing the protocol in the near future.

32. Landreth et al., *Play Therapy Interventions with Children's Problems,* 1.

33. Eliana Gil, *The Healing Power of Play: Working with Abused Children* (New York: The Guilford Press, 1991), 53.

34. Ibid., 59.

35. Ibid., 61.

36. Ibid., 63.

37. Ibid., 66.

38. Ibid., 69.

39. Ibid., 72.

40. Ibid., 81.

41. Kenneth Doka, ed., *Children Mourning, Mourning Children* (Washington, D.C.: Hospice Foundation of America, 1995).
42. Mark Speece and Sandor Brent, "The Development of Children's Understanding of Death," *Helping Children Cope with Death and Bereavement*, ed. Charles Corr and Donna Corr (New York: Springer Publishing Co., 1995).
43. Charles Corr, "Children's Understandings of Death: Striving to Understand Death," *Children Mourning, Mourning Children*, ed. Kenneth Doka (Washington, D.C.: Hospice Foundation of America, 1995).
44. Landreth et al., *Play Therapy Interventions with Children's Problems*, 135.
45. Beverly James, *Handbook for Treatment of Attachment-Trauma Problems in Children* (New York: Lexington Books, 1994), 88.
46. Mark 4:35.

Chapter 12: Treating Disruptive Behavior Problems

1. Russell A. Barkley, *Defiant Children: A Clinician's Manual for Parent Training* (New York: The Guilford Press, 1987), 10–11.
2. Walter Byrd and Paul Warren, *Counseling and Children* (Dallas: Word, Inc., 1989), 78–80.
3. Barkley, *Defiant Children*, 99–100.
4. Russell Barkley, *Attention-Deficit Hyperactivity Disorder: A Handbook for Diagnosis and Treatment* (New York: The Guilford Press, 1990).
5. George DuPaul, David Guevremont, and Russell Barkley, "Attention-Deficit Hyperactivity Disorder," *The Practice of Child Therapy*, ed. Thomas Kratochwill and Richard Morris (New York: Pergamon Press, 1991).
6. Grant L. Martin, *Critical Problems in Children and Youth* (Dallas: Word, Inc., 1992), 28.
7. Barkley, *Attention-Deficit Hyperactivity Disorder*, 47.
8. DuPaul, Guevremont, and Barkley, "Attention-Deficit Hyperactivity Disorder," *The Practice of Child Therapy*, 120.
9. Ibid.
10. Ibid.
11. Ibid.
12. Martin, *Critical Problems in Children and Youth*, 43.
13. Barkley, *Attention-Deficit Hyperactivity Disorder*.
14. See appendix A for information to obtain some of these assessment tools. Thomas Achenbach and Craig Edelbrook, *Child Behavior Checklist;* Keith Conners, *Conners Parent Rating Scale;* Stephen B. McCarney, *Attention-Deficit Disorders Evaluation Scale;* Rina Ullmann, Esther Sleator, and Robert Sprague, *ADD-H Comprehensive Teacher Rating Scale*.
15. Rudolph Moos, *Family Environment Scale* (Palo Alto, Calif.: Consulting Psychologists Press, Inc., 1994); Richard Abidin, *Parenting Stress Index* (Charlottesville, Va.: Pediatric Psychology Press, 1990); H. J. Locke and K. M.

Wallace, "Short Marital Adjustment and Prediction Tests: Their Reliability and Validity," *Journal of Marriage and Family Living* 21 (1959): 251–255.

16. DuPaul, Guevremont, and Barkley, "Attention-Deficit Hyperactivity Disorder," *The Practice of Child Therapy,* 121.

17. Barkley, *Defiant Children.*

18. Michael Gordon, *ADHD/Hyperactivity: A Consumer's Guide* (DeWitt, N.Y.: GSI Publications, 1991).

19. Grant L. Martin, *The Hyperactive Child: What You Need to Know about Attention Deficit Disorder—Facts, Myths and Treatment* (Wheaton, Ill.: Victor Books, 1992).

20. Louise F. Guerney, "Play Therapy Techniques for Learning Disabled Children," *Handbook of Play Therapy,* ed. Charles E. Schaefer and Kevin J. O'Connor (New York: John Wiley & Sons, 1983), 424.

21. Adapted from Michael Gordon, *ADHD/Hyperactivity.*

22. Karen Wells and Rex Forehand, "Conduct Disorders," *Handbook of Clinical Behavior Therapy with Children,* ed. Philip H. Bornstein and Alan E. Kazdin (Homewood, Ill.: Dorsey Press, 1985), 218–265.

23. M. Rutter, J. Tizard, and K. Whitmore, *Education, Health, and Behavior* (London: Longman, 1970).

24. P. Graham, "Epidemiological Studies," *Psychopathological Disorders of Childhood,* ed. Herbert Quay and John Werry (New York: John Wiley & Sons, 1979), 185–208.

25. Syed A. Husain and Dennis P. Cantwell, *Fundamentals of Child and Adolescent Psychopathology* (Washington, D.C.: American Psychiatric Press, 1991), 90.

26. Ibid.

27. Numbers 14:18.

28. Alan E. Kazdin, "Aggressive Behavior and Conduct Disorder," *The Practice of Child Therapy,* ed. Thomas Kratochwill and Richard Morris (New York: Pergamon Press, 1991).

29. E. B. Hook and D. S. Kim, "Prevalence of XYY and XXY Karyotypes in 337 Non-retarded Young Offenders," *New England Journal of Medicine* 283 (1970): 410–411; Husain and Cantwell, *Fundamentals of Child and Adolescent Psychopathology.*

30. Garry Landreth et al., *Play Therapy Interventions with Children's Problems* (Northvale, N.J.: Jason Aronson, Inc., 1996).

Chapter 13: Treating Anxious and Depressed Children

1. Syed A. Husain and Dennis P. Cantwell, *Fundamentals of Child and Adolescent Psychopathology* (Washington, D.C.: American Psychiatric Press, 1991), 111.

2. Walter Byrd and Paul Warren, *Counseling and Children* (Dallas: Word, Inc., 1989), 155.

3. R. Lapouse and M. A. Monk, "Fears and Worries in a Representative Sample of Children," *American Journal of Orthopsychiatry* 29 (1959): 803–818.
4. Byrd and Warren, *Counseling and Children,* 155.
5. Robert Eme and Dwight Schmidt, "The Stability of Children's Fears," *Child Development* 49 (1978): 1277–1279.
6. Richard Morris and Thomas Kratochwill, "Childhood Fears and Phobias," *The Practice of Child Therapy,* ed. Thomas Kratochwill and Richard Morris (New York: Pergamon Press, 1991), 77.
7. Ibid.
8. Isaac M. Marks, *Fears, Phobias, and Rituals* (New York: Oxford University Press, 1987).
9. L. Miller, C. Barrett, and E. Hampe, "Phobias of Childhood in a Prescientific Era," *Child Personality and Psychopathology: Current Topics,* ed. A. Davids (New York: John Wiley & Sons, 1974), 72–95.
10. American Psychiatric Association, *Diagnostic and Statistical Manual of Mental Disorders,* 4th ed. (Washington, D.C.: American Psychiatric Association, 1994).
11. Byrd and Warren, *Counseling and Children,* 155–158.
12. Some examples of the effectiveness of play therapy with fear and anxiety include Eugene Alexander, "School Centered Play-Therapy Program," *Personnel and Guidance Journal* 43 (1964): 256–261; Karen Barlow, Garry Landreth, and JoAnna Strother, "Child-Centered Play Therapy: Nancy from Baldness to Curls," *The School Counselor* 34 (1985): 347–356; Mary Ellen Milos and Steven Reiss, "Effects of Three Play Conditions on Separation Anxiety in Young Children," *Journal of Counseling and Consulting Psychology* 50 (1982): 389–395.
13. Garry Landreth et al., *Play Therapy Interventions with Children's Problems* (Northvale, N.J.: Jason Aronson, Inc., 1996).
14. Husain and Cantwell, *Fundamentals of Child and Adolescent Psychopathology.*
15. Byrd and Warren, *Counseling and Children,* 28.
16. Ibid.
17. American Psychiatric Association, *Diagnostic and Statistical Manual of Mental Disorders,* 4th ed.
18. Nadine Kaslow and Lynn Rehm, "Childhood Depression," *The Practice of Child Therapy,* ed. Thomas Kratochwill and Richard Morris (New York: Pergamon Press, 1991), 45.
19. K. H. Bauersfeld, "Diagnosis and Treatment of Depressive Condition at a School Psychiatric Center," *Depressive States in Childhood and Adolescence,* ed. A. Annell (Stockholm: Alinquist & Wiskell, 1972), 281–285.
20. Brian McConville and L. C. Boag, "Three Types of Childhood Depression," *Canadian Psychiatry Association Journal* 18 (1973): 133–138.

21. W. Reinberg et al., "Depression in Children Referred to an Educational Diagnostic Center: Diagnosis and Treatment," *Journal of Pediatrics* 83 (1972): 1065–1072.

22. Nadine Kaslow, Lynn Rehm, and Alexander Siegal, "Social-Cognitive and Cognitive Correlates of Depression in Children," *Journal of Abnormal Child Psychology* 12 (1984): 605–620.

23. National Center for Health Statistics, Department of Health and Human Services, *United States Monthly Vital Statistics* (Washington, D.C.: GPO, 1984).

24. As cited in Angela Sabates, "Rain, Rain, Go Away: Depression in Children," *Christian Counseling Today* (fall 1995): 42–45.

25. Kaslow and Rehm, "Childhood Depression," *The Practice of Child Therapy*, 46.

26. Byrd and Warren, *Counseling and Children,* 152.

27. Husain and Cantwell, *Fundamentals of Child and Adolescent Psychopathology.*

28. Byrd and Warren, *Counseling and Children,* 153.

Chapter 14: Treating Other Common Childhood Problems

1. Charles E. Schaefer and Howard Millman, *How to Help Children with Common Problems* (New York: Van Nostrand Reinhold Co., 1981), 177.

2. Ibid.

3. Walter Byrd and Paul Warren, *Counseling and Children* (Dallas: Word, Inc., 1989), 104.

4. Syed A. Husain and Dennis P. Cantwell, *Fundamentals of Child and Adolescent Psychopathology* (Washington, D.C.: American Psychiatric Press, 1991), 212.

5. Ibid.

6. Ibid.

7. Schaefer and Millman, *How to Help Children with Common Problems.*

8. Husain and Cantwell, *Fundamentals of Child and Adolescent Psychopathology.*

9. Schaefer and Millman, *How to Help Children with Common Problems.*

10. Byrd and Warren, *Counseling and Children,* 106.

11. Husain and Cantwell, *Fundamentals of Child and Adolescent Psychopathology,* 162.

12. Ibid.

13. Byrd and Warren, *Counseling and Children.*

14. Schaefer and Millman, *How to Help Children with Common Problems.*

15. Husain and Cantwell, *Fundamentals of Child and Adolescent Psychopathology.*

16. Melvin Levine, "Encopresis: Its Potentiations, Evaluation and Alleviation," *Pediatric Clinics of North America* 29 (1982): 315–330.

17. Garry Landreth et al., *Play Therapy Interventions with Children's Problems* (Northvale, N.J.: Jason Aronson, Inc., 1996).

18. American Psychiatric Association, *Diagnostic and Statistical Manual of Mental Disorders,* 4th ed. (Washington, D.C.: American Psychiatric Association, 1994).
19. Husain and Cantwell, *Fundamentals of Child and Adolescent Psychopathology,* 151.
20. Ibid.
21. Ibid., 145–146.

Chapter 15: Children and Psychopharmacology

1. R. J. Salinger, "Psychopharmacology," *Baker Encyclopedia of Psychology,* ed. David Benner (Grand Rapids: Baker, 1985), 949.
2. American Association of Christian Counselors, *1995–96 Membership Registry* (Forest, Va.: American Association of Christian Counselors, 1995).
3. Jo Ellen Patterson and Mark Magulac, "The Family Therapist's Guide to Psychopharmacology: A Graduate Level Course," *Journal of Marital and Family Therapy* 2 (1994): 151–173.
4. Ibid.
5. Joseph Biederman, "New Developments in Pediatric Psychopharmacology," *Journal of the Academy of Child and Adolescent Psychiatry* 31 (1992): 14–15; Oscar Bukstein, "Overview of Pharmacological Treatment," *Handbook of Behavior Therapy and Pharmacotherapy for Children,* ed. Vincent Van Hasselt and Michel Hersen (Boston: Allyn & Bacon, 1993), 13–27; Magda Campbell, Katherine Godfrey, and Harry Magee, "Pharmacotherapy," *Handbook of Clinical Child Psychology,* ed. Clarence Walker and Michael Roberts (New York: John Wiley & Sons, 1992), 873–902; Michael Gitlin, *The Psychotherapist's Guide to Psychopharmacology* (New York: The Free Press, 1990); and Wayne Green, "Principles of Psychopharmacotherapy and Specific Drug Treatments," *Child and Adolescent Psychiatry: A Comprehensive Textbook,* ed. Melvin Lewis (Baltimore: Williams & Wilkins, 1991).
6. Biederman, "New Developments in Pediatric Psychopharmacology," *Journal of the Academy of Child and Adolescent Psychiatry.*
7. Oscar Bukstein, "Overview of Pharmacological Treatment," *Handbook of Behavior Therapy and Pharmacotherapy for Children,* ed. Vincent Van Hasselt and Michel Hersen (Boston: Allyn & Bacon, 1993), 14.
8. Wayne Green, "Principles of Psychopharmacotherapy and Specific Drug Treatments," *Child and Adolescent Psychiatry: A Comprehensive Textbook,* ed. Melvin Lewis (Baltimore: William & Wilkins, 1991), 770.
9. Joseph Biederman and Ronald Steingard, "Pediatric Psychopharmacology," *The Practitioner's Guide to Psychoactive Drugs,* ed. Alan Gelenberg, Ellen Bassuk, and Stephen Schoonover (New York: Plenum Medical Book Company, 1991); Bukstein, "Overview of Pharmacological Treatment," *Handbook of Behavior Therapy and*

Pharmacotherapy for Children; Kenneth Gadow, "Pediatric Psychopharmacotherapy: A Review of Recent Research," *Journal of Child Psychology and Psychiatry and Allied Disciplines* 33 (1992): 153–195; Green, "Principles of Psychopharmacotherapy and Specific Drug Treatments," *Child and Adolescent Psychiatry.*

10. Biederman and Steingard, "Pediatric Psychopharmacology," *The Practitioner's Guide to Psychoactive Drugs,* 343.

11. Green, "Principles of Psychopharmacotherapy and Specific Drug Treatments," *Child and Adolescent Psychiatry,* 771.

12. Biederman and Steingard, "Pediatric Psychopharmacology," *The Practitioner's Guide to Psychoactive Drugs;* Bukstein, "Overview of Pharmacological Treatment," *Handbook of Behavior Therapy and Pharmacotherapy for Children;* and Green, "Principles of Psychopharmacotherapy and Specific Drug Treatments," *Child and Adolescent Psychiatry.*

13. American Psychiatric Association, *Diagnostic and Statistical Manual of Mental Disorders,* 4th ed. (Washington, D.C.: American Psychiatric Association, 1994).

14. Kenneth Gadow, "Pediatric Psychopharmacotherapy: A Review of Recent Research," *Journal of Child Psychology and Psychiatry and Allied Disciplines* 33 (1992).

15. Charles Popper, "Psychopharmacologic Treatment of Anxiety Disorders in Adolescents and Children," *The Journal of Clinical Psychiatry* 50 (1993): 52–63.

16. Magda Campbell and Elizabeth Spencer, "Psychopharmacology in Child and Adolescent Psychiatry: A Review of the Past Five Years," *Journal of the American Academy of Child and Adolescent Psychiatry* 27 (1988): 269–279.

17. Green, "Principles of Psychopharmacotherapy and Specific Drug Treatments," *Child and Adolescent Psychiatry.*

18. Magda Campbell, Katherine Godfrey, and Harry Magee, "Pharmacotherapy," *Handbook of Clinical Child Psychology,* ed. Clarence Walker and Michael Roberts (New York: John Wiley & Sons, 1992).

19. Garry Landreth, *Play Therapy: The Art of the Relationship* (Muncie, Ind.: Accelerated Development, Inc., Publishers, 1991).

20. Douglas Golden, "Play Therapy for Hospitalized Children," *Handbook of Play Therapy,* ed. Charles E. Schaefer and Kevin J. O'Connor (New York: John Wiley & Sons, 1983), 212–233.

21. Michael Gitlin, *The Psychotherapist's Guide to Psychopharmacology,* (New York: The Free Press, 1990), 179.

22. Biederman, "New Developments in Pediatric Psychopharmacology," *Journal of the Academy of Child and Adolscent Psychiatry,* 15.

23. L. Markowitz, "Better Therapy through Chemistry," *Family Therapy Networker* (May/June 1991): 22–31.

SUGGESTED READING

Note: Some of the following books clearly do not promote a Christian worldview in treating children. In fact, some contain material that is clearly in opposition to Scripture. Nevertheless, rather than "throwing out the baby with the bathwater," I suggest that these books contain truths that are helpful in ministering to children. I would argue that all truth is God's truth, whether revealed to a believer or not. For the sake of the children, let's use those tools that are truly therapeutic and not in opposition to the Word of God.

John Allan, *Inscapes of the Child's World: Jungian Counseling in Schools and Clinics* (Dallas: Spring Publications, 1988).

Virginia Axline, *Play Therapy* (New York: Ballantine Books, 1969).

Walter Byrd and Paul Warren, *Counseling and Children* (Dallas: Word, Inc., 1989).

Eliana Gil, *The Healing Power of Play: Working with Abused Children* (New York: The Guilford Press, 1991).

Garry Landreth, ed., *Play Therapy: Dynamics of the Process of Counseling with Children* (Springfield, Ill.: Charles C. Thomas Publisher, 1982).

Garry Landreth, *Play Therapy: The Art of the Relationship* (Muncie, Ind.: Accelerated Development, Inc., Publishers, 1991).

Garry Landreth, Linda Homeyer, Geri Glover, and Daniel Sweeney, *Play Therapy Interventions with Children's Problems* (Northvale, N.J.: Jason Aronson, Inc., 1996).

Grant Martin, *Critical Problems in Children and Youth* (Dallas: Word, Inc., 1992).

Clark Moustakas, *Psychotherapy with Children: The Living Relationship* (Greeley, Co.: Carron Publishers, 1992).

Violet Oaklander, *Windows to Our Children: A Gestalt Therapy Approach to Children and Adolescents* (Highland, N.Y.: The Center for Gestalt Development, Inc., 1988).

Kevin J. O'Connor and Charles E. Schaefer, eds., *Handbook of Play Therapy*, vol. 2 (New York: John Wiley & Sons, 1994).

Charles E. Schaefer and Kevin J. O'Connor, eds., *Handbook of Play Therapy* (New York: John Wiley & Sons, 1983).

Lenore Terr, *Too Scared to Cry: Psychic Trauma in Childhood* (New York: Basic Books, 1990).

Rise Van Fleet, *Filial Therapy: Strengthening Parent-Child Relationships through Play* (Sarasota, Fla.: Professional Resource Press, 1994).

INDEX

ABOUT THE AUTHOR

Daniel Sweeney earned a Ph.D. from the University of North Texas and an M.A. from Azusa Pacific University. He is a licensed marriage, family, and child counselor; licensed professional counselor; and registered play therapist-supervisor. Sweeney is an assistant professor of counseling at George Fox University in Portland, Oregon, and was the former assistant director of the Center for Play Therapy at the University of North Texas. He counsels in a private practice. His mentor, Dr. Garry Landreth, is recognized as a leading thinker in the play approach to counseling children. In addition to cowriting *Play Therapy Interventions with Children's Problems* (Northvale, N.J.: Jason Aronson, Inc., 1996), Sweeney has also contributed to the *Journal of Psychology and Christianity* and *Christian Counseling Today.* Sweeney conducts training seminars for both counselors and parents. Sweeney and his wife, Marla, have four children, whose ages range from four to twelve.

In play therapy, the language of children is play, and the toys are the words. A well-equipped playroom, therefore, provides a child with an environment in which a wide variety of issues and emotional expressions may be addressed. This is one of the playrooms at the University of North Texas.

Clinical supervision of counseling sessions is an integral part of the training process in play therapy. The use of one-way mirrors and videotaping as illustrated in this photo is optimum. Play therapists (and all counselors) should always participate in supervision and self-critique. There is no substitute for viewing oneself on videotape.

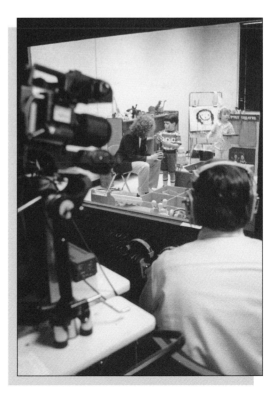

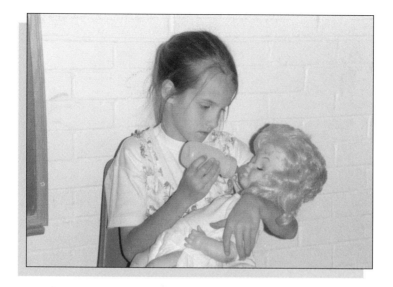

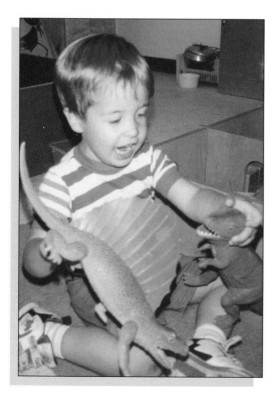

The counseling experience for children should be one that allows for children to engage in a wide variety of emotional expression. Emotions that are too threatening for a child to express verbally may be projected onto toys, providing the therapeutic distance necessary for processing issues. A child should be able to play out nurturing themes (above) and aggressive themes (below). The therapist's consistent accepting responses to all types of expression in the play provide children with the opportunity to process hurts, needs, desires, and experiences.

Contact with the therapist is facilitated through the use of toys. Children who use the stethoscope like this are not simply "playing doctor"; they are making contact with the therapist. While such play might be reenactment of an experience, a display of care and nurture, or some other theme, what may be the most important aspect is the development of the relationship between therapist and child.

The play therapy relationship includes involvement with the child as directed by the child. Children need to feel accepted and prized, and they will do so when the therapist is both verbally and nonverbally involved. The therapist is leaning over, smiling, touching the doll (and not the child, which is too intrusive), and making eye contact. Such focused attention communicates understanding and acceptance.

Puppets are important toys to include in the playroom. Children can often express more through the use of puppets because of the therapeutic distance they provide. Puppet play can give children a safe way to express feelings (particularly negative feelings) because the puppets—and not the children—are the ones expressing the feelings.

Puppets also provide a safe way to make contact with the therapist. As children express themselves by "biting" the therapist with the puppet, it is important that the emotional expression is fully accepted. This facilitates the children's acceptance of feelings that may have been frightening or confusing.

Through the use of toys, children can "play out" experiences as well as the emotions associated with those experiences. What may have been an *out-of-control* experience for the child in real life may be *controlled* within the play process. Negative experiences and the difficult-to-understand feelings that go with them (like getting an injection) can be safely addressed in play.

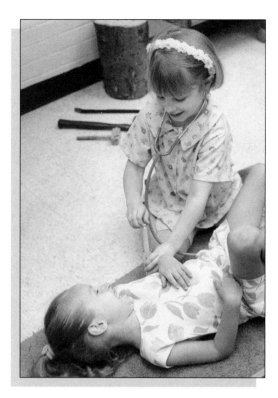

The opportunity for the child to lead the process is one of the most healing aspects of the play therapy relationship. Being in control means that the child is the producer, director, and choreographer of the play process. Handcuffing the therapist, as seen in this photo, is something I will allow. Where else can a child be self-directed and expressive so that he or she can learn self-acceptance, self-control, and self-esteem?

Group play therapy gives children the opportunity to address both interpersonal and intrapersonal issues. In play groups, children often interact with each other but will also play out their issues independently of other group members. Unlike other types of group therapy, group cohesion is not a goal in the playroom.

The group play therapist must be an excellent attendant to each child and an expert limit setter. Play is often fast and furious, and it is important for the therapist to equalize responses among children. It may be a temptation in this situation to focus on the two girls at the sandbox while the boy's quiet painting goes unnoticed.

Sandplay is another type of projective play that provides the opportunity to process intrapsychic issues without having to verbalize. This tray represents the stage of *struggle,* in which two large creatures are trying to steal the gold nugget from an army of protectors. This case involved a preteen boy who had been molested by *two* perpetrators.

This same client, in a sand tray later in the treatment process, moved toward the stage of *resolution.* The two (usually large and powerful) perpetrators are gone; there is increased organization to the tray; and it is an airport scene, representing the client's emerging sense of freedom. While in previous trays the client had always placed a miniature representing himself, in this tray he is "off flying an airplane."

Projective approaches to treatment can also be used with families. Using play in family therapy and assessment can greatly enhance communication and can be used to co-opt older children into the treatment process. Examples include the use of sandplay, as seen above in the mother-daughter counseling, and family art, as shown below. Using play with families is enjoyable and makes use of innovative projective and metaphorical techniques that can establish a greater sense of relatedness and unity.